Wholefood
BAKING

*For the sweetness in my life — my beautiful daughter
Nessie. And for Fran — no matter how tired she is after
a ten-hour day, she will have made you a rhubarb coffee
cake to have with a cup of tea when you arrive from
interstate because she loves you.*

Wholefood
BAKING

Jude Blereau

MURDOCH BOOKS

Contents

Introduction

I was lucky enough to grow up with a lot of delicious baking, mostly by my mum. Taste and place memories fly immediately to the cinnamon teacake for a weekend afternoon tea; Canadian apple roly poly with all its sticky syrup from the *CWA Cookbook* for dessert, apple pie (Ma's Apple Pie found in a magazine) and pumpkin pie. But they also include the dried apricot pie that was often in my best friend Nene's lunchbox — I would trade anything I possibly could for that, but being the wonderful friend she still is today, she would share it with me. These are all fragrant and delicious memories that I am sure have inspired my love for baking.

I believe we've become far too critical and shallow in how we view baked sweet goods with regards to our concept of healthy eating and sweetness in general, and I regularly see this when I consult or speak. Many are shocked when I suggest that there is a valid role for sweetness in a wholesome diet and many live with a fair amount of denial around sweetness.

This denial commonly manifests in an eating pattern that, while it may be considered healthy in the current fractionalised and narrow view of healthy eating, it is, I believe, imbalanced and without a shred of common sense. This is a topic well covered in my previous books. In such an eating pattern it is typical to see people binge on chocolate and especially yoghurt — denial is always an unbalanced act. I believe that to be a human is far more than to require the physical fuel and nutrients to run our body, far more than just to achieve and do. To be human is also to feel love, to be a part of family or community, to be joyful and to experience and create beauty. Food is a deeply joyful and delicious part of life, especially sweetness. I believe that we are body and soul and that we are hardwired for sweetness in all of its many forms — the sweetness of love, the smile and smell of my baby girl (now all grown up), the sweetness of my mum cooking that deliciousness for me, the sweetness of that beautiful man looking at me in the way that he does — life is sweet, and there is so much to be grateful for. I know this is why I love baking so very much — it's beautiful and it gives so much joy. And don't tell me that cake or pudding cannot heal — I've seen it. Maybe sometimes we need comforting before we can actually get on with the process of healing.

I truly believe that there is a very valid place for cake, biscuits or pie in the balanced eating of a wholesome everyday life. But, I also think that we have lost sight of what a cake, biscuit or pie truly are. I was saddened to see one of my most favourite bakers consider that her priority as a baker was not health, but flavour in a very recent book. I simply do not see why we cannot have both, and just do not believe that highly refined ingredients actually offer any flavour whatsoever and have robbed traditional baking of much of its beauty. There is now a large and wonderful world of less refined, more whole ingredients available for baking, which result in delicious, but more wholesome results, nourishing to body and soul. Put your nose to many of these 'everything old is new again' sweeteners and flours and you will notice many dimensions of flavour

— the coconut and deep caramel of palm sugars, the forest and perfumed fragrance of maple syrups and sugars, the deep and assertive aroma of buckwheat flour and the sweet earth and summer easterly winds that blow through my mind when I smell spelt flour. These, and many others, are the flours and sweeteners I use in my kitchen, and once you understand how to use them, I know you will come to love and use them also.

Basically, you can achieve a more wholesome result simply by using the less-refined versions of white wheat and spelt, and replacing refined sugar with the less-refined crystallised sugars that still retain some of their molasses, less-refined oils with unrefined, and the unstable unsaturated and polyunsaturated oils with the more stable oils such as olive, coconut, macadamia nut and the exceptionally stable butter. This is a relatively simple thing to do, and your results will be fine. But, as you go further and explore the wholemeal flours, the whole sweeteners such as rapadura sugar or maple syrups and such, things will change radically — cakes will become browner, crumb will become denser, ingredients will misbehave. In all, it will become challenging, and this book is planned as a guide for that journey. On the way I want you to keep in mind that it may be challenging at times, but well worth it. An attempt that is less than wonderful, can be still be delicious — it doesn't have to be perfect.

I would absolutely encourage you to read Ingredients and What They Do (see page 2) and Becoming A Baker — Instinct and Technique (see page 46) before you start with the recipes. Baking is a world of variables, which are only multiplied when you step away from the everyday refined ingredients. And, when your attempt is less than wonderful, go back to these pages and work out what happened — recipes are a guideline and nowhere is this more true than in the world of baking with whole and semi-refined ingredients. For example, the flour I've used here in Perth, Western Australia, will almost certainly be different from what you have access to should you live far from here. You read a little more and try it again — this is what makes you a cook or a baker. Many of you who have read my previous books will notice some differences in flour weights and the descriptions of some ingredients. While these are always heavily researched, I had not fully realised until now just how much both these aspects vary from country to country. I have looked more closely at the ingredient, spent much more time coming to know it and am very happy to settle with what you will find in these pages.

This book is not about being a purist, but rather seeking to get the best result using the most wholesome ingredients and balancing that with deliciousness. Within these pages you'll find a range of sweet goods using a wide variety of wholemeal (whole-grain) and semi-refined flours and whole and semi-refined sweeteners. Some will err towards nourishing the body, and some more towards nourishing the soul, but certainly both can be considered whole and real.

May there be much joy and sweetness in your life, and at your table.

Jude X

Ingredients
and what they do

There is now a wide range of wholesome, unrefined and semi-refined ingredients available for baking. Where possible, I prefer to use organic or biodynamic and Fairtrade — I find these have far deeper and more delicious flavours, and I know I am walking more lightly on the earth.

Sweeteners

Other than providing an obvious sweetness and flavour, sweeteners have many other important roles in baking:

TAKE INTO ACCOUNT

In essence, when a crystallised or granulated sweetener (such as cane sugar, rapadura sugar, maple sugar or palm sugar) bakes into a batter, it melts to a liquid. It may already be in a liquid form (such as maple syrup or brown rice syrup). It has no structural properties and will need to be supported by something else — eggs and flour are most commonly used.

* They add colour to the crumb and crust, as they caramelise during cooking.
* They can add crunch to the crumb when they interact with heat (in brownies, for example).
* When creaming butter and sugar, a crystallised sugar is dragged through the fat with the aid of the paddle or beater and traps air, which helps to raise and lighten the crumb (see Air and Crumb on page 52).
* As the crystals or granules melt during the cooking process, they add moisture (or add moisture in liquid form in the case of maple syrup, for example).
* They help to tenderise the crumb by inhibiting the development of gluten (as does fat) — this is why the sweetness is increased in many a low-fat product.

It's important to choose the right sweetener for the job. Knowing which sweetener to use to achieve your desired result is important. Here are a few guidelines:

* Whole (unrefined) sweeteners are strongly flavoured and can dull the colour and flavour of butter, flour and fruits. Blueberry Boy Bait (see page 131) and Rhubarb, Candied Hazelnut and Buckwheat Cake (see page 144) are good examples of using different sweeteners for a specific result.
* Very fine crystal sugars (such as muscovado sugars) melt easily on the tongue and will produce a very moist texture to the crumb.
* Crystallised or granulated sugars will trap more air when beating butter than a liquid sugar (read more about this in Air and Crumb on page 52), thus creating a lighter crumb.
* Small amounts of raw honey or brown rice syrup will give a chew to a cake crumb.

Sap sweeteners

Sap is the nourishing fluid that flows through a plant or tree and it is naturally sweet. When the roots of the tree reach deep into the ground, its sap is a rich source of minerals. Many plant saps, including birch and pine, sorghum and corn (maize), have been used throughout history. The ones most commonly available today include: cane sugar, maple syrup and maple sugar, and palm sugars.

Cane sugar

The most well known sweetener would be cane sugar — and it's a great example of what makes a food good or bad. Sugar (as with most foods) is not necessarily a *bad* thing — it really is more about what we do to it that makes it so. When you take the natural juice from sugarcane, boil, strip and refine it of all its mineral goodness, resulting in concentrated sucrose, which is then bleached, you are going to end up with a highly body-incompatible product that will simply behave like high-octane fuel in the body. It's interesting to note that a very popular health supplement is molasses, which is simply all the goodness (that is, vitamins and minerals) that has been stripped from cane sugar. Fortunately things are changing, and we are seeing a resurgence in traditional whole (unrefined) sugars.

Rapadura sugar

Rapadura (also known as panela, gur, jaggery, chanacaca and papelon) is made from sugarcane and is the most unrefined (most whole) cane sugar available. The sugarcane is pressed without heat to release the juice, which is then filtered, the fibre removed and then simmered over gentle heat to evaporate off the water. Brands vary — some are quite moist; some are quite dry. Darkly coloured and flavoured, these granules retain the valuable vitamins and minerals that are essential for the digestion of sugar, and which include calcium, phosphorus, chromium, magnesium, cobalt, copper, zinc and manganese. In its traditional home of Latin America, rapadura sugar is even considered nourishing to the body as it also contains vitamins A, C, B1, B2 and B6, niacin and iron. These minerals and vitamins, along with polyphenols, help to slow down the absorption of sugars, giving it a naturally low glycaemic index. Rapadura contains about 73–83 per cent sucrose, compared with 99 per cent sucrose in a white sugar.

The production of what we commonly know as sugar, be it white or brown, is very different from that of the rapadura process. Common sugar is boiled under vacuum (to achieve high temperatures without caramelising the sugar) to evaporate the water and sugar crystals are formed (hence, we refer to it as a crystallised sugar). All traces of molasses and goodness are separated off, and the sugar is then bleached. Any darker common sugars (packaged as brown and dark brown sugars) are simply a white sugar with carefully controlled amounts of molasses left in — or, in some cases, polyphenols and/or sugar syrup sprayed back on (see also Raw Sugar, Turbinado Sugar and Evaporated Cane Sugars on page 8).

For all its wonderful properties, one of the problems of baking with rapadura sugar is the colour and flavour that the molasses imparts — it's not always what you want. This is when I turn to the slightly more refined cane sugars, which still have varying amounts of goodness intact.

Slightly more refined cane sugars

Commonly labelled as 'Made from Unrefined Cane Sugar', these new, slightly more refined sugars are still crystallised, but much more molasses is left on during the processing path. Some are washed as well or centrifuged to remove the molasses.

A wide range of these unrefined, less-coloured sugars are available. They vary in crystal size — from the very fine icing (confectioners') and caster (superfine) sugars (known as *golden icing sugar* and *golden caster sugar* respectively) to the larger all-purpose varieties, including the robust and chunky *demerara sugar*. They also include the moist and sticky, very small sugar crystal, light to very dark brown sugars known as *muscovado*.

These slightly more refined cane sugars are never the same as the more body-compatible product that is rapadura, but used in moderation they are an excellent compromise from time to time. I am particularly fond of the golden icing and golden caster sugars as they are wonderful when you want more sweetness, less colour and less flavour than a rapadura.

Crystal size

Crystal size does matter when baking cakes and biscuits — the smaller caster (superfine) sugar dissolves more easily and is perfect when whipping with eggs to form a base for a sponge or meringue.

A slightly larger, everyday granulated or rapadura sugar can form the base of most cakes or cookies, and when beaten with butter, will help to trap the air required to give the cake or cookie a nice crumb (read more about this in Air and Crumb on page 52).

The larger demerara crystal is generally considered to have a larger amount of natural molasses left intact — hence it has a good depth of flavour and is also great as an everyday workhorse. I prefer demerara as a coating on the outside of certain cakes, biscuits and scones, where it adds delicious flavour and crunchiness.

A rapadura sugar will also add more weight to a mix — particularly in relation to cakes, so you will need to consider how you leaven the cake (see Raising Agents on pages 22–24).

Golden syrup, treacle and molasses

Sugarcane juice is traditionally boiled (under vacuum) three times — with each time, sugar crystals are removed and a progressively darker and more concentrated syrup is left. This process converts much (but not all) of the remaining sugar molecules in the sugar to an invert form — that is sucrose breaks down into fructose and glucose.

Golden syrup, from the first boiling, is rich in fructose, hence its intense sweetness. I'm not a fan of most commercial golden syrups and many are now made by mixing an uncrystallised sucrose syrup with an enzyme that converts it to an invert sugar. I far prefer the organic golden syrups — darkly coloured, luscious and knock-your-socks-off rich in flavour.

Treacle is from the second boiling, and finally blackstrap molasses is from the third. Sometimes sulphur dioxide can be used in the production (generally with young cane) and refining of sugar (to lighten the colour of the molasses and lengthen its shelf life), thus I always use unsulphured blackstrap molasses. In the organic, wholefood world this can often be called organic molasses, but a quick look at the brand website will often tell you whether or not it is sulphured (extremely rare).

For baking, it's important to know that the consistency of these syrups remains the same even when cooked — they stay how they look in the jar. When heated, they may become runnier (in a steamed pudding, for example, where the golden syrup runs down the side of the pudding), but they will give a pleasant chew to your cake or cookie.

Clockwise from top left: coconut sugar; maple syrup; rapadura sugar; golden icing (confectioners') sugar; dark muscovado sugar; brown rice syrup.

Raw sugar, turbinado sugar and evaporated cane sugars

These are all refined and crystallised sugars, but are considered to have more of the natural molasses left intact during the refining process, hence the slightly darker colour of the raw and turbinado sugars. It's important to understand though that this is not always the case in a raw sugar (even organic) and some can simply be a refined white sugar (albeit organic) with added molasses. It pays to research your brand. Demerara sugar is often used as a replacement for raw or turbinado sugars, but note that raw sugar can come in a variety of crystal sizes. Evaporated cane sugar is generally a smaller crystal, with more of the natural molasses left.

Vanilla bean golden caster sugar

I like to very finely grind ½ vanilla bean (cut off the tough woody stem first) with 210 g (7½ oz/1 cup) golden caster (superfine) sugar, then mix this with the remaining sugar from a 1 kg (2 lb 4 oz) packet and store in a glass jar. When I use this sugar, it adds more vanilla deliciousness to my baking.

Maple syrup and maple sugar

I love maple syrup. It's such a beautifully flavoured sweetener to use, and it's rich in trace minerals, including calcium. It's far cheaper to buy in bulk, but be very particular about the brand you use. I prefer organic as non-organic can contain formaldehyde traces from the pellets used in the trees to extend sap flow — this practice is not permitted under organic certification or by the Canadian Government. You can also get maple sugar, which is simply maple syrup similar to rapadura in the sense that the water is evaporated off at a low temperature and granules remain.

Palm sugar and coconut palm sugar

These are concentrated sap sugars. Palm sugar is made from the sap of the sugar palm, and coconut palm sugar is made from the nectar from the blossom of the coconut palm. They are delicious, darkly fragrant and mineral-rich sweeteners. When compared with a rapadura sugar, they are less sweet and earthier in flavour.

Grades and colours vary. Sugar palm sugars are generally darker in colour than coconut palm sugars. They are sold in a wide variety of styles: as a small log, wrapped in paper, which is generally soft, and easy to shave off thin slivers using a sharp knife; or some are set into small plastic containers — although I prefer not to use these as the sugar can be very hard. Granulated palm and coconut sugars are also becoming widely available. They look similar to a rapadura sugar, varying from a light golden colour for a coconut palm sugar to a dark brown for a sugar palm sugar.

Apart from being so delicious and mineral rich, one of the huge benefits of these sugars is that they have a low glycaemic index — yet are not fructose based. They are primarily sucrose, followed by glucose with just a small amount of fructose.

Maltose-based sweeteners

These are some of the most whole and body-compatible sweeteners. They are made by steeping grains with enzymes that break down the starches into simpler sugars. These sugars are still complex but take much longer to digest than the sugar in sap sweeteners.

Brown rice syrup (brown rice malt)

This is one of the least sweet and most whole sweeteners. It retains its syrupy consistency even when cooked, and tends to crisp when directly exposed to heat. As a result, a cake crust will be crisp and the inside a bit chewy, but it is great in biscuits, and excellent in 'creams'. It's also wonderful to drizzle over yoghurt, porridge and pancakes. Brown rice syrup is commonly used together with maple syrup. It's the perfect pairing — the maple thins out the thick rice syrup and adds a touch more sweetness.

Barley malt

This is strongly flavoured (think beer). Use as described for brown rice syrup (see above) but go easy — it's very strong.

Spelt syrup

Fairly new to the market, spelt syrup is similar to brown rice syrup and barley malt. It has a lovely mild flavour. Use as described for brown rice syrup (see above).

Amasake (amazake)

Made from fermented rice, this is a fascinating, brilliant though mostly unknown sweetener that looks like puréed rice pudding. It's made using a similar process to the syrups and malts above, but extracted at a far earlier stage. Because this is a fermented food, amasake is easy to digest and aids digestion too. Originally, rice milk was watered-down amasake.

Other whole sweeteners

There are a handful of natural, whole sweeteners that are neither sap sweeteners nor maltose-based.

Raw honey

Honey is generally the most easily available, local sweetener and almost certainly the first used by humans. It's a wonderful thing with many healthful, nourishing and healing properties. Always choose raw honey — unfiltered, unprocessed, unrefined and unheated — as it will still have all its goodness and enzymes intact. Use in any drink or foods that do not require heating. Indeed, the ancient wisdoms of Ayurveda consider it to be indigestible and toxic when heated. Remember that it's twice as sweet as sugar, so go carefully. If you do choose to use it in baking, it behaves as the maltose-based sweeteners — that is it remains as it is in the jar, and will give a delicious chew to your cake or cookie.

Stevia

The leaves of this plant have been used for centuries to sweeten and as a remedy for diabetes. Stevia is available both as a liquid, as a white powder or in a more whole form, where the leaves are ground into a fine powder. Although it's not a bad thing in its whole form, I'm not that mad about stevia. For all its intense sweetness, it has a bitter edge and it's a sweetener I just don't use.

My least favourite sweeteners: fructose

Fructose is the sugar found in fruits and can be converted from some carbohydrates during processing. As with sucrose, nature goes to a lot of trouble to protect and pad it out with a lot of other nutrients, including fibre. Fructose is not such a great sweetener. First, unlike glucose, which is digested in the gut, fructose is metabolised in the liver and this can place a large strain on that organ. Second, because it doesn't stimulate the release of insulin (that's why it's recommended for diabetics), which in turn stimulates the hormone leptin, the brain can't 'hear' the 'I've had enough, thank you' message. It's easy to keep on eating or drinking substances sweetened with fructose. Finally, fructose converts more easily to fat than glucose. Like any food, it's always going to be better when left whole — in the original apple or grape, for example. It's because of these reasons that I'm not a fan of fructose-based sweeteners. The fructose sweeteners listed below are the ones commonly available, masking as healthy sweeteners.

Agave syrup (agave nectar)

Agave has become very popular as a sweetener because it has a low-glycaemic index, which is because it has a high-fructose content. Agave is not a traditional sweetener, and was only recently developed in the 1990s. It's made by converting carbohydrate and inulin (a fructose-rich complex carbohydrate) from the agave plant's root bulb into refined fructose, in a process not too dissimilar from the production of high-fructose corn syrup (HFCS), which results in an extremely high-fructose content, commonly about 85 per cent. While there are claims of a low-heat and enzyme-aided conversion, I rarely use it, and the gloss is most certainly coming off agave as a healthy sweetener. I'm not a big fan of agave, but I do use it in small amounts from time to time because it has a lovely viscosity (slightly less thick than a brown rice syrup) and it is a nice option in things such as a dairy-free ice cream, where its viscosity helps give a smooth texture by masking the higher crystal formation due to less fat.

Fruit juice concentrates

I find fruit juice concentrates to be poor sweeteners for baking, preferring the flavour and nutrient richness of other sweeteners such as a rapadura sugar or maple syrup.

Sweeteners I would never use

High-fructose corn syrup (HFCS)

Cheap and plentiful, HFCS is the main sweetener used in commercial food products and drinks. It is refined from corn through a convoluted process that transforms glucose into fructose, resulting in a highly processed product.

Artificial and nutritive sweeteners

There is a large range of artificial sweeteners on the market, which includes: aspartame, saccharin, cyclamate and many more. I would not recommend or use any of these products.

There is also a range of products known as 'nutritive sweeteners' on the market — these *sound* natural, and so are very popular, especially because they '*are not sugar*'. One of the best-selling nutritive sweeteners are the sugar alcohols, which are pure, white and highly refined. I'm not a fan of sugar alcohols — primarily because they are *highly, highly, highly* refined and fractionalised sweeteners and do not break down in the stomach. Once in the bowels, they attract water, which can lead to fermentation of bad bacteria. Common reactions to sugar alcohols can be stomach cramping and anal leakage. It defies common sense or logic that this is better for you than a beautiful unrefined, nutrient-rich rapadura sugar or maple syrup on the grounds that 'it is not sugar'.

Flours and meals

Flour, along with eggs, is a main structural component of baked goods. The starch in flour thickens and absorbs liquid when heated, giving structure. These starches can also be from pseudo grains (such as buckwheat or quinoa) and root starches (such as arrowroot and kudzu/kuzu). Especially important is the protein in the flour — it is this that provides strength and structure to baked goods. Specifically gliadin provides extensibility and body, and glutenin provides binding and elasticity. When these are moistened with a liquid (water, or water in butter, milk, et cetera), they combine to form gluten. When the dough is manipulated (that is, stirred, kneaded and so on), an elastic web of gluten is formed. Once in the oven, the heat causes steam (from the moisture in the batter) and carbon dioxide (from leavening) to expand the dough, and the gluten web stretches and sets, helping to raise and set the cake.

Gluten flours for baking

Wheat

Wheat is one of the most popular grains for baking because of its gluten content — a well-balanced gliadin–glutenin ratio of 1:1 that will hold a good rise from the leavening; however, protein levels vary enormously in wheat, and this will impact on your result. You will find a selection of wholemeal, light wholemeal and white wheat flours on the market, but it will be their protein level that determines how you use them.

* **Hard/strong (high-protein) flour (12–14 per cent)** With a lot of gluten to promote greater elasticity, this is excellent for making pizza, pasta or bread, but it will give you tough cakes and pastry.
* **Soft (low-protein) flour (6–8 per cent)** In this category are cake flour and pastry flour, with cake flour having less protein than pastry flour. Because there is less protein, mixtures can safely include more moisture and fat, which results in a more delicious crumb, making these flours ideal for making cakes and pastry. Some brands also chlorinate the flour, which lowers the proteins and the starch — this is not done in the organic, wholefood world, and is becoming rare in most good conventional brands, but it pays to check.
* My organic unbleached white cake flour weighs in at 150 g (5½ oz) per 1 cup for one brand and 135 g (4¾ oz) for another. I work on an average weight of 135 g (4¾ oz) per 1 cup of unbleached white cake flour. Remember, there is no such thing as uniformity in the wholefood world.

Around this basic difference you will find a variety of wheat flours:

* **Baker's flour (hard/strong) (12–14 per cent)** White high-protein flour, but no reason why there couldn't be a wholemeal version.
* **Pasta and noodle flour** Mid-strength flour that produces a softer, but sturdy noodle.
* **Plain (all-purpose or general) flour (10–12 per cent)** Generally a white flour made from a blend of hard and soft flours. It is suitable for most baking, and in the commercial world often triple sieved. When you go to the supermarket and see a packet of white (or wholemeal) plain or self-raising flour, this is what it is. It can be referred to as medium–high on the packet. Unfortunately, in the organic world it is generally simply labelled as 'organic white flour' and could be a baker's flour for all you know. Most wholemeal wheat flours also fall under this category (that is, you don't really know what you've got).
* **Pastry flour (8–9 per cent)** Often referred to as medium strength.
* **Cake (soft, low protein) flour (6–8 per cent)** Often referred to as low–medium.
* **Atta ('lite') flour** A wholemeal wheat flour that has been sieved to remove some of the heavier bran — a light wholemeal so to speak.

Remember that white or wholemeal wheat flour is not the same thing as whole or white cake or pastry flour and will produce a denser end result.

I work on a weight of 150 g (5½ oz) per 1 cup of baker's flour.

*

I work on a weight of 150 g (5½ oz) per 1 cup organic white wheat flour. Similarly, I work on a weight of 150 g (5½ oz) per 1 cup organic wholemeal wheat flour.

*

I work on a weight of 135 g (4¾ oz) per 1 cup organic white cake flour. Similarly, I work on a weight of 130 g (4½ oz) per 1 cup organic wholemeal cake flour.

Wholemeal versus unbleached white

Many people think that a healthy cake means one only made from wholemeal flours. While it is true that a flour ground from a whole grain will always be more nutritious, there are times when you may want something lighter — wholemeal does not always equate to a 'healthier' product. In the organic and wholefood world, some grains, especially wheat and spelt, offer wholesome, but more refined unbleached white flours that still retain a large amount of nutrient goodness. These flours are made by grinding the whole grain, then sieving it to remove the bran and germ. Some brands remove a lot, giving you a whiter flour that is mostly endosperm (mostly starch), and some remove only a little, leaving you with white flour lightly speckled with bran and germ — a light wholemeal, so to speak. These flours are best stored in the fridge to preserve the integrity of the nutrients, especially the fat. Optimally, stone-ground flour is better than grain ground on a steel mill, as the heat from the steel oxidises the highly desirable fats.

Spelt (dinkle or farro)

Spelt (sometimes referred to as dinkle or farro in Europe) is considered to be an ancient wheat and a precursor to what we know as wheat today. While it is a gluten grain, *the gluten in spelt is more easily tolerated* and the grain is more water-soluble, which makes it far easier to digest. While spelt has a higher ratio of gliadin (body and extensibility) to glutenin (binding and elasticity) than wheat, it behaves much the same as wheat flour, but extra care needs to be taken when leavening is considered (see Baking with Wheat Versus Spelt below). Spelt flour has a darker colour than wheat flour and produces a darker crumb. Its nutrients are very evenly distributed through the berry, and thus even the starchy endosperm has a good dose of nutrients.

The spelt world does not have quite the same commercial history that wheat has, thus flours vary enormously from brand to brand. Both wholemeal and white spelt flours vary from country to country, producer to producer, and from season to season. My advice is to find a brand you like, know what they call it and stick with that. In Australia I prefer the Kialla brand for white spelt flour and Four Leaf for wholemeal spelt flour, and Demeter Mill for either.

Wholemeal spelt flour
This will vary in look, depending on whether it's been ground with a stone or steel mill, but the germ and bran should be visible.

White spelt flour
These vary enormously. Some are quite 'white' with a large amount of endosperm, some are fine with just a little germ or fibre, and some are more similar to a light wholemeal. This matters because the more 'wholemeal' your white spelt is, the more liquid it will absorb. You often need to assess your white spelt before using it. If you have a lovely white spelt with very little bran or germ (mostly endosperm), it will work well when white spelt is called for. But if it looks more like a light wholemeal, I recommend sieving the flour first through a fine sieve. This will catch most of the germ and bran, which you can discard. Measure the required quantity from the sieved flour.

Spelt flakes
Spelt flakes (also referred to as rolled spelt) are spelt kernels, groat or berries that have been steamed and rolled.

Baking with wheat versus spelt — it's all about gluten and weight
I absolutely love spelt, and this is my preferred medium for all general baking. Not only is it far easier to digest, but it also has a much sweeter and less assertive flavour than wheat. A cooked wheat batter is also more golden in colour and to me, has a more robust crumb (even when made with a cake flour) whereas a spelt crumb is softer. You will notice that many of the recipes in this book are built on spelt. But should you only have wheat and you want to use this, you need to take the following considerations into account.

What wheat flour do you have?
It's critical that you first know what you have, so you have some idea of its gluten content — and what you will have varies considerably depending on which country you live in. In Australia, most organic wholemeal and white wheat flours for baking will be an all-purpose mix of some kind — not too hard or too soft, but certainly

I work on a weight of 145 g (5¼ oz) per 1 cup of wholemeal spelt flour.

*

I work on a weight of 130 g (4½ oz) per 1 cup of white spelt flour.

*

I work on a weight of 130 g (4½ oz) per 1 cup of spelt flakes.

far harder (that is, will contain more gluten) than spelt. But this is said with fingers crossed, because there is no uniformity. You may have pastry flour (which is a lower protein) or cake flour (which has a lower protein still). The wholemeal version of both will have more gluten because of the bran and germ.

More gluten requires more liquid

Because the gliadin–glutenin ratio of wheat is different from spelt, the way that the wheat gluten behaves is very different from that of spelt. When replacing spelt flour with wheat flour, even if you are working with the substitutions given below or equal weight, you will notice better rise in the wheat product. When using a plain (all-purpose) flour (with a much higher protein than pastry or cake flour), your batter will most likely require a small amount of extra liquid. For 2 cups plain white or wholemeal wheat flour, I generally work on 60–125 ml (2–4 fl oz/¼–½ cup) of extra liquid.

Wholemeal cake flour also often requires this same little bit of extra liquid (as you have more gluten from the bran and germ, both of which also tend to absorb more liquid) but rarely with unbleached white cake flour, though batches do vary from time to time and there is no such thing as uniformity.

Conversely, when replacing a wheat recipe with spelt take into account that the gluten structure is different — softer in effect — and you won't need as much leavening (see box below). Too much and you can end up with a strong batter without the robust gluten of wheat to actually capture the air created, and you will most likely require less liquid, especially with unbleached white spelt.

Leavening when converting wheat to spelt flour

When converting wheat to spelt flour, assess the leavening on the amount of spelt. You will need to work out in cup quantity how much spelt you have — for example, when converted the amount of white spelt to equal 1 cup of white wheat flour will now weigh 150 g (5½ oz) (rather than the 130 g/4½ oz it generally does). This is in effect 15 per cent more white spelt. Leaven (add baking powder) at 1¼ teaspoons per cup, but also assess other leavening in the cake, such as eggs, creamed butter and sugar, whipped eggs, et cetera.

Converting spelt to wheat flour

Weight reflects different densities within the flour, and will vary enormously from country to country, season to season and depend on weather, growing conditions, milling, et cetera. Different densities will absorb different amounts of liquid and alter sugar and fat ratios, so they make a difference (read also Factors That Affect Crumb, page 52).

I would absolutely recommend that you keep a little book and with each new batch of flour, record the average weight for 1 cup. Once you settle on a weight, stick with it. The weights you have here in this book are what I work with, come what may, from year to year.

SPELT TO WHEAT
CONVERSION

Should your spelt to wheat
conversion batter or crumb
be too dense, know that
your wheat flour may well
be different from mine, and
reduce the amount next
time — I would go in 5 g
(⅛ oz) reductions.

WHEAT TO SPELT
CONVERSION

Should your wheat to spelt
conversion be too dense,
again, reduce the flour in
5 g (⅛ oz) reductions, and
should it be too loose (or
rise and collapse when
cooked), reduce both liquid
and leavening in the mix.

Plain (all-purpose) white wheat flour — organic or not

If you are *simply replacing the white spelt with a white wheat flour*, I would recommend you replace 1 cup of white spelt (which weighs 130 g (4½ oz) with the equal weight of white wheat flour rather than the 150 g (5½ oz) it generally weighs. But in effect this is only 86 per cent of 1 cup of white wheat flour. You have reduced the amount by 20 g (¾ oz) per 1 cup of white wheat flour. This reduction in weight will help reduce some of the gluten and absorbent qualities of plain white wheat flour. You will most likely need an extra 20–60 ml (½–2 fl oz) of liquid.

When *replacing this white wheat flour with white spelt*, you will need to increase the amount by 20 g (per 1 cup) giving you 150 g of unbleached white spelt flour (which generally weighs 130 g), which will make up for the lost gluten and the way gluten behaves. This increase in weight will help make up some of the gluten and absorbent qualities of plain white wheat flour, and you should not need to reduce your liquid quantities given in the recipe.

Plain (all-purpose) wholemeal wheat flour — organic or not

Replace 1 cup wholemeal spelt (which weighs on average 145 g/5¼ oz) with 130 g (4½ oz) only of wholemeal wheat flour (which generally weighs 150 g/5½ oz). But in effect this is only 86 per cent of 1 cup of wholemeal wheat flour, so you have reduced the amount by 20 g (¾ oz) per cup of wholemeal wheat flour but only 15 g (½ oz) less by weight of the spelt flour. It is the gluten that you have removed in that 20 g that is more important than the removal of the weight of 15 g. This reduction in weight will help reduce some of the gluten and absorbent qualities of plain wholemeal wheat flour. You will most likely need an extra 20–60 ml (½–2 fl oz) of liquid.

When *replacing this wholemeal wheat flour with wholemeal spelt*, you will need to increase your amount by 20 g (per 1 cup) giving you 165 g (5¾ oz) of wholemeal spelt flour (which generally weighs 145 g). Again, it is the increase in gluten that is more important than the 15 g of weight. This increase in weight will help make up some of the gluten and absorbent qualities of plain wholemeal wheat flour, and you should not need to reduce your liquid quantities given in the recipe.

Organic pastry flour

This has recently become available in Australia in the wholemeal option only as an American import (namely, Bob's Red Mill). On weighing this, it averages at 155 g (5½ oz) per 1 Australian cup. As a note for those of you translating from American cookbooks, the weights given for whole-wheat pastry flours vary from 110–130 g (3¼–4½ oz; adjusted for an Australian cup). This is a big difference not only in the range, but also on the 155–160 g (5½–5¾ oz) mine weighed. This will have a huge impact on your result.

The white pastry flour should weigh in at about 130 g (4½ oz) adjusted for an Australian cup. If reading American recipes calling for pastry flours, I would follow the conversions below for cake flours.

Organic cake flour

This is the closest in behaviour to spelt but slightly different. My organic unbleached white cake flours weigh in at 150 g (5½ oz) per 1 cup for one brand and 135 g (4¾ oz) for another. I work on an average weight of 135 g (4¾ oz) per 1 cup of unbleached white cake flour. The organic wholemeal weighs in at 130 g (4½ oz) per 1 cup. Remember, there is no such thing as uniformity in the wholefood world. As a note for those of you translating from American cookbooks, most American cake flours weigh in at about 125 g (4½ oz; adjusted for an Australian cup). This is a big difference.

Converting spelt flour to wheat cake flour
You should be very mindful about adding extra moisture with cake flour, so go carefully — you may not need it as it is my experience that the gluten content is very similar.

For white, replace 130 g (4½ oz/1 cup) white spelt flour with 130 g (4½ oz) of white cake flour (rather than 1 cup which weighs on average between 135 g/4¾ oz and 160 g/5¾ oz).

For wholemeal, replace 145 g (5¼ oz/1 cup) of wholemeal spelt flour with 130 g (4½ oz/1 cup) of wholemeal cake flour.

Converting wheat cake flour to spelt flour
Should your wheat to spelt conversion be too dense, reduce the flour in 5 g (⅛ oz) reductions, and should it be too loose (or rise and collapse when cooked), reduce both liquid and leavening in the mix.

For white, replace 135 g (4¾ oz/1 cup) white wheat cake flour with 135 g (4¾ oz) white spelt flour.

For wholemeal, replace 130 g (4½ oz/1 cup) wholemeal cake flour with 145 g (5¼ oz) wholemeal spelt flour.

Wheat-free and spelt-free flour options for baking

Rolled oats, oatmeal and oat flour

Oat is a high fat and sweetly flavoured grain. Rolled (also called flakes), as a meal, or as a flour, it is wonderful in baking. Considered to be low in gluten, some oats claim to be 'gluten-free', which means they have been grown and stored free from contamination with other grains. If you need to be gluten free, then you must absolutely confirm the status of the oat products you use. They may well be labelled 'wheat-free' — because they are not wheat, they are oats — but that doesn't mean they are free from any contamination with a gluten grain.

Because they are so low in gluten, and that protein is highly water-soluble, they don't contribute much to the structure of baked goods. They do, however, help to retain exceptional moisture, but too much can give a chewy and gummy consistency to the crumb. Generally it has also been my experience that you don't require as much added moisture as required with other wholemeal flours.

Stabilised rolled oats

Stabilised refers to oat kernels or groats that have been steamed before rolling. These are best lightly roasted in the oven before using to increase flavour and digestibility, but this is not essential. I prefer the more traditional rolled oat (fat and firmish) than the smaller, thinner and flakier versions.

Oatmeal and oat flour

What these two products are varies enormously from country to country and from producer to producer, which makes it very difficult for the home baker — and the recipe writer. The information that follows differs from my earlier books, because the details given to me have changed. After exhaustive research and discussions I am happy to say the following: in Australia oatmeal is generally considered to be finely ground (stabilised) oat kernels (groats), in some cases they can be rolled before grinding (thus stabilised rolled oats, ground). In texture, it equates to a wholemeal flour, but, because the oats been steamed it is not as prone to rancidity as many wholemeal flours. The oatmeal is then sieved, which removes most of the bran and germ, resulting in oat flour. In many other countries, typically the United States and Britain, oat flour is considered to be simply ground oat kernels (groats) — a much heavier product than what we know in Australia.

Barley flour and barley flakes (rolled barley)

Barley flour

I absolutely love the earthy, honest flavour of barley. As with oatmeal and oat flour, how this is made varies from producer to producer, and country to country, but it is either ground from hulled barley (with some of the hull intact) or pearled barley (with little if any hull intact, making it slightly more refined) and then sieved to remove some of the bran and germ — and in the case of hulled barley, hull too. Barley is high in protein, but too low in gluten to build good structure, so it is best mixed with other gluten flours. Look for a barley flour that has some visible bran and germ. In Australia I prefer the Four Leaf brand.

Barley flakes (rolled barley)

Made from pearled barley that has been steamed (stabilised), then rolled.

Gluten-free flours for baking

I prefer not to use commercial pre-mixed gluten-free baking flours (unless I lived in the United States where excellent mixes are available). A fundamental behaviour of gluten-free flours is that they do not like to stick together. This is the main reason that most commercial gluten-free baked goods are made with highly refined starches, such as potato, rice, tapioca and cornflour (cornstarch). When mixed with a liquid, such as water, these will stick together and help bind the mix. Xanthan gum and guar gum are commonly used to help bind and give texture to the crumb, though, again, I have never been an advocate of these. This will generally result in a carbohydrate product with a high-glycaemic index. People who turn to gluten-free flours commonly have very fragile digestive systems, and these starches will only help to feed bad bacteria in the gut, further compounding basic intestinal issues.

Below are the flours and starches I like to use and all are best used in combination (see Gluten-free Baking on page 61). Please note that brands differ in flavour and it pays to find a brand you like.

Almond meal (ground almonds)

Referred to in many books as almond 'flour', this is simply very finely ground blanched almonds.

I work on a weight of 100 g (3½ oz) per 1 cup of almond meal.

Amaranth and quinoa

I group amaranth with quinoa as they are often used interchangeably. They both have a strong, assertive flavour and are high in protein, which is wonderful, but they really bully other flavours and take over. Chocolate (especially dark) and banana stand up to bullying wonderfully — chocolate by overpowering and banana by softening — and I love to use either or both with amaranth and quinoa. Both are available as a rolled version (flakes) where the grain is steamed before rolling (stabilised), which softens their flavour, making them excellent to replace other gluten rolled and flaked grains in baking.

I work on a weight of 125 g (4½ oz) per 1 cup of amaranth flour.

Amaranth flour

A member of the *Caryophyllales* family (which includes spinach), the tiny seeds are ground to make a flour that is soft and creamy in colour with an assertive flavour — many say grassy flavours, but to me I smell earth and taste beetroot. Amaranth works wonderfully with orange.

Quinoa flour and quinoa flakes

Quinoa is part of the *Chenopodium* family, and the sacred mother grain of the mighty Inca civilisation. As a flour, it is very strong and assertive in flavour, with a strong smell of earth. Different brands are not equal — some are more bitter/earthier than others, so find a brand you like. In Australia I like Olive Green Organics.

I work on a weight of 120 g (4¼ oz) per 1 cup of quinoa flour, and 100 g (3½ oz) per 1 cup of quinoa flakes.

Chickpea flour (besan)

This is technically not a flour, but made from ground chickpeas and is incredibly handy, in small amounts, in gluten-free baking. It adds a wonderful soft and moist texture to baked goods.

Rice flour, brown or white

These are always two of my first choices in gluten-free baking and most often my foundation grain. White rice flour will give you a lighter result, though brown is perfectly fine. In some countries, notably the United States and Britain, you can get 'superfine' versions of brown rice flour; if you have this option available to you, you will get a better result. Rice flour is always best 'softened' by mixing in something very small and fatty, such as desiccated coconut or ground nuts, to help break the heaviness. For a finer and softer crumb, add a portion of arrowroot or cornflour

I work on a weight of 160 g (5¾ oz) per 1 cup of brown rice flour, and 155 g (5½ oz) per 1 cup of white rice flour.

(cornstarch). Small amounts of other gluten-free flours, such as buckwheat, amaranth or quinoa, can be included too.

Buckwheat

I work on a weight of 140 g (5 oz) per 1 cup of buckwheat flour.

Buckwheat flour is milled from unhulled buckwheat and then sieved to remove some of the outer husk, before the inner kernel (groat) and any remaining husk is milled into flour. Alternatively, it can simply be milled from the unhulled buckwheat, and then sieved of husk, some bran and germ. Buckwheat is not a true cereal grain, but rather it is related to the rhubarb and sorrel family. It is not related to and does not contain any wheat. As a flour, it has a strong, assertive and perfumed flavour and is better mixed with another flour, such as brown rice flour, to soften its flavour. Its texture can be quite gummy and it will absorb an astonishing amount of liquid.

Coconut flour

I work on a weight of 130 g (4½ oz) per 1 cup of coconut flour.

While it is not a grain flour, this is sold as and used as a baking flour. It is actually what is left when the oil has been extracted from coconut meal. It is extremely high in fibre, high in protein and gluten free. Because it's so high in fibre, too much of it in a recipe will give you a brick-like result. In small amounts, though, it provides a gorgeous flavour.

Maize (corn)

Polenta (cornmeal/maize meal)

I work on a weight of 140 g (5 oz) per 1 cup of polenta.

This is a coarse, grit-like meal made from ground corn. In many cases the skin and germ are removed to extend shelf life. Search and ask for polenta that is made from corn with the germ intact — this should be stored in the fridge to avoid spoilage.

Maize flour (corn flour/golden corn-maize flour)

This looks like a fine wholemeal flour and is a beautiful pale-yellow colour. It is also referred to as 'corn flour'. What we know as cornstarch or cornflour (the white flour used for thickening) is the white starch inside the highly refined grain (see Starches and Thickeners opposite).

Maize meal (cornmeal)

Softer than polenta, this is a mix of ground polenta and maize flour.

Millet

I work on a weight of 150 g (5½ oz) per 1 cup of millet flour.

Millet as a flour can have a strong and astringent, slightly bitter taste. Good millet and better-tasting millet flour is very fresh. Too much millet flour can give your baked goods a dry crumb. As with all wholemeal flours and semi-refined flours, millet benefits from cold storage, especially in the warmer months.

Teff

I work on a weight of 140 g (5 oz) per 1 cup of teff flour.

Teff is one of the smallest grains in the world, and I am in love with its subtle flavour and ability to give a suberb soft crumb to gluten-free baked goods.

Gums

Both xanthan gum and guar gum are commonly used in gluten-free baking to bind a crumb, and mimic gluten in providing rise and texture to the crumb. I have never been an advocate of these, and you can absolutely get good results without them. Xanthan gum is described as a polysaccharide, made by fermenting corn sugar with the bacterium *Xanthomonas campestris*. Xanthan gum's role in gluten-free baking is to give viscosity and stickiness — it helps bind the batter together.

Starches and thickeners

Cornflour (cornstarch), true arrowroot, tapioca flour and kudzu (kuzu) are all starch-based thickening agents that help to provide structure in baked goods; cocoa can also be used to provide a portion of 'flour' in gluten-free baking. While they all help to provide structure, they should not be relied on to do the whole job. It's best to use these in small portions in a gluten-free baking mix to help soften the heavier gluten-free flours and give a lighter crumb. They can also be used to thicken a custard or cream.

Kudzu (kuzu)

Made from the root of the kudzu plant, this thickener is well known for its medicinal qualities in China and Japan, where it is traditionally used to treat digestive problems, such as an upset stomach or to soothe the nerves. When used to thicken sauces, it imparts a beautiful, clear sheen to the finished sauce. It will also set soft puddings. It must be completely dissolved (generally in a little liquid) before using, and then gently brought to the boil while stirring constantly. Kudzu continues to thicken as it cools.

As a guide, 2 teaspoons of kudzu will set 250 ml (9 fl oz/1 cup) of liquid to a sauce consistency, while 2½ tablespoons will set to a soft pudding consistency. Kudzu is usually sold in lumps. To measure it, simply grind it up in a bowl using the end of a rolling pin, or using a mortar and pestle.

True arrowroot (and tapioca flour)

Similar in appearance to cornflour (cornstarch), true arrowroot comes from the root of a tropical plant and is gluten free. When purchasing, ensure the package has the word 'true' on it, as much of the arrowroot sold is actually tapioca flour. True arrowroot is a rich source of trace minerals and calcium — it is this mineral content which differentiates it from tapioca flour. It has been traditionally fed to babies and young children as it's very easy to digest — I grew up eating 'Milk Arrowroot' biscuits, as was the case for many a child. It's a great choice for baking. It does have a distinct mineral flavour to it, as you would expect, and you need to be careful when adding salt — especially when using a Celtic sea salt, which has a very strong mineral flavour, and when using both in a recipe, the salt can highlight the strong mineral flavour of true arrowroot and vice versa. I prefer to use true arrowroot as it's more nutritious, but it's fine to use the more commonly available form of tapioca flour.

Cornflour (cornstarch)

This is the finely ground endosperm of corn. It is very white and has little nutrient value. It is, however, particularly useful when some 'structure' is required in a dairy-free 'cream' or panna cotta, for example, that requires more body than a sauce — a body that true arrowroot, tapioca flour or kudzu (kuzu) just don't have.

In small portions, it is also useful as a flour, to aid binding, especially in gluten-free baking. Check the packet when you buy cornflour as it is often actually made from wheat. When using cornflour as a 'flour' in a gluten-free mix, it pays to buy an organic, GMO-free brand as I find them far lighter than the generic packets of corn 'flour' (cornstarch) found in the supermarket. They will give a far superior result. This is referred to as natural cornstarch in the United States.

Potato flour and potato starch

Potato flour

This is made from cooked, dried and ground potatoes, and has a potato flavour. It can be used as a thickener for soups, gravies and sauces, but it is a little thick for baking.

Potato starch

Be very careful when buying this, as many potato starches are actually 'flours'. This is made from the starch of the potato and looks like a very fine flour. It is used in baking, adding moisture or as a thickening agent (similar to cornstarch/cornflour). A small amount of this is invaluable in gluten-free baking, adding a soft and moist texture.

I work on a weight of 160 g (5¾ oz) per 1 cup of potato starch.

Raising agents

The action of rising a baked good is often referred to as leavening. In traditional baking, there are three main ways to raise and, thus, lighten a cake.

* **Physical leavening** This takes place when heat from the moisture in ingredients, such as butter, eggs, milk or fruit, produces steam, which expands and raises the mixture. When you cream butter and sugar together or whip eggs, you are also trapping air into the mixture. For a detailed discussion of physical leavening, see Beating to the Ribbon on page 52 and Air and Crumb on page 52.
* **Chemical leavening** This relies upon the reaction between an acid and an alkaline medium, which when mixed with moisture and heat, create carbon dioxide to lift the mixture.
* Use of yeast or sourdough.

Many commercial flours are labelled as 'self-raising', which means they have been pre-mixed with a chemical raising agent, specifically baking powder. Outside the world of wheat, very few flours (if any) offer a self-raising version — but even if they did, I would prefer to leaven the flour myself, and would recommend you do too.

Chemical leavening

Let's start with chemical leavening, as this is the one most commonly used by the home baker. We have the option of using a chemical raising agent that has been prepared for us (baking powder), or mix the acid and alkaline ourselves.

Acid and alkaline: baking powder

It's incredibly important to understand your baking powder. I recommend you take the time to do this, and form a long-term relationship with a brand you like. Many commercial baking powders use baking soda (bicarbonate of soda/sodium bicarbonate) as the choice of alkaline as opposed to potassium bicarbonate in the healthier brands (for those who want to reduce the amount of salt in their diet). I don't have a problem with a sodium bicarbonate version, but it's worth noting that potassium bicarbonate will create less carbon dioxide to lift a batter than baking soda — it has a more subtle and gentle lift, which I happen to really like.

The problem area for most (virtually all) commercial blends of baking powders is the acid — most use sodium aluminium sulphate or a phosphate aerator (also called sodium aluminium phosphate). Fundamentally they are aluminium based. This is a popular acid to use because it is slower to react with the alkali, thus more rising action takes place in the oven than in the bowl. Baking powders with these products have a noticeably bitter taste in the mouth (not to mention aluminium in the body). The healthier blends commonly use calcium phosphate as the acid.

Baking powders with no salt or aluminium are considered 'healthier' and 'fast acting', which means the chemical reaction begins at a lower temperature and on contact with moisture — but even when I leave my mix to sit for a couple of minutes or so, I have not had any problems.

Alkaline alone: baking soda (bicarbonate of soda/sodium bicarbonate)

When mixed (and thus activated) with an acid, baking soda is a sturdy lifter. Care needs to be taken when using it, though, as it will begin to react immediately when mixed with the acid and moisture. Typically, it's good to use for a batter that is immediately cooked (such as pancakes) or baked (such as a cake). Cultured buttermilk, yoghurt, sour cream, vinegar and citrus are all good choices for the acid. Baking soda is often used in recipes with natural (undutched) cocoa powder as it helps to soften the bitter acidity of the cocoa, and also reacts with that acidity to help raise the batter.

Commonly you may also see a recipe call for a small amount of baking powder and an even smaller amount of baking soda (with a corresponding acid somewhere in the ingredient list) and wonder why the recipe uses both types. Sometimes, especially in a plain cake with little flavour, adding too much baking powder to get the required lift can give a nasty aftertaste, so by adding a small portion of that sturdy lifter, baking soda, whose flavour is also balanced out by its acid activator, gives the requisite extra burst.

It's easy to tell when you or a recipe has used too much baking soda — the crumb rises aggressively in the oven with big bubbles. The crumb is what I would describe as 'spent' — it's beyond its best, and there is a noticeable bitter aftertaste in the mouth — some describe this as a soapy flavour.

HOW MUCH BAKING POWDER TO USE?

The common ratio of baking powder to flour is 2½ teaspoons per 1 cup of flour, but I find this far too much. I use 1¼ teaspoons per 1 cup of flour as a general rule and find that this amount is more than enough. Sometimes less, sometimes more given the situation, but I can also use some other, less invasive techniques to help raise the cake if needed (see Box of Tricks on page 59).

Acid alone

Cream of tartar (potassium hydrogen tartrate)
A by-product of the wine industry, cream of tartar is made from the sediment found in wine casks. Many traditional baking powders were made from one part baking soda to two parts cream of tartar. You can easily make baking powder yourself following this ratio.

Familiar home acids
Cultured buttermilk, yoghurt, vinegar, natural (undutched) cocoa powder and even molasses all help to provide acidity. I love using vinegar in this role, with a preference for apple cider vinegar. Vinegar also helps to tenderise the gluten in the flour, and helps to produce a cake with a fine crumb — particularly in cakes made without eggs.

Increasing the leavening power of baking powder

When you add vinegar to a batter leavened with baking powder, the vinegar also reacts with the alkaline, creating more carbon dioxide to lift the cake. The carbon dioxide reaction also helps to neutralise the acidic flavour of the vinegar. This is a tool I often use in plain, especially dairy-free and/or egg-free cakes, where there is no butter or egg to provide extra lift.

Gelling agents

The gelling agents agar and gelatine behave quite differently. Agar sets quickly, provides a sturdy structure and holds well at room temperature, but has a chunky texture. Gelatine, on the other hand, takes hours to set, does not hold well in hot weather, but is infinitely flexible and smoothly textured.

Agar

Also known as kanten, this is a nutrient-rich, high-fibre, zero-kilojoule gelling agent made from seaweed. It comes in flakes, powder and bars, but I prefer powder and flakes, with powder as my first choice, as they are easy to measure and give reliable results. Agar will set at room temperature and can be boiled and reheated without losing its gelling ability. I have specified powder in most recipes as it does give more reliable results. Some batches of flakes are stronger than others, and the consistency of their setting can vary enormously.

If you're worried the jelly will be too soft or too hard, test your set: when you have dissolved the flakes or powder, simply place a little in a small bowl, pop it in the fridge (or freezer) until cold. If it is too soft, add it back to the mix, along with a little more agar and cook until dissolved. If it's too firm, add more liquid and cook for a couple of minutes more.

Agar dissolves best in high-pectin juices, such as apple, but works in most fruit juices. When using flakes and powder in recipes, it needs to be dissolved slowly over a *gentle boil* and stirred frequently to stop it clumping or sticking to the base of the pan. Powder takes about 8–10 minutes from the boil, and flakes up to 25 minutes to dissolve (from the boil).

Agar will not set in distilled and wine vinegars, or in food containing large amounts of oxalic acid or acid, such as chocolate, rhubarb or spinach.

When using high-acid juices, such as lemon, lime or pineapple, double the agar.

Gelatine

Traditionally made from the skin and bones of cows, gelatine is a time-honoured way to aid digestion, especially in cooked and high-protein foods. It's one of the reasons stocks made from animal bones are so nourishing. It's very important to use gelatine that you trust — one that is made from the healthiest of cows. I prefer to use the Bernard Jensen brand, which is powdered, and it is freely available online from www.greenpastures.com.au.

HOW MUCH AGAR TO USE?

To achieve a good, but not too solid jelly, the basic equation is 3 teaspoons of agar flakes or ½ teaspoon of agar powder per 250 ml (9 fl oz/1 cup) of liquid. This is the equation I most commonly use. (For the past 12 months, however, I've had to reduce the ratio of flakes to 2 teaspoons per 1 cup, but I think this has to do with the production, and this is typical for many natural foods as they aren't subjected to uniformity that many conventional products are.)

For a very firm jelly that you want to turn out and cut into shapes, increase the amount of agar.

HOW MUCH GELATINE TO USE?

You'll need 1½ teaspoons of powdered gelatine to set 250 ml (9 fl oz/1 cup) of liquid to a wobbly consistency, and 2 teaspoons per 250 ml (9 fl oz/1 cup) for a firmer set jelly.

For leaf gelatine, you will need 5 g (⅛ oz) per 250 ml (9 fl oz/1 cup) of liquid.

Chocolate and cocoa (cacao)

Chocolate, as we know it, is the result of a long process. Seeds from the cacao tree are firstly scooped out of the large pods and left to ferment and then spread out to dry. At this stage, the beans are considered to be raw — the full flavour that is chocolate is yet to be realised. The seeds are then roasted and shelled to become what we call 'nibs', which can be left whole or broken into pieces. During roasting the flavour of cocoa is developed. Within the Raw Food movement, a view is held that raw cocoa nibs and all products that come from them are more nutritious and preferable, but this is highly contentious and hotly debated as the chocolate flavour is only fully realised from the application of heat. They do have higher levels of phytonutrients, but in my experience, a harsher flavour. At this point it's important to understand that the terms cocoa and cacao are interchangeable. The nibs are then ground to form a thick paste — this is commonly known as **cocoa liquor**, made up of cocoa butter (fat) and cocoa solids (the brown part, which can become a powder) — and in some cases vanilla and sugar is added at this stage. The cocoa liquor is then pressed to remove most of the fat (cocoa butter), and the remaining solids are ground to what we know as cocoa powder. Cocoa is a lot like coffee, quite acidic — this varies with the variety of bean, and is also increased when the fat is removed. As with coffee, the quality and variety of the bean is everything; poorer quality beans are generally more acidic.

When discussing cocoa, it pays to bear in mind that you can get as many chocolate professionals in a room together and they will all call a similar thing something different. In Europe and the United States, cocoa mass/mass/liquor refers to a product that contains both solids and fat, but this ratio can be manipulated by the producer. In Australia, cocoa mass/mass is considered to be the powder left over when the fat is removed, and cocoa solids can refer to any component of the original cocoa liquor — fat, powder, et cetera.

Cocoa nibs

Nibs are becoming widely available and add a delicious flavour and/or crunch to creams, biscuits or cakes. They are a great replacement for nuts, with a crunchier texture. Nibs are available whole and broken up (which look a little like roughly chopped nuts).

Cocoa butter

This is the pressed fat from the cocoa liquor, and it has a delicious, but subtle chocolate flavour.

Natural (undutched) cocoa powder and unsweetened dutched cocoa powder

It's important here to remember the acidity of cocoa powder is increased when the fat (cocoa butter) is removed, thus the quality of the powder is everything. Most

Clockwise from bottom right: cocoa nibs; unsweetened dutched cocoa powder; white chocolate; chocolate (70%); cocoa butter; vanilla paste, and vanilla beans.

natural cocoa powders are tart and acidic, and I would encourage you to taste them before buying, if possible, as brands vary enormously. One of the methods devised to reduce this problem was that of 'dutching', or alkalising the cocoa powder by soaking the nibs in an alkaline solution, commonly potassium carbonate, which neutralises the acid and softens the flavour. This process also changes the colour of the cocoa to a deep chocolatey red. I do love using unsweetened dutched cocoa powder, and prefer the Green & Blacks brand.

In baking, you must know which type of cocoa powder you are dealing with, as the acidity of a natural (undutched) cocoa will interact with whatever leavening you are using. You will often see a little baking soda (bicarbonate of soda/sodium bicarbonate) added to a batter when natural cocoa powder is used as it will temper the acidity and together they will create lift.

Chocolate bars and couverture chocolate

Chocolate, set in bars, is a mixture of cocoa liquor, sweetening, flavouring (such as vanilla), milk powder and an emulsifier, commonly soya lecithin. The proportions determine the mouthfeel, flavour and use. Brands certainly vary, and I am particularly interested in the sugar used. Most organic brands use raw sugar, but my favourite, the German Rapunzel brand, uses rapadura sugar, and it makes for a beautifully sweetened chocolate.

Certain chocolates must have a minimum percentage of cocoa liquor. Confusion arises when this is sometimes labelled as chocolate liquor/cocoa mass, cocoa solids or even 'cacao'. Throughout the book, you will see that when I call for a chocolate, it will have a percentage next to it with the words 'cocoa solids', but know that some brands might say any of the above words. They will mean the same thing.

The best guide for you as a consumer is the percentage number on the packet. The higher the number, the higher the percentage of cocoa liquor (chocolate liquor/cocoa mass/cocoa solids). It will be more bitter as there is less addition of sugar.

Dairy-free and vegan chocolate bars

While a dark chocolate may not necessarily include milk powder as an ingredient, many include it in the listings or as a warning as they are produced using the same machinery as that for milk chocolate. If you want a brand that absolutely has no milk product (and branded as vegan), you may like to track down the brands: Loving Earth in Australia; Tropical Source, which uses soya lecithin as an alternative, in the US; and Dagoba and Rapunzel worldwide.

Unsweetened chocolate

This is pure cocoa liquor set into a bar and, depending on the quality of the beans, can be very bitter.

Cooking (baking) chocolate

Most cooking chocolate these days is made by blending various amounts of cocoa liquor with cocoa butter, sugar and emulsifiers — typically soya lecithin. Good brands should tell you the amount of cocoa liquor and cocoa butter used, but a bar with 40 per cent cocoa liquor will behave and taste very differently from one with 70 per cent (see Chocolate Bars and Couverture Chocolate, opposite). Many have an additional amount of cocoa butter, which helps to give a smoother consistency when melted.

Semi-sweet, dark and bittersweet chocolate

The more cocoa liquor, the more intense and darkly flavoured the chocolate. Again, chocolate with a lower percentage will taste and behave very differently from one with a higher percentage. I keep a 70 per cent cocoa liquor bittersweet chocolate for general baking use — I like quite a dark and bitter edge to my chocolate, and prefer it over many of the cooking chocolates. Dark chocolate should have at least 65 per cent cocoa liquor and semi-sweet at least 56 per cent.

Milk chocolate

It's hard for me to talk about milk chocolate as I am not a fan of it. Made with milk powder, a lesser amount of cocoa liquor, plus sweetener, flavouring and emulsifier, it has a pronounced creamy mouthfeel and taste. It's lovely to see some development in the world of milk chocolate, with brands displaying ever-increasing amounts of cocoa liquor on the front.

White chocolate

Technically, this isn't chocolate, as it only contains cocoa butter (fat) — and it should most definitely be cocoa butter; beware inferior brands that are often made with hydrogenated vegetable oils — milk powder, sweetener, emulsifier and flavour (typically vanilla).

Couverture chocolate

This is made with both a high level of cocoa solids and cocoa butter (fat). This extra fat (typically 30 per cent) gives it a deliciously smooth texture that flows well with more sheen, thus it melts easily on the tongue, which means it has a more voluptuous mouthfeel. Sweetness (usually in the form of sugar), vanilla and the emulsifier soya lecithin are often added.

Compound chocolate

This is a cheap way to produce 'chocolate' using cocoa powder and vegetable oils instead of cocoa liquor and cocoa butter. I don't use this in any way.

Chocolate chips or drops

These are made with less cocoa butter so that when they heat up, they hold their shape — but in most cases, I prefer to simply chop up my favourite chocolate bar.

Flavouring agents

Herbs and spices

In the following recipes I have used vibrant, fresh organic herbs and spices — this makes an enormous difference. These multi-dimensional flavours are carried on very volatile oils, and once exposed to oxygen, can diminish quite rapidly. Where possible, freshly ground spices will give you the best results. I prefer to grate nutmeg as I use it (I have a microplane nutmeg grater), and I have been known to grind cinnamon quills in my Thermomix or electric spice/coffee grinder rather than use an old and tired packet. There are many excellent organic brands available, and ½ teaspoon of this kind (ground cardamom for example) is very, very different from a conventional or old one with far less flavour.

Vanilla

Vanilla bean seeds

The seeds contained within the vanilla bean impart a sensual, beautiful and delicious flavour. Vanilla beans should be plump and soft, not dry and hard. Generally, vanilla beans are used to infuse liquids with flavour. As a basic rule, you cut down the length of the bean, open it out flat and scrape down the bean with a small knife, collecting all the seeds. Add the seeds to the liquid, then also add the remaining bean halves. When the liquid has come to the boil (or just below), remove it from the heat and leave it to infuse. Remove the bean before using the liquid but don't throw the bean away. Give it a quick wash, then when dry, it's great to add to sugar, especially golden caster (superfine) sugar (see page 8).

Vanilla essence and extract

Vanilla is often described as an essence or an extract, and there are rules that define both. I've found that quality vanilla can be called an essence in one country, and an extract in another. I refer to it in my recipes as natural vanilla extract and I recommend you look for one that only has vanilla and alcohol and no sweeteners (generally fructose or glucose, corn syrup, glycerin, fructose or propylene glycol). I have a preference for the Nielsen-Massey and Heilala brands, and while both are expensive, you only need to use a very small amount.

Vanilla paste

This is also very handy. It is vanilla seeds suspended in a thick syrup medium, generally inulin or tragacanth. Again, I prefer to use the Nielsen-Massey or Heilala brands.

Flavouring extracts

There are many, many flavouring extracts on the market (coffee, citrus and almond, for example) and most are fake. I like to use the real ingredient where possible, but when I want to use a flavouring extract, I am very keen on Boyajian Citrus Oils and Nielsen-Massey extracts. When I travel, rather than shop for shoes and clothes, vanilla and flavouring extracts are what I seek out.

Colouring agents

Sadly, many of the commercially available colours we use are dangerous, and in Australia we continue to use many that are banned in many other countries. Most of the time I make my own — using beetroot or raspberries for pink; passionfruit or ground turmeric for a light-yellow glow; a very concentrated parsley or spinach juice for green; and blueberries for a blue/purple. If you don't have the time to make your own, there is a good range of colours made from safe and natural foodstuffs on the market, and the brands I use include: Dancing Deer Earth Grown Colors, Hullabaloo and India Tree.

Fats for baking

Fat is an important ingredient in baking, providing moisture, texture and flavour. I've included fat options for dairy-free and gluten-free baking.

Butter

Butter is the most superior of all fats for baking. This is a healthful, nourishing and stable fat, and will always give the best crumb. Butter is about 20 per cent water and milk solids, though this varies and more water means less fat. This has implications, especially when making pastry, as the more fat you have, the better the flake, and with gluten grains, the more water the more the development of the gluten, which will result in tougher crumb or pastry. French butter in particular is well known as high-fat butter and makes exceptional pastry. Butter will also provide some water to help raise your biscuit, muffin or cake. I have a preference for unsalted butter when baking, and prefer to add my own salt as needed.

Where milk solids are not tolerated, you can use ghee (though remember this is pure fat; see page 32).

SOFTENED BUTTER IN MY RECIPES

Butter when noted as softened in my recipes should be the texture of face cream.

Lard

A nourishing and stable animal fat, lard is especially good for making pastry. Being 100 per cent fat, the same above rules apply when replacing with butter (or vice versa).

When butter or ghee cannot be used

Your best option is for a naturally light coloured and delicious oil, but one that is heat stable. With a high amount of oleic acid, macadamia nut and almond oils will give beautiful results, as will the more traditional extra virgin olive oil. Remember that all olive oils (organic or not) are not equal, and choose one that is fragrant and full flavoured.

Coconut oil

In addition to the above three options, you can consider coconut oil, which is a non-animal saturated fat. Even though it is referred to as a nut, it is not, and can be used for those intolerant to macadamia nut or almond oils.

Baking with coconut oil has its limitations, though. When the cookie or cake comes out of the oven, the crumb will be soft and moist, as if made with butter, but as it cools, the crumb will toughen and restrict and will be slightly crumbly. When you use unrefined, full-flavoured (extra virgin) coconut oil, it may have a slight aftertaste also — not everyone likes this. This can be softened, as can some of the effects. Tougher texture and the tendency to be crumbly, for example, can be mitigated when you match the coconut oil with the right things — chocolate, coconut, banana and lime all tame the aftertaste, and mashed banana, in particular, helps to soften the texture and hold the crumb, as do eggs.

Having said all this, coconut oil can be fabulous in some baked goods. It's an especially good choice for muesli bars, and shines when included in mixes that have lots of fruit in them (especially banana). Served warm from the oven, cookies, cakes, pastry and puddings will all be delicious.

Finally, for those with a highly limited diet (no animal fats, no dairy, no nut oils) coconut oil is a godsend, and a piece of cake or cookie, even if crumbly and slightly more chewy, is a welcome and delicious option.

Coconut oil comes in two varieties, 'full flavour' and 'less flavour', and because some manufacturers term their coconut oil 'butter' when in fact it is an oil and not a butter, I've also included information on coconut butter to help you understand what it really is (see Creaming Butter and Sugar or Creaming Coconut Oil and Sugar in Factors That Affect Crumb on page 53).

Unrefined, full-flavoured (extra virgin) coconut oil

This will be called different things by different brands. It has the full fragrance of coconut and also retains the most nutrients. As mentioned before, when baked into a cake, it can have a strong aftertaste and not everyone likes this.

Less-flavour (virgin) coconut oil

Also called refined or flavourless but, again, it is called varying names by different brands. This oil has been deodorised (generally by running through clay) to remove the strong coconut fragrance (though some nutrient loss occurs in this process). This is a good choice when you don't want a cooked coconut aftertaste in biscuits, pastry, cakes, et cetera.

Coconut butter (spread)

This delicious spread is coconut flesh that has been ground into a paste. As it is the whole coconut, it retains all of the protein, fibre, vitamins and minerals. It's a great choice to use in nut and seed balls and energy bars, smoothies or spreads.

Storing fats

When choosing any oil, make sure it is not rancid. Oils are far less stable to light, heat and oxygen than saturated fats (butter, lard and coconut oil). A rancid oil is bitter and nasty in flavour, and not at all good for you. As a general rule, fats, especially nut oils, are best kept in a cool, dark place, especially during the hot months, but saturated fats are more stable than nut oils and don't go rancid as quickly in the warmer weather.

BAKING WITH COCONUT OIL

In my recipes, coconut oil is always unrefined, full-flavoured (extra virgin) coconut oil, unless otherwise specified.

Eggs

Eggs play many very valuable roles in baking:

* They add moisture in the form of fat and liquid.
* They add richness from the fat in the yolk.
* They bind and 'stick' ingredients together.
* They help to leaven the cake by trapping air, and supplying some water, which becomes steam when heated.
* Their protein helps give structure to a cake.

Eggs ensure a light and more beautiful finished crumb — but good news for those with egg allergies (one of the most common allergies I see), you don't have to use eggs. The finished egg-free product will not be as 'glued together' or as light, but it will still be excellent. It's easy to get away without eggs in biscuits and pastry, but it is a little more difficult in muffins and cakes — in muffins especially as there is not so much surface area to hold the cake together. Muffins and cakes made without egg tend to be slightly flatter and a little more dense than those with.

Eggs are especially valuable when using many of the very low gluten and gluten-free grains as they help bind everything together, and they can be whipped to help give more rise to the cake (by trapping air) (see Gluten-Free Baking, page 61).

Egg whites are also especially handy, adding extra protein to a cake (especially in gluten-free situations), or when whipped, they add extra lightness and air. It's good to keep in mind that sugar will increase the stability of whisked egg white (meringue).

Replacing eggs

There is a variety of ways to replace eggs, but no single substitute provides the whole package — that is, moisture, richness, binding, leavening and structure — which makes you realise how amazing the egg is.

Egg replacers

These help to mimic the leavening and binding of an egg, and do give a lovely crumb. While I'm not a great fan of them, they do have a place in highly restricted diets. Common ingredients include: potato starch, tapioca flour, leavening (calcium lactate [non-dairy], calcium carbonate, citric acid), cellulose gum and carbohydrate gum. Because egg replacers have no fat, this needs to be taken into account when using them and you will need to increase the fat from other sources.

Ground chia seeds and ground flaxseeds

Both of these become extremely viscous and gooey when combined with liquid, and will help to bind, add richness and add moisture. I far prefer chia seeds, and find they give a lighter and moister result compared to flaxseeds (linseeds).

Milks

Milk provides moisture and fat to a baked good. It's essential to take into account the fat content of the milk you choose. For example, a cake made with a full-cream, non-homogenised dairy milk will be far moister and more luscious than one made with a low-fat milk such as soy, almond or rice. In the latter cases, extra attention will need to be given to adjusting moisture in the cake — either by increasing the fat (butter, oil or egg yolk), or by making a slightly wetter mix by slightly increasing the amount of fruit. You can read more about this in Dairy-free and/or Egg-free Baking on page 58.

Milks with fat

Dairy milk

Low-fat milks should never be used as a substitute for full-cream as they behave very differently in cooking not only due to the obvious reduction in fat, but also due to the increase in protein from added milk solids. If necessary, it is wiser to substitute with a dairy-free milk (see Dairy-free and/or Egg-free Baking on page 58).

Coconut milk and coconut cream

These are a brilliant choice for flavour and fat. They need to be stirred well before use, and if cold, it is best to gently warm them, so the fat can be evenly distributed before use. Brands vary enormously, so you need to know what is good and what is not good. First, avoid low-fat options as they tend to have additives and stabilisers. Second, coconut milk and cream can have a variety of richness — the lighter milk, the richer cream and the fatty oil. I look for brands that don't have too much of the oil in them (quite a few of the organic ones do). How to tell? Place the tin in the fridge to firm up before opening — any oil will have set solid at the top. The cream will be very thick but certainly not hard, and often it is at the top of the tin (if there is no oil) or immediately underneath the hardened oil. The white and watery liquid below the cream is the milk.

Cultured yoghurt and cultured buttermilk

With a lovely acidic tang to them from lactic acid, cultured yoghurt and cultured buttermilk make exceptionally light baked goods, as the acid reacts with the alkaline in the baking powder or baking soda (bicarbonate of soda/sodium bicarbonate) to provide extra lift. That same acidity also provides a delicious tang to the result, and to my taste balances out sweetness beautifully.

They are very similar products except that they vary in the bacteria used to culture the milk, and also in their fat content. Of the two, cultured buttermilk is the lower in fat. Cultured buttermilk is essentially a by-product of making butter — cream is cultured, then made into butter, and the resulting 'buttermilk' can be used for baking.

Sadly, buttermilk today is most often low-fat milk, thickened with milk solids and then cultured — still low fat, but certainly higher in protein than the traditional

BAKING WITH DAIRY

I always use full-cream, non-homogenised, organic milk in my recipes.

*

When I call for cream, I am asking for thin (pouring or single) cream with 35 per cent butterfat.

*

When I call for yoghurt in a recipe, I mean one that has not been thickened with milk solids, which is the case for most thick or 'pot set' yoghurts.

*

When I call for labne, I am asking for real yoghurt that has had the whey dripped off it, and this process naturally thickens the yoghurt (see page 249).

REPLACING YOGHURT WITH CULTURED BUTTERMILK

Because cultured buttermilk is lower in fat than yoghurt, if replacing yoghurt with buttermilk, you will need to account for the lost fat in some way and vice versa.

version. I do think though that you need to be careful using cultured buttermilk — it's gorgeous, but its acidity can easily overwhelm some of the beautiful flavours that you have built into a cake or muffin.

No-fat and dairy-free milks

These are all best enriched with a fat of some kind — I prefer to use coconut milk if fat is needed.

Rice milk

This is a delicious and sweet-tasting milk for baking. Adding coconut milk will add much-needed fat to the rice milk, making it more usable in cake and dessert work. Remember all brands are not equal; find one that you like.

Almond milk

With a beautiful sweet taste, this is excellent for dessert work. Please, don't buy the tetra-packed almond milk. It is invariably made with almond essence, has been pasteurised and just won't produce the same result. Almond milk should always be homemade (see page 278 for a recipe).

Soy milk

Keep in mind that the quality (and that equals flavour) of the soy milk will reflect in the result. I only use Bonsoy, which is one of the more expensive brands but it is a superb soy milk and the purest available (in Australia).

REPLACING DAIRY MILK
I work on a volume of 170–185 ml (5½–6 fl oz/ ⅔–¾ cup) no-fat or dairy-free milk combined with 60–80 ml (2–2½ fl oz/ ¼–⅓ cup) of coconut milk equals 250 ml (9 fl oz/ 1 cup) of full-cream dairy milk.

Salt

....

Salt is the magic ingredient that enables the flavours in your baked goods to be tasted fully. Having said that, often when baking with organic, pure and whole ingredients, I prefer to let them speak for themselves, without the salt, and they do just fine, and I believe salt in baking is overly relied upon.

I use a Celtic sea salt in all my recipes. It is mineral-rich, so you only need very little to get a good result. Use judiciously, especially if using it together with true arrowroot (see page 21).

Some other useful ingredients

Nuts and seeds

These are useful in so many ways, as they add flavour and fat. When ground, they play many valuable roles in baking (especially gluten free):

* Adding extra fat, thus moistening the crumb, and softening heavy bran and germ.
* They literally get in between what is essentially the ground meal of a heavy grain and lighten the effect of using so much bran and germ.
* When using 'white' flours, with less bran and germ (especially starches such as arrowroot), ground nuts or seeds will stop the tendency for them to stick together (the glue effect). They can help to give texture and flakiness to the result.

With high unsaturated, mono-unsaturated or polyunsaturated fat content, nuts and seeds are very susceptible to damage from oxygen, light and heat. It is essential that nuts are not rancid. When buying from a bulk bin, taste one first, or if in a packet, I have been known to open the packet and taste before buying. I do not have a problem with this — organic seeds and nuts can be very expensive, and I expect to get a high quality, undamaged nut for that money. Nuts and seeds are best stored in the fridge.

Coconut: desiccated, shredded and flaked

Coconut in these forms is great to add flavour, texture and fat. Desiccated coconut, in particular, is also useful in the roles described for ground nuts and seeds (see above). Take care to source coconut that does not have added sulphur dioxide and is not rancid.

Dried fruit

With a rich and luscious flavour, I prefer organic, unsulphured dried fruit. It is much more expensive, so it pays to look after it — store in the fridge to protect against weevils (which love it).

Fresh fruit and vegetables

These are two of my favourite tools when baking with whole-grain flours. When they are chopped into small pieces or grated, they are invaluable in many roles in baking:

* The piece of fruit or vegetable takes up space in the batter providing what is essentially internal scaffolding. As the batter sets around it in the oven, the fruit softens, releasing moisture as an added bonus, and you are left with an air pocket.
* Very small or grated pieces can get in between the heavier bran and germ, lightening the result and providing a moist texture, especially in the mouth.
* They are brilliant in a low-fat cake, cookie or muffin as they provide moisture both from the juices that ooze out as they cook, and the soft, moist texture of the fruit itself when you bite into it.

Tools

for the wholefood kitchen

You certainly don't need a lot amount of expensive equipment to bake. Indeed, many of my most-loved cooking pieces I have bought for virtually nothing at second-hand shops. However, good equipment does make a huge difference to your results — both in ease of preparation, and in the oven. What follows is a basic equipment list, and the things I like to use.

Bowls

I can't have enough bowls — I love them, preferably china, and the prettier the better. When creaming butter and sugar or whipping eggs, a bowl that is smaller yet slightly deeper is more desirable than one that is large and wide. This helps to condense the ingredients and it allows the beater to get deep enough into the ingredients to do its thing, thus producing a better result.

Stand mixer and hand-held electric beaters

I have both, but if I had to choose, I'd probably go for the stand mixer as it gives you such a great result and you can walk away while it keeps doing the job. Small hand-held electric beaters are so easy to whip out for a little job, but a wooden spoon can easily step in to cream butter and sugar (as our mothers and grandmothers used to use) and a whisk can quickly whisk some egg whites or cream.

Wooden spoons, spatulas and whisks

Wooden spoons are not created equal, and good ones will be your favourites for years. A good one for baking — especially for creaming a butter and sugar mix — will be fairly thick, and have a flattish bottom edge, giving you more surface area for the spoon to contact the bowl. For stirring pastry creams and curds as they come to the boil, you need a wooden spoon that has no curve — simply straight across the bottom edge, which, again, will give you a large amount of surface contact as you stir.

I like the silicone spatulas that are slightly cupped — they are great for scraping down the sides of a bowl, keeping the mix together and getting it out of the bowl, and I keep a variety of sizes.

A whisk is a very personal thing, and it should fit comfortably in your hand. I use stainless steel (never non-stick) whisks for whipping through a bowl of dry ingredients to disperse and lighten, for whipping and creaming, but also for folding. I like a balloon whisk and one that is less of a balloon and more elongated. I like them slightly flexible, with thinner wires and not too stiff.

Sieves

You need a range of good-quality sieves, and I prefer these instead of the more traditional sifter. There is nothing wrong with the traditional sifter, it's just that I prefer the simple sieve and use it to sieve flours and strain all sorts of things. Look for high-quality stainless steel, in a fine and medium mesh — they will cost more but last forever, and I am a big fan of the Rosle brand (available in Australia). It's handy to have a medium-sized sieve for larger bowls, and a smaller one for smaller bowls. I tend to keep my eye out for sieves (together with natural food colouring) when I travel.

Plastic and metal dough scrapers

These are much larger than a spatula, and fit comfortably in a hand, with a thin edge and large surface area. I use plastic and metal ones for different purposes. Plastic dough scrapers often have a rounded edge and are more malleable, making them invaluable for folding egg whites into a cream base, or whipped cream into a pastry cream base, or turning batter or mix out of a bowl.

The metal dough scraper, with its straighter harder edge, is your basic tool for smoothing out the icing on the sides of a cake. Mine is stainless steel with a wooden (but it could be plastic) handle, 15 cm x 11 cm (6 x 4¼ inches), with square edges.

Both types of scrapers are great for cleaning mess on benches after pastry making.

Scales

A good set of scales is incredibly important — it is essential to know what some of your ingredients (especially flour) actually weigh. Generally, you will get what you pay for. I prefer scales that have both a metric and imperial option, and a low graduation — that is, it weighs in increments of 1 or 2 grams ($\frac{1}{32}$ or $\frac{1}{16}$ oz) — for precise measurements. Mine weighs in 1-gram increments. It should tare easily — that is, you can reset the weight to zero, and weigh more ingredients. Some now convert to measure liquids too, but I'm not fussed about that, as I prefer my liquid measures in cups.

Measuring cups: dry and liquid

These are not all equal — a cup measure varies throughout the world, so you need to check the numbers on the cup.

An Australian cup measures 250 ml (9 fl oz), an American cup is 237 ml (8 fl oz) and an English cup is 285 ml (10 fl oz). A set generally contains a 1 cup, ½ cup, ⅓ cup and ¼ cup measures, with lines marked inside also.

A liquid-measure cup is usually glass, with graduated lines to show measurements in millilitres and fluid ounces. It's incredibly handy to have a 1-cup measure and 2-cup measure for measuring liquids. When measuring a liquid, you should have your eye level with the measure — it can be very deceptive looking down on it.

You need to know what cup measure you are using, and also what the cup (and tablespoon) measure used by the particular cookbook or food magazine you are reading is.

Measuring spoons

As with measuring cups, you need to know what tablespoon measure you are dealing with. An Australian and New Zealand tablespoon is 20 ml (4 teaspoons), an English tablespoon can commonly be 20 ml or 15 ml (3 teaspoons), and an American tablespoon is 15 ml. They are essential for good baking. Also check your teaspoon is actually 5 ml. I have found some to range from 6.5–7 ml, which will impact measurements for baking powder, baking soda (bicarbonate of soda) and agar powder.

For grating and zesting

Any stainless steel grater will do, but a microplane for grating and zester for citrus will make life much easier, and give you beautiful zest.

Pastry cutter

A pastry cutter is a tool that enables you to cut the butter into the flour, keeping your hands out of the mix, thus not melting the butter. Look for sturdy stainless steel ones over the wooden handled versions with flimsy wire loops, which won't stand up to cutting cold butter.

Rolling pin

A good rolling pin is a thing of wonder. Mine is a long and thin copper one, with small wooden handles, measuring 34 cm (13½ inches) of rolling width. I love it to bits. It is a special edition by Tala (who make fabulous cooking tools) and a gift from a friend. I really love that I can put it in the freezer on a hot summer day, and the chilling makes a huge difference. Personally, I prefer heavy, long and thin pins to light and thick; if I wasn't lucky enough to have mine, I would choose a similar length and thickness of wood, without handles. I wouldn't choose marble as it is just far too heavy. Mind you, in a pinch, I've used bottles — with or without wine in them — and they have been fine also.

Palette knives

These help you keep your hands off the pastry when rolling, help to turn it, and they have about 100 million other handy uses in the kitchen, especially for cake decorating. I keep a range of sizes. I love palette knives, and prefer a blade that is not too flexible.

I keep a 10 cm (4 inch) blade (which I rarely use), a 15 cm (6 inch) blade (I use this for cake decorating) and a 25 cm (10 inch) blade for general purpose. I have straight and offset palette knives in these lengths. I love my 15 cm palette knife — both versions, straight and offset. I use these for placing icing on the side of a cake, and on top of a smaller cake. The smaller 10 cm offset is perfect for putting icing on cupcakes.

Cake and muffin tins

I prefer to cook in good old-fashioned tin or enamel-coated tin, rather than non-stick. It has been my experience that most non-stick tins stick, and I don't like my food touching the non-stick surface. You will get what you pay for, and I prefer high-quality, heavier tin, especially some of the French ones. Always look after your tin — do not scrub it once used, but soak it and gently scrub with a toothbrush if needed, and place in a warm oven to dry fully before storing. When you live by the sea, the salt can rust tin, and you might like to coat them with a little oil before storing. Stainless steel is also a great option — especially for springform cake tins. Coming onto the market is enamel coated (usually black) tin, and I am a big fan of this.

Cake tins and baking trays are another thing I shop for when travelling — I'm not going to tell you all the shapes you should have. Choose what works for you, but you will get what you pay for, so look for good-quality ones. My experience has been heavier is better.

Tart tins

These should be high-quality tin. These are generally French and are more heavy-duty, which will stop them warping in a hot oven. High-quality tart tins usually come in the following depths:

* 2.5 cm (1 inch), which is excellent for a shallow tart with a lesser amount of filling, for example, pastry cream and fresh fruit.
* 3.5 cm (1¼ inch), which is a good all-purpose depth for tarts and quiches.
* 5 cm (2 cm), which is often referred to as a deep tart tin.

Commonly, however, things vary — very often the smaller tart tins, such as a 20 cm (8 inch) diameter, measures about 2.5 cm (1 inch) deep, a 24 cm (9½ inch) about 2.5–3 cm (1–1¼ inches) deep, and the larger 26 cm (10½ inches) running to 3.5 cm (1¼ inches) deep. As a general rule, the shallower tins of about 2.5 cm (1 inch) are best for tarts, and the deeper 3–3.5 cm (1¼ inch) ones are better for pies.

Enamel-coated tin camping plates also make excellent pie tins — and they are cheap. They typically measure 17 cm (6½ inches) across the base diameter and about 21.5 cm (8¼ inches) diameter at the top by 3.5 cm (1¼ inches) deep with a 1.5 cm (⅝ inch) lip, which is fabulous for making a fancy crust on a pie.

Baking trays

As with all my bakeware, I try not to use non-stick and look for heavy-duty tin, stainless steel or enamel-coated tin. Cheap and thin trays will generally warp in the oven. I like some body and weight to my trays, and I believe they give a better result. Especially good is the tray that comes with your oven — heavy, enamel-coated tin. I am always on the lookout for baking trays at second-hand shops. I do not like the 'cushioned' baking trays either.

Silicone bakeware and silpats

I am not a fan of these at all. I don't like the way they bake, and I don't trust them. If you must use these, choose the high-quality French silicone-ware, which is very expensive, not the cheap (often Chinese) knock-offs.

A word about silpats (baking mats) and the 'need' to use these: I never have, and truly don't think they are necessary. In some instances — making tuiles (which I actually never do) — they may be handy, but I have survived for many years without them.

Rotating cake stand

These make cake decorating all so much easier. I prefer the stainless steel, heavier-duty ones to the plastic — you get what you pay for.

Piping bags and nozzles

It's very sad to see the deterioration in the quality of baking equipment these days, and one of the areas in which it is most evident is in piping (icing) bags and nozzles or tips. Many of those available in a general kitchen store are cheap (the steel in the tip will bend out of shape) and the bags are totally unsuitable to make the job easy.

Firstly, for seriously decorative nozzles (making leaves/flowers/patterns), I prefer those that do not have a screw band on them, but rather slip into a coupling. This enables you to change the tip easily mid-piping, should you so wish. I also keep simple plastic star and plain nozzles. They are cheap enough to get in sets, but it is the size 5 (5 mm/¼ inch) and size 11 (11 mm/½ inch) that I use all the time.

Secondly, the bag — I would recommend going to a wholesale business that sells to professionals and buy a high-quality bag preferably made of nylon because it is hardy and cleans well. A good all-purpose size is size 30 (30 cm/12 inches), and this size fits the aforementioned plastic star and plain nozzles perfectly, but for more decorative nozzles with a coupling, I go to a smaller bag, size 23–25 (23–25 cm/9–10 inches). For general work, you need enough room in your bag to fit the icing down the bottom near the nozzle, to be able to twist the bag, then you will need enough room left-over to hold it. Smaller bags are good only for very, very small jobs.

If you wash the bags and nozzles well after use and dry immediately with a towel and then leave to air dry, before putting them away, they will last you for a long time.

The oven

This is your defining piece of equipment and it will affect everything you bake. All ovens are different, even if they are the same make and model. There is no such thing as setting a temperature and thinking that all will be well.

For a conventional oven, an average temperature for baking is considered to be a moderate oven, 180°C (350°F/Gas 4). Here, because hot air rises, it's best to arrange the oven rack halfway or a little higher in the oven and centre your cake on the rack. Whereas in a fan-forced (convection) oven, the heat is moved around, so you will need to reduce the temperature by 15–25°C (35°F). As a general rule, 165°C (320°F/Gas 2–3) fan-forced will give you a moderate oven.

Keep in mind that fans vary too — my favourite oven at home (I have two) for baking is an old, cheap, white electric fan-forced, with two fan settings — low and high. I loved the low fan setting, which cooked cakes beautifully at 165°C but it eventually broke (and could not be fixed as it was so old and the parts weren't available anymore). After that sad day, my oven would only set to high and I have had to lower the oven temperature to 150°C (300°F/Gas 2) for the same cake and time. My much more expensive, flashier stainless steel oven has only one fan setting — fast — and I need to set the oven temperature to about 147°C (300°F/Gas 2) for the same cake and time.

Consider also any hot spots in your oven. Mine at home is hotter on the right-hand side, and I often have to position my cake well to the left (for a lighter cake when I do not wish to open the oven halfway through the cooking time) or turn it during the cooking process.

Many people use an oven thermometer to measure the actual temperature of their oven, and this is a good tool. It does not, however, in any way replace your instincts or your eyes. A good measure for oven temperature is that a muffin recipe should take 30–35 minutes to cook.

Becoming a baker
— instinct and technique

Baking is so much more than simply following a recipe — it's about understanding the many variables that affect and impact on what you are wanting to achieve. Baking is not black and white — it includes the entire spectrum of grey in between. My daughter is an excellent and adventurous cook, but a bit hesitant when it comes to baking. When I ask her why, I discovered it's because of all those mystical grey tones that she has not yet had time to experience and learn. It is these that make baking successful. The following tips are a combination of instinct and technique, and it is mastering these over many other things that will make you a successful baker.

Know your oven

Other than a good understanding of technique this is the most important rule of baking. You have to get to know your oven and form a relationship with it — you must learn how it cooks and rely on this. When faced with a new oven, you must keep your eyes on your food (through the glass door) every 10 minutes or so to see what is going on and adjust the temperature if necessary. Don't think I always get it right either — at home yes, but recently when doing a class and dealing with a new (to me) oven, biscuits were burnt as I was so busy I couldn't keep my eyes on the oven.

Finally, always preheat your oven. Uncooked pastry or cake batter must go into an oven at temperature, and not to do so is a major cause of failure in many situations.

Read through the recipe before you start and work in sequence

Recipes are written describing a sequence — this is especially important in baking. Baking is primarily about trapping air or creating gas to raise a cake or biscuit, and once done, you can't simply let it sit there while you line your tin or sieve your flour. Get in the habit of reading through the recipe before you begin, and work in the sequence suggested.

Line your tin

As noted in the tools section, I'm not a fan of non-stick — and I find they always stick regardless. Lining your tin protects your cake from sticking and allows it to come out easily. I was brought up with three methods:

* Buttering the tin and then dusting it with a fine layer of flour.
* Rubbing butter on brown paper and cutting the paper to fit the tin.
* Saving the foil wrappers of blocks of butter (lined with waxed paper) and cutting them to fit the tin.

We now turn to a non-stick baking paper to line our tins, but like so many things these days, this can be fraught with issues also. You want to look for a baking paper actually coated with silicone rather than quilon. The main concern regarding quilon is that it is a chemical containing the heavy metal chrome, which can become toxic when baked, but because it is a cheaper option, it is more commonly used. Mind you, silicone also has its issues, as often organotins are used with silicone, and again concerns have been raised about the safety of these. I choose to use a silicone-coated, high-grade, unbleached, biodegradable baking paper (If You Care brand), which can be used a number of times.

How to line a round cake tin

I like to line the base and side of a round cake tin using the one sheet of baking paper. This method works best for tins up to 24 cm (19½ inch) in diameter but is adequate for 26–28 cm (10½–11¼ inch) diameter round tins too — you just lose a bit of coverage on the sides.

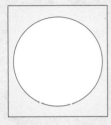

Take a sheet of baking paper that is long enough to cover the base and go up the side of the tin.

Fold the sheet of baking paper in half, then quarters, then a triangle.

Place the point of the triangle in the centre of the tin and press into the tin base, making a visible crease where it meets the tin edge. Then mark the paper with a pencil where it lines up with the top edge of the tin.

Remove the triangle from the tin and cut along the top edge mark.

Make two cuts down to the crease that you made with your finger.

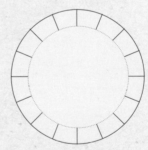

Open up the triangle to reveal a circle. Lightly grease the tin, then line with the circle of baking paper, pressing the sides into the edge.

Cooking your cake

Cooking times in a recipe are always a guideline — your baked good is a bit like your baby, you need to keep an eye on it. Check on your cake after about 15 minutes or so, and at frequent intervals by looking at it through the oven door (turn the light on). Things happen, it won't be exactly the same twice, even a slight difference in ingredients (for example, weight of flour) can affect how it cooks that day. If your oven is too hot, your cake will cook on the outside before the inside is done. You can tell a lot of things by simply looking at it through the door — if the top darkens very quickly or if the edges are well cooked but the centre very wet, you may need to lower your oven temperature a bit. After about two-thirds of the expected cooking time, you can open the oven door ever so slightly (I call it a stealth move) and very gently touch the centre with your fingertips to feel how it's going. If it's very uncooked, but the top or edges are very dark, you will need to reduce the oven temperature.

How to tell when your cake is cooked

Cakes made with less-refined ingredients are much more dense than traditional cakes, and some, especially those with a large amount of wholemeal grain or fruit, can take a long time to cook, so moderate and steady is better than fast and hot. Never hurry a cake — that is, raise the oven temperature. Larger cakes may need to cook at a lower temperature even still. Learning to tell when a cake is cooked is something that takes a little experience, but in general:

* When you look at the cake, it should be evenly coloured, and depending on the flour, a light golden colour.
* When you touch the centre of the cake with your fingertips, it should be slightly springy, but sturdy underneath. You are using just the tip of your fingers to feel and 'listen' to the cake.
* When inserting a cake tester or skewer in the centre of the cake, it should come out clean, and the cake should pull away ever so slightly from the sides of the tin.
* As the cake cooks, it may crack — even slightly — and this crack should be evident in the centre of the cake as well as the edges. The heavier the cake, the smaller and lighter these cracks will be.
* Traditional cakes made with large amounts of fat tend to be glossy when cooked, so as you reduce the amount of fat, you can expect a reduction in the amount of sheen.
* The finished colour or tone of the top of the cake should be uniform. In low-fat and very low fat cakes, this will appear as a drying out of colour and uncooked batter looks wetter. In gluten-free cakes, this drying out is often accompanied by a noticeable sandiness in appearance.

Measuring a cup of flour

Measuring by weight is the most accurate way to measure flour. What 1 cup of flour may actually weigh depends on a lot of things — where and how it was grown, or how it has been milled, or you may have packed your cup too densely, or left air pockets in your cup measurement. It's one of the main reasons recipes often don't work as you'd like them to. If you end up with too little flour in the cup, you won't have quite the structure you were wanting, and if too much, the result will be too dry. *It's far easier and more consistent to weigh*, but there will be times you won't be able to do that — and goodness knows our mothers and grandmothers never did and still made beautiful cakes.

Measuring a cup of flour is a skill — make sure the flour is in a wide-mouth container, such as a cloth bag, canister or paper bag, that you can fit the cup into easily. The flour should not be compacted, but soft — if my flour is in a bag, I tend to give it a little shake. If it's in a canister, you can loosely aerate it a little with a fork. Using your measuring cup, scoop up enough flour to fill the cup to overflowing — that is, heaped. Do not press on the flour with your hand or a knife to pack it down. Using a butter knife, sweep straight across the top of the cup, levelling it. When I do measure by cup, I know that I will then have to also rely on the look of the batter and the consistency and be prepared to adjust it as needed.

To sieve or not to sieve

Sieving is a method of aerating flour (and often cocoa) and for breaking up any lumps in it. It is also a method of blending some dry ingredients together — for example, flour, baking powder and/or baking soda (bicarbonate of soda). I certainly don't sieve as a consistent rule. I don't sieve when:

* I have fruit in the cake — which most of my everyday cakes do.
* I use wholemeal flours.

I do sieve when:

* The crumb is the only show in town — that is, there is no fruit to help aeration.
* Baking soda (bicarbonate of soda) is used, I sieve it into the dry ingredients, as it is often clumpy and must be finely and evenly distributed.
* Cocoa powder is used, as it is often very clumpy.

When I don't sieve, I do still break up the flours and aerate them by whisking. Add all your dry ingredients to the bowl — usually flours, raising agent, dry sweetener or coconut — then whisk through to break up any lumps and to combine the ingredients.

Folding

This is a gentle method of mixing ingredients together, and is often used when mixing a heavier ingredient into a lighter one (for example, folding flour into whipped eggs and sugar), or when mixing a light, airy ingredient into a heavy one (for example, folding whipped egg whites into a batter). I use different tools to fold — preferring a whisk for folding flour into whipped eggs and sugar, and a plastic dough scraper for folding egg whites into a cream base, or whipped cream into a pastry cream base.

Folding is best done in a large bowl with good surface area that gives you room to manoeuvre. The action of folding is a gentle movement around the edge of the bowl and angling downward to the bottom. As you reach the bottom (and pick up some of the flour that tends to sink down), you are now angling up and folding this over the mix. It is also important to start with a small amount of the mixture being added — a small amount of whipped egg white to a batter (this will help to loosen what is a heavy mixture, before continuing on), or a small amount of flour being added to whipped eggs and sugar. The goal of folding is to keep the air that you have gone to a lot of trouble to trap intact.

Beating to the ribbon

This term is used to describe the point at which eggs and sugar beaten together are ready. When you lift the whisk, the batter should fall and fold onto itself 'as a ribbon' and hold that ribbon shape for about 10 seconds before dissolving. Usually by the time it has reached this stage, it has also tripled in volume.

Turning your batter into the cake tin

Most often, you have gone to a lot of trouble to incorporate air into your batter and you need to take care when turning that batter into the cake tin. Rather than spooning your batter into the tin, it's better to tip the bowl and use a spatula to encourage it to flow into the tin — especially when you are relying on air from whipped eggs and sugar, or creamed butter and sugar, with or without the addition of eggs.

Factors that affect crumb

WHAT IS CRUMB?
Crumb is how we describe the texture of baked goods — the better the crumb, the better it will feel in the mouth.

Air and crumb

Basically, the more air you can incorporate into the batter, the lighter textured (and more delicious) will be the crumb and thus the result. In addition to chemical leavening (see page 23) we can incorporate air into a batter in the following ways.

Adding eggs

Because eggs have a degree of moisture in them, they will, simply by beating with a fork and adding to the batter, provide more rise as the small amount of water in them turns to steam. This is more applicable in a muffin or cake — you can easily mimic this action in a biscuit (that doesn't require too much rise) with a touch of baking powder.

Creaming butter and sugar or creaming coconut oil and sugar

As an electric beater moves through softened butter and sugar granules, a drag is created through the butter — this incorporates air into the butter. The mix is noticeably lighter and creamy in texture. We can do this by hand using a wooden spoon, or with the flat paddle attachment of a stand mixer. The longer the creaming time, the more air you can incorporate into the resulting batter and it pays to take this time to beat volume into the butter and sugar if you are adding eggs, as they will curdle less. As this happens, the butter will lighten in colour considerably as air is incorporated. Any granulated sugar works well — including rapadura, palm and maple sugar. It's important to keep in mind that regular refined white sugars are a much finer crystal than rapadura, so rapadura will never dissolve as completely as refined sugars when being creamed into butter.

You can also cream butter and maple syrup and still get some excellent air, but it won't be quite as good. When you cream coconut oil, you must first ensure you have the right texture of coconut oil. Coconut oil is best for creaming when it is a soft (not quite set hard), gooey consistency, and will be a cloudy white colour. Because it is pure fat and because of the way it responds to temperature, coconut oil can go from being rock hard (when very cold) to liquid (when too hot) very quickly. If your coconut oil is too liquid, place it in the fridge to firm up — not the freezer — and leave until it is whitish and softly set. If in the dead of winter, it is too hard, I would suggest you melt it and then do the same thing — it's very difficult to thaw it out to the correct consistency as you end up with some bits melted on the outside and some rock hard on the inside. Keep in mind you will always get a better result with butter, as it retains a far more stable consistency for beating than coconut oil.

Adding egg/s to the creamed butter and sugar

By simply adding an egg or eggs to creamed butter and sugar (or coconut oil and sugar) we add more opportunity for rising. But, by beating it and creaming it with the butter and sugar well, we can trap even more air, resulting in a light and delicious crumb. Once the butter and sugar are 'creamed' (and maximum air is incorporated), eggs are added, one at a time. It can be tricky adding egg/s into creamed butter and sugar. Firstly, eggs contain some water, and you are emulsifying this water into the butter mix. It is very important that you only add one egg at a time, and beat the mixture until the egg is fully incorporated.

Secondly, eggs are best at body temperature, if they are too cold, they (along with any cold air flowing over the mixture as you beat) can cause the butter to harden, and appear 'curdled'. You don't want this to happen, as you will lose the air you have worked so hard to include. This curdling effect is more pronounced in winter, and I would recommend if it does happen, that you wrap a warm cloth around the bowl

Any butter for creaming should be soft — that is the consistency of face cream.

Coconut oil is best for creaming when it is a soft (not quite set hard), a gooey consistency, and will be a cloudy white colour.

(and as it cools, re-warm it), make sure your eggs are slightly warm (holding them in your hand works well), and if all else fails, sit the bowl in a bath of warm water, just long enough to soften — not melt — the butter, then take it out and continue beating. As the ratio of egg to butter increases, this curdling effect is more marked, and adding a small amount — 1 tablespoon — of the flour mix halfway through will help.

Whipping eggs and sugar

Using a hand-held whisk or whisk attachment fitted to your stand mixer, whisk the whole eggs and sugar until thick and to the ribbon (see page 52). A fine crystal sugar works best here — I use a golden caster (superfine) sugar, but I've also had good results with rapadura sugar.

Whipping egg whites and folding into a batter

Simply by whipping egg whites and folding them into a batter, we can include more air, and produce a lighter texture and crumb. It's important to use a dry, spotlessly clean, and fat-free bowl to whip egg whites so they reach their full volume potential. And remember that warm or room temperature egg whites will beat better than cold ones.

You can also separate the eggs in a mix, and beat the egg yolks and sugar until thick and creamy, then fold in the whipped egg whites. This is an especially handy trick in many a gluten-free cake.

Fat and crumb

Fat helps to condition and moisten the flour, especially the heavy bran and germ (and sometimes hull) you find in many unrefined flours. You see this commonly in many commercial wholemeal 'healthy' cake or bar options that soak the paper bag with fat (usually oil). The fat from eggs and butter will give a superior crumb, oil is good, and while you can use coconut oil, it will give you a more crumbly and constricted crumb when the baked good has cooled or is cold (see Coconut Oil in Fats for Baking on page 32). While my example of the commercial cake is extreme, as your percentage of wholemeal flour increases, so should your consideration of the amount of fat used. If you want high percentages of wholemeal flours and low fat at the same time, you will need to consider how to incorporate moisture into the finished cake. By far the best option is to consider the amount of fruit used — it will provide moisture, flavour and sweetness. You can chop, grate or stew the fruit. You may also need to include more liquid into the batter. As a general rule, the higher the percentage of wholemeal flour used, the more liquid needs to be added — this is because they absorb lots more moisture than a simple unbleached, starchy white flour.

But, you also need to consider the flour you are using: spelt and oat are more water soluble, and oats will add their own moisture to the cake, so it can be easy to add too much; brown rice, amaranth and quinoa are very heavy and absorb a lot; and starches require very little.

Once the batter has come together, it's best to let it sit for a couple of minutes — it will thicken as it absorbs the liquid — and then add more liquid if necessary. The finished batter needs to be slightly 'wetter' than normal, especially if it is a heavy grain. This is not something that you pick up immediately — too wet and the finished cake can rise and collapse as it cools; too stiff and the cake will be dry. It is here you need to take notice of the finished batter and equate that to the result. A recipe is a guideline only because every time you bake factors beyond your control come into play. This is entirely normal and everyone does 'get it' — it just takes a little time and practice.

In pastry or quick 'biscuits', such as scones, rubbing a fat into the flour helps to coat the flour and thus protects it from gluten development when liquid is added, giving you a lighter crumb. This technique can also be used to great success when baking with protein-rich wholemeal wheat flour, where the butter is creamed into the flour and dry ingredients. This technique, pioneered by the amazing baker Rose Levy Beranbaum results in an exceptionally soft and delicious crumb, and I use it in the Pretty Buttermilk Cake (see page 172).

Moisture and crumb

The right amount of liquid, especially in a muffin and cake, also helps to determine the crumb. If you have too much liquid, the cake will rise in the oven and collapse at the sides and centre as it cools. Commonly, there will also be a dense and stodgy section at the base of the cake. If there is too little liquid, rising will be compromised by the weight of the flour, and, again, you can end up with that dense, stodgy cake at the base.

Are you using fruit? If so, the amount and water content of the fruit you use also needs to be taken into account. The amount of watery juices, from berries, plums, peaches, et cetera, that will weep into the batter as it cooks is far greater than apples, pears or bananas.

As a general rule, a batter made with less-refined flours should not be at all clumpy, moist but not at all runny and a wooden spoon should be able to move through the batter without too much resistance. If it is a thick stodgy gloop in the bowl, it will be far too thick and heavy for any rising to take place, and you, as a baker, may choose to add extra yoghurt or milk to the batter to loosen it to a better consistency — no matter what the recipe might say.

Also keep in mind that generally gluten-free batters with a high percentage of heavier flours (such as brown rice, quinoa, amaranth, et cetera) should be very moist, slightly runny even, as the flours will continue to suck up moisture, even when in the oven.

Mixing, beating and crumb

Get in the habit of not overbeating or overworking your gluten cake batters or pastry as you will develop the gluten and end up with a tough crumb. Try to stir with a light touch, and make each stir count. When adding liquid, try to assess how it's looking and think ahead — don't keep stirring it if it's obviously sucking up all the milk, and is a thick, clumpy mix; add more milk as needed.

STORING YOUR BAKED GOODS

All baked goods are best stored in an airtight container in a cool, dark place. As many of the recipes in this book include large amounts of fresh fruits or vegetables, when the weather is warmer, it is best to store these in the fridge, otherwise they will go mouldy very quickly. The same is true for biscuits and cakes based on butter. Frosted plain crumb cakes can happily sit out at room temperature, covered with a cake dome, and biscuits in a tin, but when the weather is hot, the butter can quickly become rancid, leaving a nasty flavour. The fridge will be better, but remember to leave them to sit a little time at room temperature before eating for the cold butter to relax and deliciousness to be fully realised.

Specialised baking
— *dairy free, egg free and gluten free*

No matter what your restriction, there is always a wholesome, natural and real alternative. What matters is that you have a good understanding of ingredients and technique. Knowing how ingredients work is important so you can manipulate that behaviour to gain the desired results. Being lateral in your approach is essential, and knowing how to use technique will help to deliver those results — always nourishing deliciousness.

Dairy-free and/or egg-free baking

Dairy milk, yoghurt and cultured buttermilk are easy ingredients to replace, but without the large range of opportunities to include air provided by butter and/or eggs, we need to consider how to achieve a delicious, light crumb. This is especially true if you cannot use either butter or eggs. Biscuits and pastry are easy as they don't rely on so much air for their texture, and even just a pinch of baking powder can do wonderful things. (For a detailed discussion on dairy-free pastry, see page 224.) It's muffins and cakes you need to consider — you can only keep adding so much chemical leavening until you end up with a nasty aftertaste, and it takes less than you think. There are many ways to create air without butter and eggs, and in this section we explore some of the best ways.

Replacing butter

I would never recommend using margarine, or any of the numerous vegan oil-based shortenings. No matter how 'natural' and 'healthy' they sound, they are highly processed products and the fats are very damaged. I would recommend the following replacements.

Ghee versus butter

Butter is made up of fat, milk protein and water, and in most cases it is the milk protein (casein) that is not tolerated. When you remove the water and milk solids, you are left with the pure butterfat — commonly known as ghee. I would always recommend ghee as your first option as it is the most nourishing and will give you the best result — you don't necessarily need to immediately choose coconut oil or oil. Remember to reduce the amount of ghee by 20 per cent as it is pure fat when replacing the butter and to add that 20 per cent back in liquid (see Replacing Butter, Oil or Ghee in Fats for Baking on page 32). If you can tolerate egg, add this to the creamed ghee and sugar and beat well.

Coconut oil

Choosing coconut oil allows you to incorporate air through creaming the solid oil with sugar (see page 53). If you can tolerate egg, add this to the creamed oil and sugar and beat well.

Oils

You can still get great results using oils, and if eggs are allowed, you can build an enormous amount of air into a cake by creaming whole eggs and sugar, or egg yolks and sugar, then whipping the egg whites to fold through. When eggs are not tolerated, your technique changes from a wet to dry one — essentially stir together and mix. Delving into the Box of Tricks (see page 59) now becomes very important.

Replacing milk, yoghurt and cultured buttermilk

Dairy milk can easily be replaced with rice or almond milk mixed with a percentage of coconut milk to add fat and body (see No-fat and Dairy-free Milks on page 36).

Replacing yoghurt and cultured buttermilk is also very easy. Simply add 2 teaspoons of vinegar (I like apple cider vinegar) to 250 ml (9 fl oz/1 cup) rice or almond milk and leave it to sit for a few minutes.

Replacing eggs

While the crumb of an eggless cake will never be the same, it can still be very good. For a detailed discussion on egg replacement see page 34.

Consider technique

Technique can be invaluable in helping to provide air to the crumb. Other than the suggestions in the Box of Tricks (see page 59), if you are able to cream sugar and fat, do so, and if you are able to use eggs, make full use of the opportunity to whip sugar and eggs together to the ribbon (see Beating to the Ribbon on page 52).

Box of tricks

In addition to the previous tips, I use a variety of ingredients to help raise, lighten, and add extra fat and interest to the crumb.

Fruit

Chopped or grated fruit is invaluable in dairy-free and egg-free baking. The fruit takes up space in the batter providing what is, essentially, internal scaffolding. As the batter sets around it in the oven, the fruit softens, releasing moisture as an added bonus, and you are left with a beautiful air pocket. (Read more about this in Fresh Fruit and Vegetables in Some Other Useful Ingredients on page 37.)

Acid

You can increase the leavening power of the baking powder in your batter by adding a little vinegar or by using something that is naturally acidic, such as yoghurt, cultured buttermilk or kefir milk (a cultured milk; see page 276). This extra acid reacts with the alkaline in the baking powder, creating a little more carbon dioxide to help lift.

Apple cider vinegar is an especially useful ingredient — a little helps to tenderise the gluten in the flour, producing a more tender crumb. I work on 2 teaspoons of vinegar per 250 ml (9 fl oz/1 cup) of milk.

Finely chopped nuts and desiccated coconut

While these two ingredients don't technically lift the batter in any way, they do help to separate the flour and give a less dense result. They are especially useful in plain cakes made from 'whiter' flours and starches, such as arrowroot, where they can mitigate the tendency of the flours to stick together — that is, the glue effect. They both provide fat, flavour and texture to a crumb, and that fat is especially useful when using more wholemeal flours, as the fat can get between the bran and germ, resulting in a moister and more luscious mouthfeel.

Gluten-free baking

There is a contemporary view that gluten-free baking is healthier baking. I don't agree with this, as I don't believe that wheat and other gluten grains are necessarily unhealthy, and many of the gluten-free baked goods on offer are made with highly refined ingredients. Gluten free certainly does not equal healthy and wholesome.

There are many issues in true gluten-free baking — you cannot simply replace gluten ingredients with gluten-free ingredients and expect a similar result. Real gluten-free grain flours are often heavier (especially brown rice flour — 160 g/5¾ oz to a cup versus 145 g/5¼ oz for wholemeal spelt flour); have an assertive flavour (especially quinoa, buckwheat and amaranth); starches used to soften the crumb can also end up giving a gummy result and a cake that collapses (as there is too little structure); and finally the lack of gluten makes rising tricky. The less surface area and height there is, as in biscuits and pastry, the easier it is to replace gluten grains.

When you are choosing a gluten-free flour to replace the gluten flour, it is best to use a variety of flours (with some starches) to make up your total quantity — forming the flavour and crumb profile that you are after. A good everyday example, with a mild flavour and a crumb profile that is sturdy yet light, is the composition of the 2 cups flour for the Classic Gluten-Free Muffin (see page 124). Of the 2 cups, 1¼ is made up of my favourite gluten-free base flour, brown rice flour, which has a mild and delicious flavour. Quinoa (or amaranth) flour makes up another ¼ cup, but no more than that as it is too high a protein (but this will add structure to the muffin) and too strong a flavour. A ¼ cup true arrowroot will lighten the flour (while still providing mineral nourishment) and help to bind the flours together. Finally the ¼ cup desiccated coconut (or finely ground nuts) will get in between the heavy brown rice and quinoa flour, adding delicious flavour and fattiness. When you look at the Pumpkin, Cheddar, Rosemary and Sage Gluten-Free Scones (see page 76), the flavour profile has more of the stronger flavoured grains (quinoa — or amaranth — and buckwheat respectively), which is easily overcome with the pumpkin, cheese and herbs. It would (and indeed does) taste terrible as a sweet muffin mix. True arrowroot provides lightness (a softer crumb), helps to bind the flours together, and the addition of cornflour (rather than more arrowroot) provides moistness to the high percentage of whole grain flours (especially the ½ cup quinoa flour) as well as further lightening the crumb.

As discussed in Gluten-free Flours for Baking (see page 18) I don't like to use gums to stick my gluten-free baked goods together or mimic gluten to aid the rise — you can get great results without gums. The following are the things you need to consider.

Binding it together

Eggs are one of the best ways to bind a gluten-free mix together — you can get away with a lot when you use an egg or two. If you can't use egg, egg replacer will give you the added bonus of a light and fluffy result, or for a purer approach, chia or flaxseeds will help also (read more about these in Replacing Eggs on page 34).

Raising it

Without gluten or a gum to trap the gas produced by baking powder, or baking soda (bicarbonate of soda) and acid, it can be very tempting to just keep adding more of the chemical leavening to aid rise. But, as discussed in Dairy-free and/or Egg-free Baking (see page 58), you can only keep adding so much before you get a nasty aftertaste.

Technique can be a wonderful tool to use instead. Creaming butter and sugar and adding eggs, or if butter cannot be used, creaming coconut oil and sugar (see Fats for Baking on page 31), or whipping eggs and sugar to the ribbon (see page 52) are all excellent tricks. It is when you cannot use eggs that things become trickier, and I turn to the same Box of Tricks (see page 59) that I use in dairy-free and/or egg-free baking.

But equally important to consider is that in some very restricted instances (gluten, dairy and egg free) you may be wiser to be lateral in your thinking — something small with less surface area, such as a muffin or cupcake, may be a better option than a cake.

Adding extra protein

It also pays to remember that protein helps to give structure to a cake — when present, the protein in gluten-free flours is very different to that of wheat, spelt, barley and oats, and starches have none. Eggs are absolutely invaluable in this role, and incorporating extra egg whites (whipped) gives the added advantage of extra air. High-protein amaranth and quinoa, and ground nuts are also good in this capacity.

Recipes

Scones

and drop scones

In Australia, we know scones as something fairly white and fluffy,
served warm spread with jam and cream. I love a good scone, white
and all — but I have a particular love for the American scone, which
they call a biscuit. Still made with refined white flour, they are bound
with egg and more similar to what I knew as a rock cake when growing
up — and usually nowhere near as light and fluffy as the Australian
scone. I tend to make something that falls between the two, using
less-refined flours for integrity and flavour, more butter and I prefer
not to bind with egg. Having said this, any time you add
an egg, you will be rewarded with a better crumb.

A scone with more integrity

Scones as we know them are fluffy from the light refined flour and leavening — trying to replicate this with heavier unrefined white and whole flours by adding extra leavening will simply result in a nasty aftertaste. You could add egg, but I am happy to let them be what they are — not quite as high, and I use a small amount of baking powder and baking soda (bicarbonate of soda) to give me a nice crumb. I also don't add salt, preferring to allow the full flavour of the grain to come through.

Because the kind of scones I like and make don't need too much rise, and don't have a large surface area, they are a perfect place to use the very low gluten grains, such as oat and barley. Indeed, the scone descends from the Celtic bannock, a heavy flatbread made from barley or oatmeal, and the wedge cut from the bannock was known as a scone.

In this section you'll find a range of scones all using less-refined and wholesome flours. You can make them plain to top with your choice of delicious jams, creams and spreads or take them down the American rock cake path and enrich and flavour them with fresh and dried fruits.

All scones are at their best eaten as fresh from the oven as possible or warm on the day. Any leftovers freeze brilliantly — to reheat, place the frozen scone in a low to moderate oven to thaw and warm.

BAKING NOTES

Scones are exceptionally easy and quick to put together, but there are some basic rules that can't be broken:

- Cold butter is a critical ingredient in a scone, helping to give a tender and soft crumb. Its job is to encase the flour, thus forming a barrier when moisture is added. If the butter is too warm, or is melted by your hands, the flour will absorb the butter instead, leading to a tough crumb. This is especially important with any percentages of wholemeal flour as they carry a higher gluten load. A food processor, pastry cutter or a light (and cold) hand make for good scones. I prefer to use a pastry cutter, as I can work in one bowl, thus less washing up. When the weather is hot, it's a good idea to chill the measured flour/s beforehand.

- Never overwork the butter into the flour, stop when you have a range of sizes — from coarse breadcrumbs to a few pea- or bean-sized pieces. If you work it too much, you run the risk of the butter melting and being absorbed into the flour. Food processors are notoriously easy for overworking butter, so while I prefer not to use them for scones, if you do, take care to pulse the mix a few times, checking it carefully.

- When adding the milk, do not overmix the dough. I like to use a large serving spoon, and the aim is to bring the mix together with as little gentle stirring as possible. Pouring the milk evenly over the dry ingredients helps. Once you turn the dough out onto a lightly floured surface, do not knead or play with it, but gently coax or push it into the shape you want.

- Place the scones on the baking tray next to each other, which helps support them, and they will rise more.

- Any time you use wheat flour, you will need a bit more milk. Read more about this in Baking with Wheat Versus Spelt on page 14.

- Sugar is more important in gluten-free scones as it helps mask the strong earthy flavour of the grains.

- I prefer to reconstitute dried fruit as this stops it sucking moisture from the dough.

- All the mixes you find here will be slightly wetter than a traditional scone dough.
- Any time you add an egg, you will get a better crumb, but you will need to reduce the liquid a little.
- You can add a glaze to the cooked scone as desired.

Dairy-free scones

I prefer the texture that butter gives to a scone, but you can make most of the following scone recipes in this chapter dairy free by increasing the apple cider vinegar and replacing the milk, cultured buttermilk and butter with the following:

80 ml (2½ fl oz/⅓ cup) macadamia nut or almond oil
1 tablespoon apple cider vinegar
125 ml (4 fl oz/½ cup) rice milk
125 ml (4 fl oz/½ cup) coconut milk

Place the oil and vinegar in a small bowl. To a cup measure, add the two milks in equal proportions to get 185 ml (6 fl oz/¾ cup). Add this to the oil and vinegar and mix together. Add to the dry ingredients. Take care not to overmix as this is the main cause of heavy scones. Add the extra milk as needed — the mix should form into a moist, but not at all sloppy dough.

The amount needed will vary: about 185 ml for white spelt, a couple of tablespoons more with 50% wholemeal (though any oatmeal will reduce that amount), the full cup if it's 100% wholemeal. Finally, if you've made a mistake and it's too moist to form into a firm dough for cutting, simply drop the batter in tablespoonfuls onto the tray — you will still end up with a delicious, viable scone, just a little odd looking.

A classic scone

EGG FREE / WHEAT FREE / CAN BE DAIRY FREE
MAKES 12

This is the closest I come to a classic scone — a 'normal' scone my daughter would say! As the weather cools, I would serve these for morning or afternoon tea, with good-quality jam and cream. These bake up to a beautiful golden colour, with the taste of butter shining through, even more so when using wheat.

260 g (9¼ oz/2 cups) unbleached white spelt flour, plus extra,
    for patting out
2 teaspoons baking powder
1½ tablespoons rapadura sugar
½ teaspoon baking soda (bicarbonate of soda)
1 teaspoon apple cider vinegar
125 ml (4 fl oz/½ cup) milk
125 ml (4 fl oz/½ cup) cultured buttermilk or yoghurt
100 g (3½ oz) very cold unsalted butter, cut into rough 1 cm
    (½ inch) pieces

Preheat the oven to 200°C (400°F/Gas 6). Line a baking tray with baking paper.

Place the flour, baking powder and sugar in a bowl and sieve in the baking soda. Mix through with a whisk to combine the ingredients and break up any lumps of flour.

Place the vinegar in a cup measure, add the two milks in equal proportions to get 185 ml (6 fl oz/¾ cup). Set aside.

Using your fingertips or a pastry cutter, cut the butter into the flour until the mixture resembles coarse breadcrumbs — some bits should be the size of a pea. Add the 185 ml of milk mixture (or the 250 ml (8 fl oz/1 cup) if using wheat flour) and mix with a large spoon to just combine — take care not to overmix as this is the main cause of heavy scones. Add the extra milk as needed. The mix should form into a moist, but not at all sloppy, dough.

Lightly flour the lined tray, then turn the dough out onto it. Pat (don't knead) the dough into a rough circle or rectangle about 2.5 cm (1 inch) thick. You may need to lightly flour your hands. Using a sharp, floured knife, cut into 12 wedges or rectangles (you may well need to re-flour the knife in between cuts) and use the knife to slightly separate each wedge or rectangle so there is a small gap in between each. Don't worry if they fall out of shape a bit — that is part of their charm.

Bake for 15–20 minutes or until golden and lightly browned and just cooked in the middle (you can break one open to check). Serve warm.

VARIATIONS

Dairy free: See page 67.

*

Orange zest and currant: Add the finely grated zest of 1 orange and 75 g (2½ oz/½ cup) currants to the dry ingredients and whisk through. I like to plump up the currants in the juice from the orange beforehand, but they are fine to add dry.

A scone with more goodness

EGG FREE / WHEAT FREE / CAN BE DAIRY FREE
MAKES 12

As you move away from white flour and incorporate more wholemeal, you can expect a denser result, which gives more depth of flavour with a bit of chew. Using 50 per cent each of white and wholemeal will give you a flavoured and nourishing scone, but one that is still fairly light.

130 g (4½ oz/1 cup) unbleached white spelt flour, plus extra,
  for patting out
73 g (2½ oz/½ cup) wholemeal spelt flour
67 g (2¼ oz/½ cup) oatmeal
2 teaspoons baking powder
1½ tablespoons rapadura sugar
½ teaspoon baking soda (bicarbonate of soda)
1 teaspoon apple cider vinegar
125 ml (4 fl oz/½ cup) milk
125 ml (4 fl oz/½ cup) cultured buttermilk or yoghurt
100 g (3½ oz) very cold unsalted butter, cut into rough 1 cm
  (½ inch) pieces

Preheat the oven to 200°C (400°F/Gas 6). Line a baking tray with baking paper.

Place the flours, oatmeal, baking powder and sugar in a bowl and sieve in the baking soda. Mix through with a whisk to combine the ingredients and break up any lumps of flour.

Place the vinegar in a cup measure, add the two milks in equal proportions to get 185 ml (6 fl oz/¾ cup). Set aside.

Using your fingertips or a pastry cutter, cut the butter into the flour until the mixture resembles coarse breadcrumbs — some bits should be the size of a pea. Add the 185 ml of milk mixture and mix with a large spoon to just combine — take care not to overmix as this is the main cause of heavy scones. Add the extra milk as needed. The mix should form into a moist, but not at all sloppy dough.

Lightly flour the lined tray, then turn the dough out onto it. Pat (don't knead) the dough into a rough circle or rectangle about 2.5 cm (1 inch) thick. You may need to lightly flour your hands. Using a sharp, floured knife, cut into 12 wedges or rectangles (you may well need to re-flour the knife in between cuts) and use the knife to slightly separate each wedge or rectangle so there is a small gap in between each. Don't worry if they fall out of shape. Bake for 15–20 minutes or until golden and lightly browned and just cooked in the middle (you can break one open to check). Serve warm.

BAKING NOTE

Incorporating some oatmeal into the equation will also add a wonderful moistness to the scone.

VARIATION

Dairy free: See page 67.

Lemon-glazed blueberry scones

EGG FREE / WHEAT FREE / CAN BE DAIRY FREE
MAKES 12

These scones are about adding flavour and goodness to the classic recipe. Rather than continuing to use higher amounts of leavening to aid rise when percentages of wholemeal grain are used, I prefer to use fruit to help lighten the slightly denser texture of the crumb.

130 g (4½ oz/1 cup) unbleached white spelt flour, plus extra,
    for patting out
145 g (5¼ oz/1 cup) wholemeal spelt flour
2 teaspoons baking powder
1½ tablespoons rapadura sugar
finely grated zest of 1 small lemon
½ teaspoon baking soda (bicarbonate of soda)
1 teaspoon apple cider vinegar
125 ml (4 fl oz/½ cup) milk
125 ml (4 fl oz/½ cup) cultured buttermilk or yoghurt
100 g (3½ oz) very cold unsalted butter, cut into rough 1 cm
    (½ inch) pieces
155 g (5½ oz/1 cup) fresh blueberries

Lemon glaze
2 tablespoons brown rice syrup, or to taste
2 tablespoons lemon juice (you may need more depending
    on the acidity of the lemon)

Preheat the oven to 200°C (400°F/Gas 6). Line a baking tray with baking paper.

Place the flours, baking powder, sugar and lemon zest in a bowl and sieve in the baking soda. Mix through with a whisk to combine the ingredients and break up any lumps of flour.

Place the vinegar in a cup measure, add the two milks in equal proportions to get 185 ml (6 fl oz/¾ cup). Set aside.

Using your fingertips or a pastry cutter, cut the butter into the flour until the mixture resembles coarse breadcrumbs — some bits should be the size of a pea. Add the blueberries and toss through to evenly distribute. Add the 185 ml of milk mixture and mix with a large spoon to just combine — take care not to overmix as this is the main cause of heavy scones. Add the extra milk as needed. The mix should form into a moist, but not at all sloppy dough.

Lightly flour the lined tray, then turn the dough out onto it. Pat (don't knead) the dough into a rough circle or rectangle about 2.5 cm (1 inch) thick. You may need to lightly flour your hands. Using a sharp, floured knife, cut into 12 wedges or rectangles (you may well need to re-flour the knife in between cuts) and use the knife to slightly separate each wedge or rectangle so there is a small gap in between each. Don't worry if they fall out of shape a bit — that is part of their charm. Bake for 15–20 minutes or until golden and lightly browned and just cooked in the middle (you can break one open to check).

VARIATION

Dairy free: See page 67.

Meanwhile, for the glaze, place the rice syrup and lemon juice in a small bowl and mix together well — taste and adjust the lemon juice as needed.

Drizzle the warm scones with the glaze to serve.

Cherry and vincotto wedges

EGG FREE / WHEAT FREE / CAN BE DAIRY FREE
MAKES 12

I love vincotto as a dark liquid sweetener, made from the must of grapes. Dried cherries have a flavour like chocolate, but with far more depth. When paired with the luscious, dark velvet of vincotto and vanilla, good things happen. This is the scone I want to eat on an autumn morning with coffee — a scone with a deep flavour and a slight chew from the oatmeal.

130 g (4½ oz/1 cup) unbleached white spelt flour, plus extra,
    for patting out
73 g (2½ oz/½ cup) wholemeal spelt flour
67 g (2¼ oz/½ cup) oatmeal
2 teaspoons baking powder
1½ tablespoons rapadura sugar
½ teaspoon baking soda (bicarbonate of soda)
1 teaspoon apple cider vinegar
125 ml (4 fl oz/½ cup) milk
125 ml (4 fl oz/½ cup) cultured buttermilk or yoghurt
100 g (3½ oz) very cold unsalted butter, cut into rough 1 cm
    (½ inch) pieces
100 g (3½ oz/½ cup) vincotto cherries (see page 273)
125 ml (4 fl oz/½ cup) vincotto, for drizzling

Preheat the oven to 190°C (375°F/ Gas 5). Line a baking tray with baking paper.

Place the flours, oatmeal, baking powder and sugar in a bowl and sieve in the baking soda. Mix through with a whisk to combine the ingredients and break up any lumps of flour.

Place the vinegar in a cup measure, add the two milks in equal proportions to get 185 ml (6 fl oz/¾ cup). Set aside.

Using your fingertips or a pastry cutter, cut the butter into the flour until the mixture resembles coarse breadcrumbs — some bits should be the size of a pea. Add the cherries (don't worry if there's a bit of liquid) and toss through to evenly distribute. Add the 185 ml of milk mixture and mix with a large spoon to just combine — take care not to overmix as this is the main cause of heavy scones. Add the extra milk as needed. The mix should form into a moist, but not at all sloppy dough.

Lightly flour the lined tray, then turn the dough out onto it. Pat (don't knead) the dough into a rough circle or rectangle about 2.5 cm (1 inch) thick. You may need to lightly flour your hands. Using a sharp, floured knife, cut into 12 wedges or rectangles (you may well need to re-flour the knife in between cuts) and use the knife to slightly separate each wedge or rectangle so there is a small gap in between each. Don't worry if they fall out of shape a bit — that is part of their charm.

Bake for 15–20 minutes or until golden and lightly browned and just cooked in the middle (you can break one open to check).

Remove from the oven and leave to cool for a couple of minutes before drizzling with the vincotto. Serve warm.

VARIATION
Dairy free: See page 67.

Peach and nectarine oat and barley scones

EGG FREE / WHEAT FREE / LOW GLUTEN / CAN BE DAIRY FREE
MAKES 12

These scones are not designed for cutting and using as a base for jam and cream — or indeed any topping. The low level of gluten means it will just crumble apart. Instead we sandwich layers of scone with the most delicious maple and vanilla-scented dried peach and nectarine spread, and rely on the low gluten levels to give us the most amazingly light and tender crumb. The warmth of maple syrup and dried fruits matches and enhances the sweet flavour of barley beautifully. If desired, you can top these with cinnamon and a little rapadura sugar.

65 g (2¼ oz/½ cup) unbleached white spelt flour, plus extra,
    for patting out
82 g (2¾ oz/¾ cup) barley flour
100 g (3½ oz/¾ cup) oatmeal
2 teaspoons baking powder
1½ tablespoons rapadura sugar
½ teaspoon baking soda (bicarbonate of soda)
1 teaspoon apple cider vinegar
125 ml (4 fl oz/½ cup) milk
125 ml (4 fl oz/½ cup) cultured buttermilk or yoghurt
100 g (3½ oz) very cold unsalted butter, cut into rough 1 cm
    (½ inch) pieces
½ cup dried peach and nectarine spread (see page 274) or your
    favourite jam (to make it yourself, see page 271)

Preheat the oven to 190°C (375°F/ Gas 5). Line a baking tray with baking paper.

Place the flours, oatmeal, baking powder and sugar in a bowl and sieve in the baking soda. Mix through with a whisk to combine the ingredients and break up any lumps of flour.

Place the vinegar in a cup measure, add the two milks in equal proportions to get 185 ml (6 fl oz/¾ cup). Set aside.

Using your fingertips or a pastry cutter, cut the butter into the flour until the mixture resembles coarse breadcrumbs — some bits will be the size of a pea. Add the 185 ml of milk mixture and mix with a large spoon to just combine, taking care not to overmix as this is the main cause of heavy scones. Don't be alarmed if it looks quite moist — this is because it is so low in gluten, and is best as a soft, loose mix.

Lightly flour the lined tray and place half of the dough in the centre. Do your best to pat the soft dough into a circle about 16 cm (6¼ inches) round and 1–1.5 cm (½–⅝ inch) thick. You may need to flour your hands a little. Gently and evenly spread the peach and nectarine spread over the dough to the edges. Place the remaining dough on top — it's best to just dollop the dough over and gently spread out with your floured fingertips as best as possible.

Using a sharp, floured knife, cut the circle into 10–12 wedges (you may need to clean and re-flour the knife between cutting). Use the knife to slightly separate each wedge so there is a small gap between each. It doesn't matter if they lose some shape or collapse a little — it will just make a more interesting and delicious result.

Bake for 15–20 minutes or until golden and the dried fruit spread is lightly caramelised. Serve warm.

BAKING NOTE

If you want to make this recipe dairy free, you will notice that the amount of vinegar is less than previous recipes (see pages 67–73). Butter protects gluten from developing (read more about this in Fat and Crumb on page 54) so when using oil, larger amounts of vinegar are also used to break down the gluten. With such low gluten, too much vinegar would simply make the scones crumble to pieces. If making this dairy free, you may actually use a little less milk.

Dairy free

Replace the milk, cultured buttermilk or yoghurt and butter with the following (but note the vinegar quantity remains the same):

80 ml (2½ fl oz/⅓ cup) macadamia nut or almond oil

1 teaspoon apple cider vinegar

125 ml (4 fl oz/½ cup) rice milk

125 ml (4 fl oz/½ cup) coconut milk

Place the oil and vinegar in a small bowl. To a cup measure, add the two milks in equal proportions to get 185 ml (6 fl oz/¾ cup). Add this to the oil and vinegar and mix together. Add to the dry ingredients. You may find you may not need to add the extra milk.

Pumpkin, cheddar, rosemary and sage gluten-free scones

GLUTEN FREE
MAKES 16 GENEROUS SCONES

With the robust and fragrant flavours of sage and rosemary, and the sweetness of cheese and pumpkin, using a broader range of the more assertively flavoured gluten-free flours works well. This is a delicious, brightly coloured scone, held together by both the egg, and the moist pumpkin. I have also made these without the egg and, while not as puffy, they were still awesome.

80 g (2¾ oz/½ cup) brown rice flour, plus extra, for patting out
60 g (2¼ oz/½ cup) quinoa flour
35 g (1¼ oz/¼ cup) buckwheat flour
35 g (1¼ oz/¼ cup) teff flour, or 38 g (1¼ oz/¼ cup) millet flour
30 g (1 oz/¼ cup) cornflour (cornstarch)
30 g (1 oz/¼ cup) true arrowroot
2 teaspoons baking powder
½ teaspoon baking soda (bicarbonate of soda)
1 tablespoon rapadura sugar
a generous pinch of sea salt and freshly ground black pepper
1 tablespoon finely chopped rosemary
2 tablespoons chopped sage
100 g (3½ oz/1 cup) grated sharp cheddar cheese
1 teaspoon apple cider vinegar
250 g (9 oz/1 cup) cooked mashed pumpkin (winter squash)
1 egg, at room temperature
1½ tablespoons milk
1½ tablespoons cultured buttermilk
100 g (3½ oz) very cold unsalted butter, cut into rough 1 cm
  (½ inch) pieces

Preheat the oven to 190°C (375°F/Gas 5). Line two baking trays with baking paper.

Sieve all of the flours, starches, baking powder and baking soda into a mixing bowl. You may well be left with some bits in the base of the sieve — just tip those into the bowl. Add the sugar, salt, pepper, rosemary, half of the sage and half of the cheese and whisk through to evenly distribute.

Place the vinegar, pumpkin, egg and 1 tablespoon each of the milk and buttermilk in a small bowl and mix together well.

Using your fingertips or a pastry cutter, cut the butter into the flour until the mixture resembles coarse breadcrumbs — some bits will be the size of a pea, this is fine. Add the wet mix and stir well — your mix will be moist, but it should look as if you can form it into a soft dough. I generally only need to use 2 tablespoons of the milk and buttermilk combined,

but add the extra milk and buttermilk if you feel it is needed. Leave the mixture to sit for 5 minutes in the bowl as the moisture will be absorbed by the flours and it will be easier to handle.

Lightly flour the lined trays and place half of the dough in the centre of each. Pat each to form a rough circle about 16 cm (6¼ inches) round and 2.5 cm (1 inch) thick. You may need to lightly flour your hands. Using a sharp, floured knife, cut each circle into eight wedges (you may need to clean and re-flour the knife between cuts). Use the knife, or a palette knife, to slightly separate each wedge so there is a small gap between each. It doesn't matter if they lose some shape or collapse a little, or if they're not perfect circles.

Sprinkle each circle with the remaining sage and cheese and bake for 15–20 minutes or until golden and lightly browned and just cooked in the middle (you can break one open to check). Serve warm.

Gluten-free drop scones

GLUTEN FREE / CAN BE DAIRY FREE / CAN BE EGG FREE
MAKES 12

It's not easy being gluten free, and it's certainly not at all easy being a whole-grain gluten-free scone. Many of the gluten-free flours are earthy and extremely assertive in flavour, and not always what one wants in a scone. Hence, in the following recipes you will note a move to the mellow flavour of brown rice flour and teff, with a small portion of chickpea flour to velvet things out, and very small percentages of starch in the form of potato starch and true arrowroot to lighten the crumb. You will also notice more sugar — this is to mask some of that assertive flavour. The role of egg is invaluable in binding gluten-free scones, but if you cannot use them, chia is a good replacement. It does, however, have its own earthy flavour, thus you'll notice the chia comes with some apple purée (banana would also be good) to add a bit more fruity flavour and moisture.

The gluten-free scone mix is best moist — this, and the use of butter, will give you a better crumb, and because it's too moist to pat out as a dough, the mix is best dropped by tablespoonfuls onto the tray (hence the name). The egg batter (but not the chia seed batter) does sit brilliantly in an airtight container in the fridge overnight, and has the added bonus of firming up, so if you want to make them into a classic scone shape, this is the way to do it.

160 g (5¾ oz/1 cup) brown rice flour
30 g (1 oz) teff flour
30 g (1 oz) chickpea flour (besan)
30 g (1 oz/scant ¼ cup) potato starch
30 g (1 oz/¼ cup) true arrowroot
2 teaspoons baking powder
2 tablespoons rapadura sugar

finely grated zest of 1 lemon
60 ml (2 fl oz/¼ cup) cultured buttermilk
60 ml (2 fl oz/¼ cup) milk
2 eggs, at room temperature
110 g (3¾ oz) chilled butter, cubed

Preheat the oven to 190°C (375°F/ Gas 5). Line a baking tray with baking paper.

Sieve the flours, starches and baking powder into a mixing bowl. You may well be left with some bits in the base of the sieve, just tip those into the bowl as well. Add the sugar and lemon zest and whisk through to evenly distribute.

Place the milks and eggs in a small bowl and whisk together.

Using your fingertips or a pastry cutter, cut the butter into the flour until the mixture resembles coarse breadcrumbs — some bits should be the size of a pea.

Add the wet mix to the flour mix, and stir well — your mix will be quite moist, this is as it should be. Visually divide the mix into 12, and drop about 1 tablespoonful of mixture for each scone onto the tray, leaving some room in between them.

Bake for 15–20 minutes or until golden and lightly browned and just cooked in the middle (you can break one open to check).

Dairy free

Replace the butter with 125 ml (4 fl oz/½ cup) macadamia nut or almond oil and use 80 ml (2½ fl oz/⅓ cup) coconut milk with 1 teaspoon apple cider vinegar added. Mix the oil, vinegar, coconut milk and eggs together and add to the dry ingredients.

Egg free and dairy free

Omit the egg. Increase the coconut milk to 160 ml (5¼ fl oz) and combine with 2 teaspoons of ground chia seeds and 2 tablespoons of apple purée in a small bowl and whisk together. Leave to sit for 10–15 minutes, at which time it should be lovely and thick. Combine this mixture with the oil and vinegar in the dairy-free variation above.

Biscuits, bars and crackers

This is a good place to begin your experience as a baker, as you can get a feel for how different flours and combinations of flours work, without worrying too much about rising (and thus crumb) and holding a cake together. They are all easy to make and keep well — perfect for Homemaking 101.

Biscuits and bars

Biscuits and bars are the wonderful small delicious somethings for morning or afternoon tea, but please don't be fooled by those homey-looking ones you see on the supermarket shelves. They are a tragedy, with hydrogenated fats and fake ingredients aplenty — an illusion. They needn't be like that. Taking just a small amount of time to whip up, one batch of dough can create a plentiful supply of biscuits and bars that keep well. They are the workhorse of the baking world. They can be sturdy and transportable — indeed, given the chance, Mum would still bake a batch of biscuits to post to her grandchildren. That's a powerful love medicine.

Because they don't have a large amount of surface area, this is a wonderful place to use some of the lower-gluten grains, such as oat and barley, and gluten-free grains. In this section you'll find a broad range of biscuits and my favourite, the Oat and Barley Fig Pillows (see page 84) — there's something for all occasions.

BAKING NOTES

- I like using oil more often than butter when making biscuits, as it gives a crispier result. If you want a biscuit that is softer, thicker and has more chew, I would suggest you use butter. Coconut oil is a good choice for a very thin biscuit, but I wouldn't suggest it for a thicker one, as while it may be lovely warm, the crumb will compact when cool.

- If using butter, the dough must be chilled at all times. Once made, form the dough into a disc, place in an airtight plastic bag and leave until set and well chilled — this may take overnight with some dough. When rolling the dough, especially when the weather is hot, you may need to slide a baking tray under the dough and place it in the freezer to set up a little before continuing on. When stamping out the dough, a well-chilled dough will ensure the shape is held. Use a palette knife to slide under the stamped biscuit shape, pick it up and place it on a tray — thus keeping your hands off the shape and risking stretching it and warming it with your body heat.

- If you want the biscuit to hold its shape (especially important with stamped biscuits), chill the biscuits on the tray before placing in the oven. The more butter in the dough, the more important all these points are.

- When adding flour to wet ingredients (or creamed butter and sugar), only just beat enough to incorporate the flour — don't overwork.

World peace bar

DAIRY FREE / EGG FREE / WHEAT FREE / CAN BE GLUTEN FREE IF USING NON-CONTAMINATED OATS
MAKES 24

I came across a recipe by the wonderful baker Dorie Greenspan called World Peace Biscuits. They were a dark chocolate sablé and I was instantly hooked. I'm sure they were delicious (they looked divine) but all I could imagine was the sugar driving people nuts, and felt something a little more nutrient dense, but just as delicious, would nourish and fit the bill. I think some of our leaders might make better decisions if they had a piece of this for morning tea at their meetings rather than embarrassing pretend muffins. It keeps brilliantly, but if you find it has softened over a couple of days (that's the oats) place it back into a moderate oven for 10–15 minutes and it will crisp up again.

2 teaspoons ground chia seeds
80 ml (2½ fl oz/⅓ cup) macadamia nut, almond or coconut oil
60 ml (2 fl oz/¼ cup) brown rice syrup
1 teaspoon natural vanilla extract

Filling
160 g (5¾ oz/1 cup) pitted dates, finely chopped
90 g (3¼ oz/1 cup) dried nectarines, roughly chopped
125 ml (4 fl oz/½ cup) apple or pear juice
1 tablespoon lemon juice

Dry mix
150 g (5½ oz/1½ cups) rolled oats (not too dry is best)
67 g (2¼ oz/½ cup) oatmeal
1 teaspoon baking powder
40 g (1½ oz/¼ cup) sunflower seeds, roughly ground
35 g (1¼ oz/¼ cup) pumpkin seeds (pepitas), roughly ground
25 g (1 oz/¼ cup) desiccated coconut
37 g (1¼ oz/¼ cup) rapadura sugar

Preheat the oven to 180°C (350°F/Gas 4). Using one piece of baking paper, line a 20 cm (8 inch) square baking tin, cutting in the corners to fit. This will enable you to lift it out easily.

For the filling, place the dates, nectarines and apple juice in a small saucepan. Cover with a lid, bring to a very gentle simmer and cook for 10 minutes or until the dried fruit has softened. Add to a blender with the lemon juice and process until fairly but not perfectly smooth.

Place the ground chia seeds in a bowl with 80 ml (2½ fl oz/⅓ cup) of water. Mix and set aside to thicken.

For the dry mix, place the oats on a baking tray and roast in the oven for 5–10 minutes or until just fragrant, and ever so lightly coloured. Turn into a mixing bowl, add all of the other dry ingredients and whisk through to evenly distribute. Set aside.

Add the macadamia nut oil, brown rice syrup and vanilla extract to the chia mix, and whisk together. Add this mixture to the dry mix and combine well.

Press half of the oat mixture into the base of the tin. Very gently — I prefer to use a fork — evenly dot the date mix over the oat mixture and then very gently spread it out so the oat mixture is covered. With your fingers, sprinkle the remaining oat mixture over the date mixture and use a fork to evenly distribute, pressing down gently as you do so. Wash and dry your hands (this will make them not stick) and gently but firmly press down on the topping to even it out.

Bake for 30–35 minutes or until well cooked, golden and slightly crispy at the edges. This needs to be well cooked. Remove from the oven and cool in the tin for 20 minutes before cutting into rectangles and serving.

Store in an airtight container in a cool, dark place, or in the fridge if the weather is hot.

Oat and barley fig pillows

WHEAT FREE / LOW GLUTEN
MAKES 16

Have I told you I love fig pillows? They were one of the first things I knew I wanted to include when I set out on this book journey. Barley and oat are perfect here and match the delicious figgyness wonderfully. This pastry will crisp up as it cools from the oven, but because it contains oats, it will also soften a little over the days — simply crisp up in a moderate oven for a few minutes. Yes, it can be a tricky and fussy pastry to roll when the weather is warmer, but persevere — it's worth the effort. I haven't included an egg-free option as the egg is essential to hold the low-gluten pastry together.

110 g (3¾ oz/1 cup) barley flour, plus extra, for rolling
50 g (1¾ oz/½ cup) oat flour
½ teaspoon baking powder
80 g (2¾ oz) unsalted butter, softened
75 g (2½ oz/½ cup) rapadura sugar
1 egg, at room temperature
1 teaspoon natural vanilla extract

Filling
225 g (8 oz/1½ cups) dried figs, chopped into small pieces
finely grated zest of 1 large lemon
1½ tablespoons vincotto or 1 tablespoon rapadura sugar
1 teaspoon natural vanilla extract
35 g (1¼ oz/⅓ cup) roasted pecans, finely chopped

For the filling, place the figs in a small saucepan with 185 ml (6 fl oz/¾ cup) of water. Bring to a gentle boil, then turn off the heat and leave to sit for 1 hour or until the figs have soaked up all the water — it's fine to leave overnight too. When ready to use, finely chop the figs, return to the pan or small bowl and add the lemon zest, vincotto, vanilla extract and pecans. Mix together and set aside.

Place the flours and baking powder in a small bowl and whisk through to evenly distribute the ingredients and lighten.

Using a stand mixer fitted with the paddle attachment, cream the butter and sugar, scraping down the sides from time to time, until light and fluffy. Add the egg and beat until creamy. Add the vanilla extract and flours and beat on very low speed until the flour is just incorporated into the egg mix and you have a dough. Divide the dough in half, form each piece into a rectangle about 12 cm x 6 cm (4½ x 2½ inches), place each into a plastic bag and chill for 1–2 hours. It is important that the dough is well chilled.

Preheat the oven to 180°C (350°F/Gas 4). Line two baking trays with baking paper.

To roll, work with one rectangle at a time (and keep the remaining pastry in the fridge). This is a very fragile dough and you may have to give it a couple of minutes in the freezer to firm up during the process. Roll between two sheets of baking paper into a 40 cm x 14 cm (16 x 5½ inch) rectangle, lightly flouring as you go. As the pastry becomes bigger, it will stick to the paper. Lift off the paper, sprinkle the dough with a little flour, then replace the paper. Gently turn the whole thing over (paper and all) and repeat with the paper underneath. If you don't do this, the pastry will just stick to the paper and won't get any bigger. If at any time the pastry tears and does not peel from the paper easily, put it in the freezer for a couple of minutes to chill and firm up. Trim the pastry to get a neat rectangle measuring 40 cm x 14 cm, then place in the freezer to chill for a couple of minutes.

With the shorter (14 cm) side facing you, lay half of the filling 2 cm (¾ inch) in from the left edge down the length of the pastry. The width of the filling should measure 5 cm (2 inches). Using the paper as a support, lift the paper along the left side, folding over the 2 cm edge of pastry inwards to your right. Gently peel the paper off.

Again, using the paper to support the pastry, lift the paper along the right edge of the pastry and fold the pastry to the edge. Pat gently to seal the pastry at the edge. Leaving the paper still on, roll the biscuit log over to your right, placing it seam side down. Peel the paper gently from what is now the top of the log. Refrigerate the log and repeat with the remaining pastry and filling.

Cut each log into eight pieces and move them (I use a palette knife) to one of the trays. Again, if they are too soft to move, give them a quick chill before transferring. Bake for 20–25 minutes or until golden and the pastry changes from feeling soft under your fingertips (like an uncooked cake) to firm. The pieces should be very golden at the edges and are best well cooked.

Remove from the oven and leave on the trays to firm up for 10 minutes, then move to a wire rack. Do not leave on the trays to cool, as they will sweat underneath and the biscuit will become soggy. Leave to completely cool before eating, and you will notice that the pastry will have crisped up.

Store in an airtight container in a cool, dark place, or in the fridge if the weather is hot.

BAKING NOTE

It is best not to over-flour this dough as you roll, and to only use barley flour for rolling as oat flour will become gooey and sticky. Once rolled out, simply slide it onto a baking tray and place it in the freezer for a couple of minutes or so. It will be much easier to handle when it is well chilled.

Peanut Anzacs

WHEAT FREE
MAKES 30

Food and smell can imprint a memory like nothing else can, and for me, peanut biscuits take me back to where I grew up on Angelo Street, in South Perth, and over the road from where I lived to my godmother's house. Peanuts are so protein rich, and it's sad to see so many people reluctant to eat them because of the allergic reaction they can trigger. I believe that this is in part due to the shocking way we farm and process our peanuts, and any peanut you use should only ever be organic. Enriched with wholemeal flour and oats, this is a simple, easy, homey and protein-rich biscuit.

65 g (2¼ oz/½ cup) unbleached white spelt flour
73 g (2½ oz/½ cup) wholemeal spelt flour
1 teaspoon baking powder
50 g (1¾ oz/½ cup) rolled oats
¼ teaspoon sea salt
70 g (2½ oz/½ cup) roasted peanuts (skins removed), halved
125 g (4½ oz) unsalted butter, softened
75 g (2½ oz/½ cup) rapadura sugar
1 egg, at room temperature

Preheat the oven to 180°C (350°F/Gas 4). Line two baking trays with baking paper.

Place the flours, baking powder, oats, salt and peanuts in a small mixing bowl, and whisk through to evenly distribute the ingredients and break up any lumps.

Using a stand mixer fitted with the paddle attachment, beat the butter and sugar, scraping down the sides from time to time, until light and fluffy. Add the egg and beat until creamy. Add the flour and, on very low speed, beat until the flour is just incorporated into the egg mix and has come together. Chill the dough.

When the dough is firm to the touch, scoop up 1 heaped teaspoon at a time, quickly roll into a ball and place on the trays, leaving plenty of room in between each. When the tray is full, flatten each with a fork to about 6 cm (2½ inch) rounds. If the dough has become too soft (this is because the butter is melting), place the tray in the fridge to firm up the dough rather than adding flour to the fork. Also, the biscuits should be firm, and well chilled before going into the oven.

Bake for 10–12 minutes or until very golden at the edges — this biscuit should be well cooked to help give it a lovely crispy result. Remove from the oven and cool on wire racks.

Store in an airtight container in a cool, dark place.

Christmas crescents

WHEAT FREE / EGG FREE / LOW GLUTEN
MAKES 40

Every country seems to have its own version of a buttery and rich shortbread, enriched with nuts and dredged with icing sugar. With so little gluten, these biscuits crumble naturally. I like using maple syrup here — its flavour and fragrance enhances the result. Rather than simply sweet, these are fragrant and deeply flavoured. Perfect with a cup of tea.

    100 g (3½ oz/1 cup) roasted pecans or 160 g (5¾ oz/1 cup)
        roasted almonds (skins on)
    135 g (4¾ oz/1 cup) oatmeal
    110 g (3¾ oz/1 cup) barley flour
    a pinch of fine sea salt
    finely grated zest of 1 lemon
    180 g (6¼ oz) unsalted butter, softened
    125 ml (4 fl oz/½ cup) maple syrup
    2 teaspoons vanilla paste or natural vanilla extract
    75 g (2½ oz/½ cup) golden icing (confectioners') sugar, for dusting

Place the nuts in a food processor and pulse until they are finely ground to a meal. Add to a mixing bowl along with the oatmeal, barley, salt and lemon zest and whisk through to evenly distribute the ingredients and break up any lumps.

Using a stand mixer fitted with the paddle attachment, beat the butter and maple syrup, scraping down the sides from time to time, until light and fluffy. Add the vanilla paste or extract and flour mixture and beat on very low speed until the flour is incorporated and it comes together to form a dough. Place in an airtight container and chill for 1 hour.

Preheat the oven to 180°C (350°F/Gas 4). Line two baking trays with baking paper.

Scoop up 1 heaped teaspoon at a time, quickly (because the large amount of butter in the dough will react to your body heat) roll into a thick rope in your hands, about 4 cm (1½ inches) long. Form into a crescent and place on a tray. Alternatively, you can just place them on the trays as balls — their shape will relax a bit as they bake. Remember, if the weather is hot, chilling the dough before rolling makes them easier to shape, and chilling again before baking helps them hold their shape during cooking.

Bake for 12–15 minutes or until just golden along the edges.

Remove from the oven and cool on the trays for 5 minutes, then gently dip the tops of each in the icing sugar and place on a wire rack. If they are still too fragile, leave to cool a little longer before doing this.

Store in an airtight container in a cool, dark place for up to 8 days.

A simple and plain biscuit for many reasons

WHEAT FREE
MAKES 60 BISCUITS OR 30 SANDWICHED BISCUITS

This is designed as a plain biscuit to sandwich together (à la Monte Carlo) or simply to have by itself. Brown rice syrup gives this biscuit its subtle flavour and texture — crisp on the outside and not too chewy in the centre. This is definitely a biscuit, with no hint of cakeyness that egg often gives. Even when chilled this is a soft dough — thanks to the brown rice syrup — and while you probably could chill it as a disc and roll it out, I don't think you'd get the lovely neat edges that cutting from the chilled log gives. You can always add a little citrus zest to the dough and make a citrussy filling for extra zing.

260 g (9¼ oz/2 cups) unbleached white spelt flour
1¼ teaspoons baking powder
⅛ teaspoon fine sea salt
125 g (4½ oz) unsalted butter, softened
75 g (2½ oz/½ cup) rapadura sugar or 70 g (2½ oz/½ cup)
    granulated coconut palm sugar
1 egg, at room temperature
2 tablespoons brown rice syrup
1 teaspoon vanilla paste or natural vanilla extract

Filling
150 g (5½ oz/1 cup) golden icing (confectioners') sugar
1 teaspoon vanilla paste
15 g (½ oz) unsalted butter, softened
1 tablespoon milk (a dairy-free option here would be fine)
1 teaspoon freshly squeezed lemon juice
½ teaspoon finely grated lemon zest
85 g (2¾ oz/¼ cup) raspberry jam (to make it yourself,
    see page 271)

BAKING NOTE

Make sure this dough is well chilled before rolling out and if it is very warm, it's a good idea to put the tray in the freezer after rolling so the butter sets before cooking. They will spread out in the oven so don't place them too close together.

Place the flour, baking powder and salt in a bowl and whisk through to distribute the ingredients evenly and break up any lumps.

Using a stand mixer fitted with the paddle attachment, beat the butter and sugar, scraping down the sides from time to time, until light and fluffy. Add the egg, brown rice syrup and vanilla paste or extract and beat until creamy. Add the flour mix and beat on low speed until the flour is just incorporated into the egg mixture and has come together.

Form the dough into a rough log shape on a sheet of baking paper, then roll up in the paper to form a log about 32 cm (12¾ inches) long and 4 cm (1½ inches) in diameter. With the log still wrapped in paper, cover with plastic wrap — make sure it is well sealed so the dough does not dry out — and refrigerate for 1 hour.

Preheat the oven to 180°C (350°F/Gas 4). Line two baking trays with baking paper.

Unwrap the dough, cut into 5 mm (¼ inch) thick slices and place on the trays at least 3 cm (1¼ inches) apart.

Bake for 12–15 minutes or until lightly golden at the edges.

Remove from the oven, cool on the trays for 10 minutes before gently moving to a wire rack — they will crisp up as they cool.

For the filling, sieve the icing sugar into a small bowl. Add the vanilla paste, butter, milk and lemon juice and zest and mix vigorously with a wooden spoon until deliciously creamy.

When the biscuits are completely cool, spread half of the biscuits with a small amount of jam. Spread the filling on the remaining biscuits, then sandwich together the pairs.

Store in an airtight container in a cool, dark place for 4–5 days. Unfilled biscuits will keep for 10 days.

Almond, coconut and maple syrup biscuits

DAIRY FREE / EGG FREE / WHEAT FREE
MAKES ABOUT 50

This recipe can be used as a classic dairy-free and egg-free biscuit. Made with coconut oil, the result has a great crispy texture; when made as a thicker biscuit (not rolled out, but simply formed), it is still fine. The coconut oil flavour does come through but is a divine combination with maple syrup, and even better with chocolate and hazelnuts or almonds added. This is a quick, simple and easy recipe. They are also delicious sandwiched with Creamy Chocolate and Coconut Fudge Frosting (see page 253) or the Dark Chocolate and Coconut Ganache (made with dairy-free dark chocolate, see page 265).

BAKING NOTE

To make this nut free, replace the nuts with ½ cup finely chopped cocoa nibs.

130 g (4½ oz/1 cup) unbleached white spelt flour
145 g (5¼ oz/1 cup) wholemeal spelt flour
½ teaspoon baking powder
a pinch of fine sea salt
80 g (2¾ oz/½ cup) roasted almonds (skins on) or roasted
    hazelnuts (skins removed), finely ground
100 g (3½ oz) dark chocolate (70%), finely chopped (optional)
125 ml (4 fl oz/½ cup) maple syrup
125 ml (4 fl oz/½ cup) coconut oil (must be liquid but not too cool
    or it will set)
2 teaspoons natural vanilla extract

Place the flours, baking powder, salt, nuts and chocolate (if using) into a bowl and whisk together to evenly distribute the ingredients and break up any lumps — the nuts, especially, can tend to stick together due to their oil content.

Place the maple syrup, coconut oil and vanilla extract in a small bowl and whisk together. Add to the dry ingredients and mix until it comes together. Divide the dough in half, roughly flatten each into a 13 cm (5 inch) disc, and place each in a sealable plastic bag to chill for 1 hour.

Preheat the oven to 180°C (350°F/Gas 4). Line two baking trays with baking paper.

Roll one piece of dough at a time between two sheets of baking paper. This is a very easy dough to roll, and you won't need extra flour (see Baking Notes). As the pastry becomes bigger, it will stick to the paper. Lift the paper off and replace the paper — this breaks its seal. Gently turn the whole thing over (paper and all) and then repeat with the paper underneath; if you don't do this, the pastry will just stick to the paper and won't get any bigger. Roll until the pastry is about 25 cm (10 inches) in diameter, but it is more important that it is about 3–4 mm (⅛ inch) thick. Stamp out the biscuits using a 4–4.5 cm (1½–1¾ inch) biscuit cutter, and use a palette knife to move the biscuits to the trays. Re-roll the scraps and cut out more biscuits.

If you want drop biscuits, do not chill the dough, but rather scoop up 1 heaped teaspoon at a time, roll into a ball and place on a tray. Gently press to flatten slightly.

Bake for 12–15 minutes or until golden at the edges. Remove from the oven and cool on the trays for 5 minutes before gently moving to a wire rack. If sandwiching with a filling, wait until they are absolutely cool before doing so.

Store in an airtight container in a cool, dark place for up to 2 weeks. Be sure not to store them in the fridge as this will harden the coconut oil and damage the texture of the biscuit.

BAKING NOTES

- Take care not to grind the roasted nuts too fine or coarse.

- This is a lovely dough to roll, but it most certainly has a temperature sweet spot — neither too cold or too warm. It will come out of the fridge very firm, so leave it to relax for about 5 minutes before working with it. When the dough is very cold or if the weather is chilly, you may get a few cracks at the edges in the beginning if you roll too aggressively, so just go gently and it will become easier as the dough warms. Again, if the weather is very cold, I sometimes put my hands on it to warm the fat, and thus soften the dough. If the weather is hot, the oil will melt too quickly, and you may have to place it back in the freezer to chill for a moment or two. Don't be tempted to use any flour. To make the dough easier to handle, just pop it back in the fridge. The pastry should give a very slight resistance when rolling and needs to have some chill to hold the coconut oil. The pastry shouldn't be at all oily.

- I have specified spelt for this recipe as it produces a far lovelier biscuit with a nicer flavour and softer texture than wheat.

- When making these with chocolate, ensure the nuts are absolutely cool or the chocolate may melt.

- I use a 4 cm (1½ inch) round biscuit cutter or you could use a small 4.5 cm (1¾ inch) heart-shaped cutter.

Rugelach

WHEAT FREE / EGG FREE
MAKES 24

This is definitely my kind of sweet something — not too sweet, ever so slightly savoury and full of flavour. I tried it out for the first time last Christmas and it was fabulous with a cup of tea or coffee. I've suggested two fillings here and two rolling methods to make either slices or crescents. Each filling will make one batch or you could make half of each filling and do both!

Dough
120 g (4¼ oz) unsalted butter, softened
100 g (3½ oz) cream cheese, at room temperature
1 tablespoon rapadura sugar
145 g (5¼ oz/1 cup) wholemeal spelt flour
small amount of unbleached white spelt flour, for rolling

Cinnamon sugar
2 tablespoons light brown sugar (or rapadura)
2 teaspoons ground cinnamon

Dried apricot, raisin and roasted pecan filling
90 g (3¼ oz/½ cup) dried apricots, finely chopped
90 g (3¼ oz/½ cup) raisins, finely chopped
50 g (1¾ oz/½ cup) roasted pecans, finely chopped

Dried cherry, dark chocolate and roasted macadamia nut filling
200 g (7 oz/1 generous cup) vincotto cherries (see page 273),
    finely chopped (some of the delicious sauce can be included)
150 g (5½ oz/1 cup) roasted unsalted macadamia nuts,
    finely chopped
40 g (1½ oz) dark chocolate (no more than 70%), finely chopped

For the dough, using a stand mixer fitted with the paddle attachment, beat the butter, cream cheese and sugar, scraping down the sides of the bowl from time to time, until creamy. Add the flour and gently beat until just combined. At this stage, this is a very soft dough. Scoop it into a plastic bag, and do your best to shape it into a small rectangle about 12 cm x 10 cm (4½ x 4 inches). Seal and leave in the fridge for 1–2 hours or until firm — overnight is best.

For the cinnamon sugar, combine the ingredients in a bowl and set aside.

For the dried apricot, raisin and roasted pecan filling, place the apricots and raisins in a small saucepan with 125 ml (4 fl oz/½ cup) of water. Cover with a tight-fitting lid and cook over low heat for 10 minutes — take care that steam does not escape. Turn off the heat and leave until cool. Use a fork to mash the fruits together. The pecans will be sprinkled over the filling when assembling.

For the dried cherry, dark chocolate and roasted macadamia nut filling, combine all of the ingredients in a bowl and set aside.

To make slices Take the cold dough from the fridge and halve. Working with one piece at a time, and keeping the other in the fridge, roll out a piece between two sheets of paper (you may need a little extra flour for rolling, but try not to use too much — if it is cold, it shouldn't need it) to a rectangle about 22 cm x 18 cm (8½ x 7 inches) and 4–5 mm (¼ inch) thick. As the pastry becomes bigger, it will stick to the paper. Lift the paper off (sprinkle with a small amount of flour if needed) and replace the paper. Gently turn the whole thing over (paper and all) and then repeat with the paper underneath; if you don't do this, the pastry will just stick to the paper and won't get any bigger. Trim to a neat rectangle measuring 20 cm x 17 cm (8 x 6½ inches), then turn the pastry, still on the paper so that the longer side faces you.

Gently spread half of the filling all over the rectangle, going right to the edges. Sprinkle 2½ teaspoons of the cinnamon sugar evenly over the top. (If using the apricot, raisin and roasted pecan filling, then scatter the roasted pecans evenly over the top.)

Using the paper to help you (it is better that the dough is still chilled), roll the dough tightly from the longest side facing you into a log. Sprinkle the paper with 2½ teaspoons of the cinnamon sugar, then roll the log over it so it is covered. Place the log (paper and all) on a baking tray in the freezer to chill for at least 10 minutes. It is very important that the dough be well chilled before cutting to keep its shape, but not at all frozen or it will destroy the cell structure of some of the ingredients. Repeat with the remaining dough, filling and cinnamon sugar.

Preheat the oven to 180°C (350°F/Gas 4). Line a baking tray with baking paper.

Remove the logs from the freezer and cut each into 12 slices about 1.5 cm (⅝ inch) thick. Place on the tray and bake for 25 minutes or until lightly golden. Remove from the oven. Cool on the trays for 10 minutes, then move to a wire rack. Store in an airtight container for 1 week, or if the weather is very hot, keep it in the fridge.

To make crescents Preheat the oven to 180°C (350°F/Gas 4). Line a baking tray with baking paper.

Take the cold dough from the fridge and cut it in half. Working with one piece at a time, and keeping the other in the fridge, roll out a piece between two sheets of paper (you may need a little extra flour for rolling, but try not to use too much — if it is cold, it shouldn't need it) to a circle about 25 cm (10 inches) in diameter — the pastry should be about 2–3 mm (1/16–1/8 inch) thick. It might be a bit tricky, but it is doable. As the pastry becomes bigger, it will stick to the paper. Lift the paper off, sprinkle with a small amount of flour if needed, and replace the paper. Gently turn the whole thing over (paper and all) and then repeat with the paper underneath; if you don't do this, the pastry will just stick to the paper and won't get any bigger. Trim so you have a neatish circle. Cut into 12 wedges, as if you are cutting a cake but don't move the pieces.

Sprinkle the entire circle with 2½ teaspoons of cinnamon sugar. Spread the filling to form a ring, about 1.5 cm (⅝ inch) wide and 2 cm (¾ inch) in from the edge of the circle — you are not covering the entire circle. If the pastry is beginning to soften too much at this stage, slip a baking tray underneath it and place it in the freezer to chill for 5 minutes. Repeat with the remaining pastry, filling and 2½ teaspoons of cinnamon sugar.

Starting with the wide end, roll up each wedge and place it on the tray. Sprinkle with the remaining cinnamon sugar. Bake for 25 minutes or until lightly golden. Remove from the oven. Cool on the tray for 10 minutes, then move to a wire rack. Store in an airtight container for 1–2 weeks, or in the fridge if the weather is very hot.

BAKING NOTES
- Cultured butter is absolutely delicious in this dough.
- To tell if the rugelach are ready, you should be able to hear the fats sizzling as you're taking the tray out of the oven if you place your ear near enough — this indicates a good temperature.

Busy girl's emergency biscotti

WHEAT FREE / DAIRY FREE
MAKES ABOUT 20–25

A not too sweet, fairly heavy-duty biscotti to dip into tea or coffee and hold starvation at bay while another fire is put out. All sorts of good things will work in this recipe: garam masala, cardamom and orange zest would be lovely additions, and in the chocolate vein: cocoa nibs, dark chocolate with dried cherries and glacé ginger.

65 g (2¼ oz/½ cup) spelt flakes
145 g (5¼ oz/1 cup) wholemeal spelt flour
75 g (2½ oz/½ cup) rapadura sugar
1 teaspoon ground cinnamon
½ teaspoon baking powder
180 g (6¼ oz/1 cup) dried fruits (I used 90 g/3¼ oz dried figs,
    45 g/1½ oz raisins and 45 g/1½ oz dried apricots)
160 g (5½ oz/1¼ cups) lightly roasted nuts (skins removed)
2 eggs, at room temperature
1 teaspoon natural vanilla extract
60 ml (2 fl oz/¼ cup) extra virgin olive oil

BAKING NOTES

• It is important that the dried fruit is of the best quality and not too dehydrated — leathery fruit will give you a dry, chewy result. Look for moist, plump dried fruits. You will also need to assess its size and cut it accordingly; if the fruit is large, such as figs, cut it into thick slices. Apricots, peaches and nectarines can be left as is — they look so lovely as a nice slice of fruit in the biscotti. Nuts also can go in whole.

• I like to use a mixture of nuts: 75 g (2½ oz/½ cup) hazelnuts, 55 g (2 oz/½ cup) walnuts or pecans, and 30 g (1 oz/¼ cup) pistachios.

Preheat the oven to 180°C (350°F/Gas 4). Line a 1 litre (35 fl oz/4 cup) capacity loaf (bar) tin with baking paper overhanging at the sides — a slightly shallower tin is better than deeper.

Place the spelt flakes on a baking tray and lightly roast in the oven for 5–8 minutes.

Place the spelt flakes, flour, sugar, cinnamon, baking powder, dried fruits and nuts in a bowl and combine well.

Whisk the eggs, vanilla extract and oil together, add to the dry ingredients and mix to just combine. Spoon into the tin and smooth over the top.

Bake for 30–35 minutes (this will depend on the depth and dimensions of your tin) or until a skewer inserted into the middle comes out clean. Immediately lift the loaf (using the baking paper to do so) out onto a wire rack and leave to cool for 10–15 minutes.

Reduce the oven temperature to 170°C (325°F/Gas 3).

Move the warm loaf to a cutting board. Using a sharp knife (not a serrated one), cut the loaf into slices about 1 cm (½ inch) thick — I find these hold much better thick than thin. If you find it is too crumbly, leave it to cool just a little longer. Lay the slices in a single layer on a baking tray and return to the oven for 10–15 minutes or until they look as if some toasting (ever so slight) has taken place. Turn the biscotti over and bake for another 8–10 minutes. Remove from the oven and move to a wire rack to cool.

Store in an airtight container in a cool, dark place for up to 3 weeks (although I have found some that I'd forgotten after 5 weeks and they were still good!).

Quinoa everyday biscuits

GLUTEN FREE / DAIRY FREE
MAKES ABOUT 50

This is a great everyday gluten-free biscuit, dense with whole grains, dried fruit and seeds. It's also delicious with added dark chocolate — indeed chocolate and quinoa are soul mates. This is a great template recipe from which you can do a lot of things. A defining principle of this biscuit is the amount of rapadura sugar you use — with more sugar it will become soft and slightly chewy as it appears here in this recipe, but with less it makes a sturdier dough to roll as in the Quinoa, Cocoa Nib and Hazelnut Chocolate Sandwiches (see page 97).

50 g (1¾ oz/½ cup) quinoa flakes
60 g (2¼ oz/½ cup) quinoa flour
80 g (2¾ oz/½ cup) brown rice flour
70 g (2½ oz/½ cup) buckwheat flour
80 g (2¾ oz/½ cup) potato starch
150 g (5½ oz/1 cup) rapadura sugar
1 teaspoon baking powder
85 g (3 oz/½ cup) sultanas, roughly chopped
55 g (2 oz/½ cup) dried fruit (nectarines or apricots),
    finely chopped
25 g (1 oz/¼ cup) desiccated coconut
2 tablespoons lightly toasted sesame seeds
2 eggs, at room temperature
170 ml (5½ fl oz/⅔ cup) extra virgin olive oil
2 tablespoons brown rice syrup
2 teaspoons natural vanilla extract

Place the quinoa flakes, flours, potato starch, sugar, baking powder, dried fruit, coconut and sesame seeds in a mixing bowl and whisk through to evenly distribute the ingredients and break up any lumps.

Place the eggs, oil, brown rice syrup and vanilla extract in a bowl and whisk until combined. Add to the dry ingredients and mix with a wooden spoon until it comes together as a dough. Turn into an airtight container and chill for at least 1–2 hours or overnight.

Preheat the oven to 180°C (350°F/Gas 4). Line two baking trays with baking paper.

Scoop up 1 heaped teaspoon of dough at a time, roll between your palms and form into a ball. Place on a tray and flatten down ever so lightly, leaving room for them to spread.

Bake for 22–25 minutes or until golden. Remove from the oven and cool on the trays for 5–10 minutes before gently moving to a wire rack.

CHOCOLATE CHIP

Omit the apricot and sultanas and add 100 g (3½ oz) finely chopped dark chocolate (70%).

Quinoa, cocoa nib and hazelnut chocolate sandwiches

GLUTEN FREE / DAIRY FREE
MAKES ABOUT 50 SANDWICHED BISCUITS

Quinoa lends a wonderful earthiness to these delicious biscuits. You can present this biscuit a couple of ways. By itself it makes a small, but not too rich something delicious — perfect, for example, with a hot chocolate. But, when sandwiched with the Creamy Chocolate and Coconut Fudge Frosting or the Dark Chocolate and Coconut Ganache (made with dairy-free dark chocolate), it becomes rich and sophisticated, with a wonderful play of flavour between the cocoa nibs and chocolate in the filling.

75 g (2½ oz/¾ cup) quinoa flakes
60 g (2¼ oz/½ cup) quinoa flour
80 g (2¾ oz/½ cup) brown rice flour
70 g (2½ oz/½ cup) buckwheat flour
80 g (2¾ oz/½ cup) potato starch
113 g (4 oz/¾ cup) rapadura sugar
1 teaspoon baking powder
55 g (2 oz/½ cup) cocoa nibs, broken into small pieces if whole
75 g (2½ oz/½ cup) roasted hazelnuts (skins removed),
    finely ground
2 eggs, at room temperature
170 ml (5½ fl oz/⅔ cup) olive oil
2 tablespoons brown rice syrup
2 teaspoons natural vanilla extract
½ quantity creamy chocolate and coconut fudge frosting
    (see page 253), or 2 quantities dark chocolate and
    coconut ganache (see page 265)

Place the quinoa flakes, flours, potato starch, sugar, baking powder, cocoa nibs and hazelnuts in a mixing bowl and whisk through to evenly distribute the ingredients and break up any lumps.

Place the eggs, oil, brown rice syrup and vanilla extract in a small bowl and whisk until combined. Add to the dry ingredients and mix with a wooden spoon until it comes together as a dough. Turn into an airtight container and chill for 1–2 hours or overnight. The longer the better as it allows the cocoa nibs to infuse flavour into the dough.

Preheat the oven to 180°C (350°F/Gas 4). Line four baking trays with baking paper.

Roll one-quarter of the dough at a time. Form the dough into a rough disc and roll between two sheets of baking paper. As the pastry becomes bigger, it will stick to the paper. Lift the paper off and replace the paper — this breaks its seal. Gently turn the whole thing over (paper and all) and then repeat with the paper underneath; if you don't do this, the pastry will just stick to the paper and won't get any bigger. Roll until the pastry is about 22 cm

BAKING NOTES

- These are best rolled nice and thin as they are a dense biscuit. The pastry should give resistance when rolling and it will only do this when it is cold enough. Don't be tempted to use extra flour to help it roll. Instead, if it is very warm, place it in the fridge or freezer until the pastry firms up enough.

- Don't add salt as it clashes with the rapadura sugar.

- For an extra chocolate hit, you could add 80 g (2¾ oz) dark chocolate (I like 70%), but make sure it is very finely chopped as it makes it hard to roll the dough otherwise.

(8½ inches) in diameter, but it is more important that it is about 3–4 mm (⅛ inch) thick.

Stamp out the biscuits using a 4.5 cm (1¾ inch) heart-shaped biscuit cutter, and use a palette knife to move them to the trays. Re-roll the scraps and cut out more biscuits.

Bake for 10 minutes or until the edges are golden. Remove from the oven and cool on the trays for 5 minutes before gently moving to a wire rack.

To put together, fill a piping (icing) bag fitted with a 5 mm (¼ inch) star nozzle with the frosting or ganache and pipe a little onto half of the biscuits, then sandwich with the remaining biscuits.

Sandwiched biscuits will keep for up to 1 week, but will soften slightly, in a cool, dark place, or in the fridge if the weather is hot. Unfilled biscuits will keep in an airtight container in a cool, dark place for up to 3 weeks.

Crackers

Crackers are ridiculously expensive to buy, and I'm hoping that once you've given these a try, you will find how cheap and easy they are to make. They keep exceptionally well. All crackers need to be well cooked, and a hotter oven is better than a cooler one.

Brown rice, chia and sesame seed crackers

DAIRY FREE / EGG FREE / CAN BE GLUTEN FREE IF WHEAT-FREE TAMARI USED
MAKES ABOUT 64

These are wonderful gluten-free crackers with a lot of flavour. I've included chia seeds and sesame seeds because, apart from their nutrient density, they give the cracker texture and lightness, and stop the mixture from being too gluey.

55 g (2 oz/¼ cup) uncooked brown rice
2 teaspoons whey or 1 teaspoon yoghurt
160 g (5¾ oz/1 cup) brown rice flour, plus 2 tablespoons extra,
    for kneading
80 g (2¾ oz/½ cup) potato starch
½ teaspoon baking powder
2 tablespoons chia seeds
2 teaspoons wheat-free tamari
60 ml (2 fl oz/¼ cup) natural unrefined sesame oil
2 tablespoons sesame seeds

BAKING NOTES
• Take care to use a natural unrefined sesame oil. It is widely available, a lovely golden colour and lightly scented with sesame. It is not the roasted (darkly coloured) sesame oil.
• These are dense crackers and need to be cooked well. If after 20 minutes the centres are still damp, continue baking until they are no longer damp, rather than increasing the oven temeperature.

Place the rice in a small bowl with 250 ml (9 fl oz/1 cup) of water and the whey. Leave to soak at room temperature for 6 hours or overnight.

Rinse the rice and drain well. Pat dry with a tea towel, then place in a small saucepan with 125 ml (4 fl oz/½ cup) of water. Cover and bring to the boil over medium heat. As soon as it comes to the boil, reduce the heat to as low as possible and cook for 40–45 minutes. Check if there is any water left by tipping the pot on an angle about 5 minutes before the end of the cooking time. If so, continue to cook until there is no water left. When it is ready, small steam holes should appear on the surface. Remove from the heat, keep covered and leave until cool. If the weather is hot, leave to cool for 15 minutes before placing in an airtight container in the fridge. You should have 125 g (4½ oz/⅔ cup) of cooked rice.

Add the rice to a food processor and process for a few seconds until it is a thick, but chunky pudding consistency. Add 125 ml (4 fl oz/½ cup) of water and the remaining ingredients, except for the sesame seeds and the extra brown rice flour. Process until it comes together.

Preheat the oven to 180°C (350°F/Gas 4). Line two baking trays with baking paper — you will need to bake these in batches.

Place the extra brown rice flour and the sesame seeds onto a work surface. Place the dough on this and knead lightly until the flour and seeds are all incorporated. The dough should become noticeably less sticky as you gently knead it. Separate into two balls, cover with a tea towel (not plastic wrap, which won't let it breathe) and leave to sit for 10 minutes — this is an important step for this cracker as it dries the dough out a little and makes it easy to roll.

Working with one ball of dough at a time, roll the dough out between two sheets of baking paper into a rough rectangle about 32 cm x 26 cm (12¾ x 10½ inches) and about 2 mm (¹⁄₁₆ inch) thick — you should not need extra flour. If you find the dough sticking, it is too moist, so leave it to dry a little longer. As the pastry becomes bigger, it will stick to the paper. Lift the paper off and replace the paper. Gently turn the whole thing over (paper and all) and then repeat with the paper underneath; if you don't do this, the pastry will just stick to the paper and won't get any bigger. Cut the dough lengthways into thirds so you have three strips about 32 cm x 9 cm (12¾ x 3½ inches). Cut each strip into long triangles, measuring about 4 cm (1½ inches) at the base — you should get about 32 from each ball of dough. Use a palette knife to move the triangles to the trays. Prick each cracker five to six times with the tines of a fork.

Bake for 20 minutes or until the edges are light golden and dry. Remove from the oven and cool on the trays for 10 minutes, then move them to a wire rack.

Repeat for the remaining dough.

Store in an airtight container in a cool, dark place for up to 2 weeks.

BROWN RICE, CHIA AND FENNEL CRACKERS

Replace the sesame oil with 60 ml (2 fl oz/¼ cup) extra virgin olive oil, and replace the sesame seeds with with 1½ tablespoons fennel seeds.

BROWN RICE, CHIA AND ROSEMARY CRACKERS

Replace the sesame oil with 60 ml (2 fl oz/¼ cup) extra virgin olive oil, and replace the sesame seeds with 2 tablespoons finely chopped rosemary (leaf removed from woody stalk). Sprinkle with good-quality Celtic sea salt before baking.

Clockwise from bottom left: barley, wheat and rosemary crackers; brown rice, chia and sesame seed crackers; cornmeal, spelt, parmesan and cheddar crackers; and oat and seed crackers.

Oat and seed crackers

EGG FREE / WHEAT FREE / CAN BE GLUTEN FREE IF NON-CONTAMINATED OATS ARE USED
MAKES ABOUT 50

These crackers are my versions of Scottish oat cakes, and they are divine served with cheese, quince paste or even chutney will do the job wonderfully. Dulse flakes add a mineral-rich hit, with a sharp and savoury nuance of flavour — they're a great addition to a lunchbox.

270 g (9½ oz/2 cups) oatmeal
¼ teaspoon fine sea salt
¼ teaspoon baking powder
1 teaspoon rapadura sugar
2–3 twists of freshly ground black pepper
40 g (1½ oz/¼ cup) sunflower seeds, roughly ground
½ teaspoon dulse flakes (optional)
30 g (1 oz) unsalted butter
2 tablespoons extra virgin olive oil

Preheat the oven to 190°C (375°F/Gas 5). Line two baking trays with baking paper — you may need to bake these in batches.

Place the dry ingredients in a mixing bowl.

Place the butter and 150 ml (5 fl oz) of water in a small saucepan and bring to the boil, stirring until melted. Add to the dry ingredients with the oil. Mix well and divide into two balls, cover with a tea towel and leave to sit for 10–15 minutes. The dough does not need to be cold, and will quite possibly still be warm in your hands when you go to roll it — this is fine.

Working with one ball of dough at a time, roll out the dough between two sheets of baking paper (you won't need any extra flour) to a circle about 30 cm (12 inches) in diameter or until the dough is 2–3 mm (¹⁄₁₆–⅛ inch) thick. As the pastry becomes bigger, it will stick to the paper. Lift the paper off and replace the paper. Gently turn the whole lot over (paper and all) and then repeat with the paper underneath; if you don't do this, the pastry will just stick to the paper and won't get any bigger. Use a cutter to stamp out into desired shapes — I like to use a 4.5 cm (1¾ inch) round cutter, which gives me 20 rounds from the first roll — and place on the trays. Re-roll the scraps and cut out more biscuits, but then throw the scraps out after the second rolling. Repeat with the remaining pastry. Lightly prick the crackers with the tines of a fork.

Bake for about 20 minutes for 2–3 mm thick crackers, or about 15 minutes for 1.5 mm thick ones, or until lightly golden at the edges — these crackers must be well cooked. Remove from the oven and cool on the trays for 10 minutes before using a spatula or palette knife to move them to wire racks.

Store in an airtight container for up to 1 month in a cool, dark place.

BAKING NOTES

- I've made these crackers with butter and oil. You will get a more delicate flavour if you use all butter, but it will be more crumbly. If you want to do so, omit the oil and use 90 g unsalted butter (in total). I like the more complex flavour from olive oil, but it can leave it a bit edgy — chutney, quince paste and cheese are great to offset this.

- Roll to your desired thickness. I like these 2–3 mm (¹⁄₁₆–⅛ inch) thick, but others prefer a slightly snappier and crunchier cracker rolled to about 1.5 mm (¹⁄₁₆ inch) thickness.

- In Australia, I prefer to use the Four Leaf oatmeal, which is made from stabilised rolled oat groats, ground to a meal (read more about this on pages 17–18). Some other brands I suspect are made from ground rolled oats and are very dry. If you find your mix crumbling, this is most likely the case. You can remedy this by adding a little more water (just a sprinkle) to the mix to moisten it up.

Barley, wheat and rosemary crackers

DAIRY FREE / EGG FREE
MAKES ABOUT 64 LARGE CRACKERS

These are insanely delicious and very good. With an earthy and robust flavour, they're just what you want with some good cheese and a glass of wine. I've specified wheat flour here, as it gives the gluten required to make a good cracker. You can do this in a mixer with the dough attachment, but it's just as easy to do by hand, and that means less washing up.

110 g (3¾ oz/1 cup) barley flour
150 g (5½ oz/1 cup) wholemeal wheat flour
2 teaspoons finely chopped rosemary
1 teaspoon fine sea salt, plus extra, for sprinkling
2–4 twists of freshly ground black pepper
60 ml (2 fl oz/¼ cup) extra virgin olive oil
1 tablespoon polenta (cornmeal), for dusting
35 g (1¼ oz/¼ cup) plain (all-purpose) white wheat flour, for rolling

Place the barley and wholemeal wheat flours, rosemary, salt and pepper in a mixing bowl and whisk through to combine and evenly distribute the ingredients.

Place 125 ml (4 fl oz/½ cup) of water in a small bowl with the oil and add this to the dry ingredients. Use your hands to mix it together. You may need to add a little extra water, but no more than 2 tablespoons, to make a moist, but not at all wet dough. Turn onto a work surface and knead the dough for 5–8 minutes or until smooth. Separate into four balls, place in a bowl and cover with plastic wrap (not a tea towel or they will dry out) and leave to sit for 30–60 minutes. If the weather is hot, leave them to sit in the fridge.

Preheat the oven to 210°C (415°F/Gas 6–7). Sprinkle two baking trays with 1 teaspoon of polenta, so that it is evenly covered — you may need to bake these in batches.

Sprinkle a work surface with a small amount of plain white wheat flour. Working with one ball of dough at a time (make sure to keep the others covered until you use them), roll out the dough to a circle about 33 cm (13 inches) in diameter and about 1–1.5 mm (¹⁄₁₆ inch) thick. Roughly cut into 16 wedges like you would cut a cake (they will be large triangles). Prick each cracker about five or six times with the tines of a fork. Use a palette knife to move them to the trays. Sprinkle each cracker with a pinch of salt.

Bake for 8–10 minutes or golden along the edges — keep your eyes on these as they can go from ready to overcooked very quickly. Remove from the oven and cool on the trays for 10 minutes, then move to a wire rack.

Repeat with the remaining dough.

Store in an airtight container for up to 2 weeks.

Cornmeal, spelt, parmesan and cheddar crackers

WHEAT FREE / EGG FREE
MAKES ABOUT 50

What sells as cornmeal is varied indeed. I am calling for flour that has a bit of both grit and soft flour — in Australia, it's called cornmeal or maize meal. When I can't find that, I mix a fifty–fifty ratio of gritty polenta with a corn flour (also known as yellow/golden corn/maize flour).

145 g (5¼ oz/1 cup) wholemeal spelt flour
140 g (5 oz/1 cup) cornmeal (maize meal)
¼ teaspoon sea salt
½ teaspoon baking powder
70 g (2½ oz) cold unsalted butter, cut into 1 cm (½ inch) pieces
50 g (1¾ oz/½ cup) grated parmesan or pecorino cheese
50 g (1¾ oz/½ cup) grated sharp cheddar cheese
125 ml (4 fl oz/½ cup) cultured buttermilk

Place the flour, cornmeal, salt, baking powder and butter in a food processor and process for 1 minute or until the mixture resembles fine breadcrumbs. Add the cheeses and buttermilk and pulse until the mixture comes together. Remove the dough from the processor and form into two balls. Place in separate plastic bags, slightly flatten the balls, seal and leave to sit in the fridge for 30 minutes.

Preheat the oven to 190°C (375°F/Gas 5). Line two baking trays with baking paper — you may need to bake these in batches.

Working with one ball of dough at a time and keeping the remaining dough in the fridge, roll the dough out between two sheets of baking paper to a circle about 30 cm (12 inches) in diameter. You should not need extra flour. As the pastry becomes bigger, it will stick to the paper. Lift the paper off and replace the paper. Gently turn the whole thing over (paper and all) and then repeat with the paper underneath; if you don't do this, the pastry will just stick to the paper and won't get any bigger. Using a biscuit cutter, stamp out crackers — I use a 4.5 cm (1¾ inch) round cutter, which gives me about 25 crackers from each ball of dough. You can re-roll the scraps, but you may find the dough crumbles a little, which is fine. Use a palette knife to move the crackers to the trays, then prick each cracker three times with the tines of a fork. Bake for 15 minutes or until the edges are just golden. Remove from the oven and cool on the trays for 10 minutes, then move to a wire rack.

Repeat with the remaining dough.

Store in an airtight container in a cool, dark place for up to 2 weeks.

Muffins

Being a muffin used to be an honourable thing — quick to put together, a not too sweet treat to pack and go. Alas, they are now embarrassingly enormous, flavourless, rich in refined carbohydrate, damaged oils and sugar, pretending to be food. I actually find myself feeling sorry for them. I have firm views on muffins and am of the belief that they should be rich in fruit, and that chocolate has absolutely no place whatsoever in them or anywhere near them! As my daughter often reminds me, this is entirely my own personal taste and if you love a muffin with chocolate, then well and good. I just feel it sweetens a muffin too much, especially white chocolate — there are far better ways to use chocolate.

It all starts with a muffin

Muffins are the perfect place to develop your wholefood baking experience, following on from biscuits, bars and crackers. Here, you have the opportunity to learn how different variables can produce such differing results, affecting rise and crumb. Technically, muffins are made by whisking together some cooled, melted butter (or oil), milk, vanilla and possibly an egg (the wet mix) and adding this to the flours, sugar and raising agent (the dry mix) and stirring the mix as little as possible to bring it all together — simple. You will get a perfectly decent crumb.

But, if you like a fluffier crumb that could possibly win competitions, you can cream the butter and sugar, add your egg (see Classic Earth Market Muffins, Egg free on page 113) and then add the flour and milk alternately to make a batter before folding in the fruit. That's not what I do, but I thought I should at least let you know and give you the opportunity to explore.

Fruit: cutting, moisture and combinations

Fruit is how I choose to incorporate moisture, sweetness and some leavening in a muffin. How you cut the fruit matters, and the best way depends upon what it is. Remember that the fruit will shrivel as it cooks, and it is for this reason that I like to cut fruit into good-sized chunks, so when you eat the muffin you actually bite through fruit.

Drier fresh fruits

* **Apple** Peeled or unpeeled, apple has little moisture and needs to be cut into small chunks, about 5 mm–1 cm (¼–½ inch) in size.

* **Banana** Cut into quarters (lengthways) and sliced about 1 cm (½ inch) thick.

* **Pear** Peeled or unpeeled and roughly cut into 1 cm (½ inch) pieces.

* **Rhubarb** Sliced about 1–2 cm (½–¾inch) thick.

Wetter fresh fruits

Moist fresh fruit (such as berries) should be partnered with a firmer fresh fruit (such as apple or banana) to provide structure to the muffin (read more about this in Some Other Useful Ingredients on page 37).

* **Berries** Larger berries chopped if desired. If berries are frozen, do not thaw.

* **Mango** Peeled and roughly diced into 1 cm (½ inch) pieces.

* **Pineapple** Peeled, core removed and chopped into 5 mm–1 cm (¼–½ inch) pieces.

* **Stone fruit and figs** Cut into or roughly chopped into 1 cm (½ inch) pieces.

Dried fruits

You have to carefully consider the role of dried fruit in a muffin and how much dried fruit you use as it can suck moisture out of the batter as it cooks, especially when used in conjunction with wholemeal flours. If you are just finely chopping a small amount (up to ½ cup) and adding the dried fruit (such as sultanas or figs) to the mix or partnering them with a dried fruit such as apple, it would be best to have a slightly wetter batter than normal or a higher ratio of fat. Alternatively, you could reconstitute them in a little liquid (even a good port/vincotto or fruit juice) before using. If adding small amounts of dried fruits (as above) to a muffin with mashed and cooked fruit or vegetable (such as stewed apple or pumpkin), they will be fine.

But, if using a dried fruit as your only fruit, it would be best to reconstitute the fruit in water before using — enough to allow it to become very moist, plump and more of its original self — 200 g (7 oz) of dried apricots/peaches/nectarines/et cetera will be ample once it has been reconstituted. Drain off any remaining liquid and roughly chop, then add to the dry mixture and toss through with your hands to evenly distribute.

BAKING NOTES

The basic muffin recipe has variables and you should take these into account:

- You can use spelt or wheat (read more about this in Baking With Wheat Versus Spelt on page 14). When using wheat flour, especially plain (all-purpose), you will use more milk, about 60 ml (2 fl oz/ ¼ cup) more.

- I use 400 g (14 oz) fruit, weighed in its whole form, but if I want more of a yummy treat (especially when using plums and figs, which I love) I up the amount to 500 g (1 lb 2 oz). This will give you a divine muffin, but one that may collapse a little in all its fruity glory when warm.

- You can add ¼ cup chopped nuts or seeds. If adding nuts, make sure they are roasted first to enrich the flavour. You can increase the amount, but it will produce a slightly denser muffin.

- You can add 25 g (¾ oz/¼ cup) desiccated coconut, which adds texture, fat and flavour, and works well with tropical fruits such as mango and pineapple, without needing to add any extra milk. If you add nuts and coconut, you may need to add a small amount of extra milk as well.

- If you want a less fruity muffin and more of a traditional 'cakey' muffin, you can reduce the amount of fruit to about 200 g (7 oz). You can increase the amount of butter to a maximum of 100 g (3½ oz), which will be about 80 ml (2½ fl oz/⅓ cup) of pure fat. This ensures you have enough actual fat for a good crumb, as there will be less fruit to mask any problems. If using oil, keep it at 80 ml (2½ fl oz/ ⅓ cup); you will also need to add an extra 1–2 tablespoons of milk.

- I use rapadura sugar in these recipes as it's the least-refined, most-whole cane sugar available and fairly cheap. Other options include coconut palm sugar, raw or demerara sugar. When using a liquid sugar, such as maple syrup, it will make the batter more 'runny' in the bowl (see Baking Notes, page 115).

- Add spices as desired.

- Muffins are best eaten warm from the oven or on the day they are made. Once cool, they freeze brilliantly. To reheat, place the frozen muffins directly into a warm oven to thaw.

- The muffin tin I use is a standard 80 ml (2½ fl oz/⅓ cup) capacity.

Topping the muffin

Toppings on muffins add further flavour and texture. For the best results, match the flavours to complement the fruit used. Use the recipes on the left as basic guides, changing the nuts and spices to suit. Nuts are not roasted as they will do so in the oven. These toppings make enough to top 10 muffins.

How much liquid to add?

You will notice that many of the muffin recipes call for a mix of cultured buttermilk (or yoghurt) and milk as I find that too much buttermilk overwhelms the full flavour of the fruit. But you can use only buttermilk; keep in mind, the extra acid from the increased amount of the buttermilk means the crumb will be slightly more fragile.

Many things impact on the amount of milk and/or buttermilk you need to add:

* The classic muffin made with 50 per cent each of white and wholemeal spelt flour will, on average, use about 185 ml (6 fl oz/¾ cup) milk, plus 1–2 tablespoons, or about 185 ml (6 fl oz/¾ cup) milk with 100 per cent white spelt. As you remove egg, you will generally use 250 ml (9 fl oz/1 cup) milk, and at times may need an extra 2 tablespoons — this is because you are making up for the liquid in the egg. From time to time, though, even spelt flours weighed in the bowl will ask for more liquid — this is the nature of less-refined flours.
* The classic muffin made with wheat (make sure you read about Baking With Wheat Versus Spelt on page 14) will use about 250 ml (9 fl oz/1 cup) milk, and extra without egg.
* If the fruit is mashed or collapsing (for example, mashed banana or very ripe plums), you can expect to use about 60 ml (2 fl oz/¼ cup) less milk in the batter, as the moisture from the fruit moves immediately into the batter.
* Including other flours will also affect the amount of milk required; adding oatmeal or rolled oats to a wheat or spelt base will reduce the amount needed, whereas quinoa or amaranth will increase it.

Determining how much milk and/or buttermilk you need to add is made so much easier if you measure your flours by weight.

You are looking for a batter that moves smoothly and freely over the spoon as you mix, but is not at all runny. A batter that is not moist enough will tend to be clumpy with little free-flowing movement as you stir. A good way to know if your batter is too moist is if the muffins come out of the oven puffed and lovely, but then collapse as they cool.

CINNAMON AND NUT TOPPING

Combine 70 g (2½ oz/ ½ cup) roughly chopped raw nuts (either hazelnuts, walnuts or pecans), 1 teaspoon ground cinnamon, 2 tablespoons desiccated coconut and 2 tablespoons rapadura sugar in a bowl.

MACADAMIA NUT, COCONUT AND PALM SUGAR TOPPING

Combine 70 g (2½ oz/ ½ cup) roughly chopped raw macadamia nuts, 2 tablespoons desiccated coconut and 2 tablespoons granulated coconut palm sugar in a bowl.

Classic Earth Market muffins, revisited

WHEAT FREE / CAN BE DAIRY FREE
MAKES 9–10 GOOD-SIZED MUFFINS

This is my Classic Earth Market Muffin revisited and infinitely variable. I always made these without egg, but I must admit that I have grown to like the lightness an egg provides. The use of 50 per cent wholemeal and 50 per cent unbleached white flour produces a nutrient-dense but lighter muffin.

1 quantity cinnamon and nut topping or macadamia nut,
    coconut and palm sugar topping (opposite)
400 g (14 oz) fruit (weighed whole), prepared

Dry mix
130 g (4½ oz/1 cup) unbleached white spelt flour
145 g (5¼ oz/1 cup) wholemeal spelt flour
2½ teaspoons baking powder
75 g (2½ oz/½ cup) rapadura sugar or raw sugar

Wet mix
125 ml (4 fl oz/½ cup) milk
125 ml (4 fl oz/½ cup) cultured buttermilk, kefir milk
    (see page 276) or yoghurt, plus extra, as needed
1 egg, at room temperature
1 teaspoon natural vanilla extract
80 g (2¾ oz) unsalted butter, melted and cooled a little

Preheat the oven to 180°C (350°F/Gas 4). Place paper cases into a 12-hole muffin tin. Have your topping prepared too.

For the dry mix, place the flours, baking powder and sugar in a bowl and stir through with a whisk to lighten and break up the flours and sugar clumps. Add the fruit (except if using berries) and stir gently to distribute evenly.

For the wet mix, place equal amounts of the two milks in a measuring cup to make 185 ml (6 fl oz/¾ cup). Add this to the egg, vanilla extract and butter and whisk together in a small bowl.

Add the wet mix to the dry mix and gently mix together taking great care not to overmix and work the batter. Add the remaining mixed milks as needed (and gently fold through berries if using).

Spoon the batter into the prepared muffin tin and generously sprinkle with the topping. Bake for 30–40 minutes or until golden. Remove from the oven, cool in the tin for 10 minutes, then turn out and move to wire racks.

DAIRY FREE

Replace the butter, milk and cultured buttermilk with:
125 ml (4 fl oz/½ cup) rice milk
125 ml (4 fl oz/½ cup) coconut milk, plus extra, as needed
80 ml (2½ fl oz/⅓ cup) macadamia nut or almond oil
2 teaspoons apple cider vinegar

Place equal amounts of the milks in a measuring cup to make 185 ml (6 fl oz/¾ cup). Add this to the egg, vanilla extract, oil and vinegar.

BAKING NOTES

Using this recipe as a template, you can play around with it — I've given some of my favourite variations of other ratios and mixtures of flours below:

- Light and fluffy 260 g (9 oz/2 cups) unbleached white spelt flour.

- A little bit chewy 130 g (4½ oz/1 cup) unbleached white spelt flour, plus 73 g (2½ oz/½ cup) wholemeal spelt flour, plus 50 g (1¾ oz/½ cup) rolled oats.

- 100 per cent wholemeal — moist and more chewy 145 g (5¼ oz/1 cup) wholemeal spelt flour, plus 67 g (2¼ oz/½ cup) oatmeal, plus 50 g (1¾ oz/½ cup) rolled oats.

- High protein 130 g (4½ oz/1 cup) unbleached white spelt flour, plus 60 g (2¼ oz/½ cup) quinoa flour, plus 50 g (1¾ oz/½ cup) quinoa flakes.

Classic Earth Market muffins, egg free

EGG FREE / WHEAT FREE / CAN BE DAIRY FREE
MAKES 9–10 GOOD-SIZED MUFFINS

The addition of an egg is not essential for a good muffin. To make up for the loss of egg, increase the butter to 100 g (3½ oz) (which is about 80 ml/2½ fl oz/⅓ cup of pure fat). I would also suggest you use the creaming method, which will produce a better rise and crumb. The milk will go up to about 250 ml (9 fl oz/1 cup) plus 2 tablespoons (more if using wheat flour). If you are in a rush and simply can't be bothered to cream the butter and sugar, you can, of course, use the wet-to-dry method.

1 quantity cinnamon and nut topping or macadamia nut,
   coconut and palm sugar topping (see page 110)
130 g (4½ oz/1 cup) unbleached white spelt flour
145 g (5¼ oz/1 cup) wholemeal spelt flour
2½ teaspoons baking powder
125 ml (4 fl oz/½ cup) milk
125 ml (4 fl oz/½ cup) cultured buttermilk, kefir milk (see page 276)
   or yoghurt, plus 60 ml (2 fl oz/¼ cup), as needed
100 g (3½ oz) unsalted butter, softened
75 g (2½ oz/½ cup) rapadura sugar
1 teaspoon natural vanilla extract
400 g (14 oz) fruit (weighed whole), prepared

Preheat the oven to 180°C (350°F/Gas 4). Place paper cases into a 12-hole muffin tin. Have your topping prepared too.

Place the flours and baking powder into a bowl and stir through with a whisk to lighten and break up the flours.

Place equal amounts of the milks in a cup measure to make 185 ml (6 fl oz/¾ cup).

Using a stand mixer fitted with the paddle attachment, beat the butter and sugar until light and fluffy, scraping down the sides from time to time. Add the vanilla extract, half of the flour mixture and half of the mixed milks. Beat gently until just incorporated. Add the remaining flour mixture and remaining mixed milks and beat gently until just combined. Assess the consistency — it is now that you should add the extra buttermilk, and it should be moist enough to easily fold through the fruit in the next step. Remove the bowl from the stand and gently fold through the fruit by hand. The batter should not look at all clumpy or runny, but it should move smoothly and freely over the spoon as you mix.

Spoon the batter into the muffin tin and generously sprinkle with the topping. Bake for 30–40 minutes or until golden. Remove from the oven, cool in the tin for 10 minutes, then turn out and move to wire racks.

WET-TO-DRY METHOD

Follow the technique given for the Classic Earth Market Muffins, Revisited (see page 111), adding extra milk as needed.

DAIRY FREE

Replace the milk, cultured buttermilk and butter with:
2 teaspoons apple cider vinegar
125 ml (4 fl oz/½ cup) rice milk
125 ml (4 fl oz/½ cup) coconut milk, plus 60 ml (2 fl oz/¼ cup), as needed
80 ml (2½ fl oz/⅓ cup) coconut, macadamia nut or almond oil

Add the vinegar to the mixed milks. If you want to use coconut oil, you can still use a creaming technique (read more about this in Air and Crumb on page 52). If using a liquid oil such as warm coconut, macadamia nut or almond, do this mix with a classic wet-to-dry method.

Classic Earth Market muffin — egg, butter and dairy free

WHEAT FREE / EGG FREE / DAIRY FREE
MAKES 9–10 GOOD-SIZED MUFFINS

Taking eggs and dairy out of a muffin does have an impact, and you need to structure things a little differently. The high omega-3 chia seed can come in very handy here — ground and left to sit in warm water, it will thicken and mimic the richness, moisture and bind of an egg.

1 quantity cinnamon and nut topping or macadamia nut,
 coconut and palm sugar topping (see page 110)
1 teaspoon ground chia seeds
400 g (14 oz) fruit (weighed whole), prepared

Dry mix
130 g (4½ oz/1 cup) unbleached white spelt flour
145 g (5¼ oz/1 cup) wholemeal spelt flour
1¼ teaspoons baking powder
75 g (2½ oz/½ cup) rapadura sugar
¾ teaspoon baking soda (bicarbonate of soda)

Wet mix
1 teaspoon natural vanilla extract
80 ml (2½ fl oz/⅓ cup) macadamia nut or almond oil
125 ml (4 fl oz/½ cup) rice milk
125 ml (4 fl oz/½ cup) coconut milk
2 teaspoons apple cider vinegar

Preheat the oven to 180°C (350°F/Gas 4). Place paper cases into a 12-hole muffin tin. Have your topping prepared too.

Mix the ground chia seeds with 45 ml (1½ fl oz) of warm water, stir and leave to thicken.

For the dry mix, place the flours, baking powder and sugar into a bowl. Sieve the baking soda into the bowl and stir through with a whisk to lighten and break up the flours and sugar clumps. Add the fruit (except if using berries) and stir gently to distribute evenly.

Combine the chia mix and all of the wet mix ingredients in a bowl and whisk together.

Add the wet mix to the dry mix and gently mix together taking great care not to overmix and work the batter. Add extra milk as needed (and gently fold through berries if using).

Spoon the batter into the muffin tin and generously sprinkle with the topping. Bake for 30–40 minutes or until golden. Remove from the oven, cool in the tin for 10 minutes, then move to wire racks.

Maple syrup, pear and ginger muffins

WHEAT FREE / CAN BE DAIRY FREE
MAKES 9–10 GOOD-SIZED MUFFINS

When made with maple syrup, magic is transferred to a muffin as the syrup perfumes it with a luscious scent. The crumb also colours differently and is softer.

1 quantity cinnamon and nut topping (see page 110)
400 g (14 oz) ripe but firm pears (I like bartlett or packham),
    peeled, cored and roughly cut into 5 mm–1 cm (¼–½ inch)
    pieces
50 g (1¾ oz) glacé ginger, finely chopped

Dry mix
130 g (4½ oz/1 cup) unbleached white spelt flour
145 g (5¼ oz/1 cup) wholemeal spelt flour
2½ teaspoons baking powder
½–1 teaspoon ground cinnamon
⅛ teaspoon ground cloves (optional)

Wet mix
125 ml (4 fl oz/½ cup) milk
125 ml (4 fl oz/½ cup) cultured buttermilk, kefir milk
    (see page 276) or yoghurt, plus extra, as needed
1 egg, at room temperature
1 teaspoon natural vanilla extract
80 g (2¾ oz) unsalted butter, melted and cooled a little,
    or 80 ml (2½ fl oz/⅓ cup) macadamia nut or almond oil
125 ml (4 fl oz/½ cup) maple syrup

Preheat the oven to 180°C (350°F/Gas 4). Place paper cases into a 12-hole muffin tin. Have your topping prepared too.

For the dry mix, place the flours, baking powder and spices in a bowl and stir through with a whisk to lighten and break up the flours and sugar clumps. Add the pear and ginger and stir gently to distribute evenly.

For the wet mix, place equal amounts of the two milks in a measuring cup to make 185 ml (6 fl oz/¾ cup). Add this to the egg, vanilla extract, butter and maple syrup and whisk together in a small bowl.

Add the wet mix to the dry mix and gently mix together taking great care not to overmix and work the batter. Add the remaining mixed milks as needed.

Spoon the batter into the muffin tin and generously sprinkle with the topping. Bake for 30–40 minutes or until golden. Remove from the oven, cool in the tin for 10 minutes, then turn out and move to wire racks.

BAKING NOTE

Because the sweetness is in a liquid form, this batter will be more liquid than normal, which is fine. All granulated sugars ultimately melt when in the oven and provide part of the liquid in a batter — here you get to see it in the raw batter.

DAIRY FREE

Replace the milk and cultured buttermilk with:
2 teaspoons apple cider vinegar
125 ml (4 fl oz/½ cup) rice milk
125 ml (4 fl oz/½ cup) coconut milk, plus extra, as needed

Add the vinegar to the wet mix ingredients in the jug.

Roasted pumpkin, balsamic onion and feta muffins

WHEAT FREE / CAN BE DAIRY FREE
MAKES 9–10 GOOD-SIZED MUFFINS

This is a delicious slightly sweet–sour muffin and a wonderful choice to serve with soup. Finely chopped chives or spring onions (scallions) would both make fine additions, and you can top the muffins with a good melting cheese if desired.

1 x 200 g (7 oz) piece of butternut, jap or kent pumpkin
    (winter squash), skin on
1 tablespoon extra virgin olive oil
2 teaspoons finely chopped rosemary
35 g (1¼ oz/¼ cup) pumpkin seeds (pepitas)

Dry mix
130 g (4½ oz/1 cup) unbleached white spelt flour
145 g (5¼ oz/1 cup) wholemeal spelt flour
2½ teaspoons baking powder
good pinch of sea salt and 2–3 twists of freshly ground
    black pepper
1 teaspoon dulse flakes
1 tablespoon finely chopped rosemary
⅓ cup balsamic onions (see page 280)
80 g (2¾ oz) feta cheese, chopped into 1 cm (½ inch) pieces

Wet mix
125 ml (4 fl oz/½ cup) milk
125 ml (4 fl oz/½ cup) cultured buttermilk, kefir milk
    (see page 276) or yoghurt, plus extra, as needed
1 egg, at room temperature
80 ml (2½ fl oz/⅓ cup) olive oil or 80 g (2¾ oz) unsalted butter,
    melted and cooled a little

Preheat the oven to 180°C (350°F/Gas 4). Place paper cases into a 12-hole muffin tin.

Rub the pumpkin with the oil and place on a baking tray, then sprinkle with the rosemary. Roast for 40 minutes or until cooked and the edges are slightly caramelised. Remove from the oven and leave to cool for 10 minutes. Roughly cut the pumpkin into chunks, discarding the skin.

For the dry mix, place the flours, baking powder, salt, pepper, dulse flakes and rosemary in a bowl and stir through with a whisk to lighten and break up the flours. Add the balsamic onions, feta and pumpkin and lightly stir through (with your hands is ideal) to evenly distribute.

For the wet mix, place equal amounts of the two milks in a measuring cup to make 185 ml (6 fl oz/¾ cup). Add this to the egg and oil and whisk together in a small bowl.

Add the wet mix to the dry mix and gently mix together taking great care not to overmix and work the batter. Add the remaining mixed milks as needed. Spoon the batter into the muffin tins and sprinkle with the pumpkin seeds.

Bake for 35–45 minutes or until lightly golden. Remove from the oven, cool for 10 minutes in the tin, then remove and cool on wire racks.

Dairy free

If tolerated, replace the feta cheese with 80 g (2¾ oz) of goat's chevre or young sheep's cheese. If not, replace the cheese with ½ cup roasted vegetables (such as eggplant/aubergine or capsicum/pepper) to make up for mouthfeel.

Replace the milk and cultured buttermilk with:

2 teaspoons apple cider vinegar

125 ml (4 fl oz/½ cup) rice milk

125 ml (4 fl oz/½ cup) coconut milk, plus 1 tablespoon extra, as needed

Add the vinegar to the wet mix ingredients in the jug.

Plum, fig and hazelnut muffins

WHEAT FREE / CAN BE DAIRY FREE
MAKES 9–10 GOOD-SIZED MUFFINS

I adore the combination of fresh fig and plum, and you'll notice 500 g (1 lb 2 oz) of fruit in these muffins. They are abundantly generous in lusciousness and when broken, the jewelled brilliance of the fruit spills out. They're very, very good and the perfect thing to have with a cup of tea.

1 quantity cinnamon and hazelnut topping (see page 110)
400 g (14 oz) plums, halved, stoned and quartered
100 g (3½ oz) fresh figs, ripe but not at all squishy, peeled
    and halved or quartered depending on size

Dry mix
130 g (4½ oz/1 cup) unbleached white spelt flour
145 g (5¼ oz/1 cup) wholemeal spelt flour
2½ teaspoons baking powder
75 g (2½ oz/½ cup) rapadura sugar
75 g (2½ oz/½ cup) hazelnuts, roasted and skins removed
    and roughly chopped

Wet mix
125 ml (4 fl oz/½ cup) milk
125 ml (4 fl oz/½ cup) cultured buttermilk, kefir milk
    (see page 276) or yoghurt, plus extra, as needed
1 egg, at room temperature
1 teaspoon natural vanilla extract
80 g (2¾ oz) unsalted butter, melted and cooled a little, or
    80 ml (2½ fl oz/⅓ cup) macadamia nut or almond oil

BAKING NOTE

I love the deeply scarlet santa rosa or old-fashioned laroda plums in these muffins — I find they have both flavour and perfume. If you can't find these, any red plum (mariposa, blood or satsuma) will be fine. I wouldn't bother with the yellow plums as they just don't have the same flavour.

DAIRY FREE

Replace the milk and cultured buttermilk with:
2 teaspoons apple cider vinegar
125 ml (4 fl oz/½ cup) rice milk
125 ml (4 fl oz/½ cup) coconut milk, plus extra, as needed

Add the vinegar to the wet mix ingredients in the jug.

Preheat the oven to 180°C (350°F/Gas 4). Place paper cases into a 12-hole muffin tin. Have your topping prepared too.

For the dry mix, place the flours, baking powder, sugar and nuts in a bowl and stir through with a whisk to lighten and break up the flours and sugar clumps. Add the plums and stir gently to distribute evenly.

For the wet mix, place equal amounts of the two milks in a measuring cup to make 185 ml (6 fl oz/¾ cup). Add this to the egg, vanilla extract and butter and whisk together in a small bowl.

Add the wet mix to the dry mix and gently mix together taking great care not to overmix and work the batter. Add the remaining mixed milks as needed and gently fold through the figs. Spoon the batter into the prepared muffin tin and generously sprinkle with the topping. Bake for 30–40 minutes or until golden. Remove from the oven, cool in the tin for 10 minutes, then turn out and move to wire racks.

Pumpkin pie muffins

WHEAT FREE / CAN BE DAIRY FREE
MAKES 9–10 GOOD-SIZED MUFFINS

I often add a handful of finely chopped glacé ginger into this as well — too much ginger is never enough ginger for me — but you could also grate 1 teaspoon of fresh ginger into the mix.

1 quantity cinnamon and pecan or walnut topping (see page 110)
250 g (9 oz/1 cup, firmly packed) mashed pumpkin (winter squash)

Dry mix
130 g (4½ oz/1 cup) unbleached white spelt flour
145 g (5¼ oz/1 cup) wholemeal spelt flour
2½ teaspoons baking powder
75 g (2½ oz/½ cup) rapadura sugar
2 teaspoons ground cinnamon
1 teaspoon ground ginger
⅛ teaspoon ground mace
⅛ teaspoon ground cloves
50 g (1¾ oz/½ cup) pecans or walnuts, roasted (see page 280)
     and roughly chopped
105 g (3½ oz/½ cup) dried figs, cut into 5 mm (½ inch) pieces

Wet mix
60 ml (2 fl oz/¼ cup) milk
60 ml (2 fl oz/¼ cup) cultured buttermilk, kefir milk (see page 276)
     or yoghurt, plus extra, as needed
1 egg, at room temperature
1 teaspoon natural vanilla extract
80 g (2¾ oz) unsalted butter, melted and cooled a little
     or 80 ml (2½ fl oz/⅓ cup) macadamia nut or almond oil

Preheat the oven to 180°C (350°F/Gas 4). Place paper cases into a 12-hole muffin tin. Have your topping prepared too.

For the dry mix, place the flours, baking powder, sugar, spices and nuts in a bowl and stir through with a whisk to lighten and break up the flours and sugar clumps. Add the dried figs and stir to distribute evenly.

For the wet mix, place the two milks in a measuring cup to make. Add this to the egg, vanilla extract, butter and mashed pumpkin and whisk together in a small bowl.

Add the wet mix to the dry mix and gently mix together taking great care not to overmix and work the batter. Add the extra buttermilk as needed.

Spoon the batter into the prepared muffin tin and generously sprinkle with the topping. Bake for 30–40 minutes or until golden. Remove from the oven, cool in the tin for 10 minutes, then turn out and move to wire racks.

Summer zucchini, oven-dried tomatoes, basil, feta and olive muffins

WHEAT FREE / CAN BE DAIRY FREE
MAKES 9–10 GOOD-SIZED MUFFINS

This is a very forgiving recipe, and you can add extras as desired — ground seeds, finely chopped spring onions (scallions) or chives are all delicious. Change the ingredients as you please — some roasted or grilled eggplant (aubergine) or capsicum (pepper) instead of tomatoes are excellent.

I prefer to dry the tomatoes myself and this produces a softer, but more densely flavoured result than many commercial ones. I recommend you at least triple this oven-dried tomato recipe to use in salads and lunches. They will keep in an airtight container in the fridge for up to 1 week.

60 g (2¼ oz) feta cheese, chopped into 1 cm (½ inch) pieces
70 g (2½ oz/¾ cup) grated cheddar cheese
80 g (2¾ oz/½ cup) pine nuts

Oven-dried tomatoes
8–10 cherry tomatoes, halved
5 basil leaves, torn
pinch of sea salt and freshly ground black pepper
1 tablespoon extra virgin olive oil

Dry mix
130 g (4½ oz/1 cup) unbleached white spelt flour
145 g (5¼ oz/1 cup) wholemeal spelt flour
2½ teaspoons baking powder
good pinch of sea salt and freshly ground black pepper
1 teaspoon dulse flakes
1 zucchini (courgette) (about 150 g/5½ oz)
¼ cup roughly chopped basil
2 tablespoons grated parmesan or pecorino cheese
40 g (1½ oz/¼ cup) pitted Kalamata olives, roughly chopped

Wet mix
125 ml (4 fl oz/½ cup) milk
125 ml (4 fl oz/½ cup) cultured buttermilk, kefir milk
   (see page 276) or yoghurt, plus 1 tablespoon extra, as needed
1 egg, at room temperature
80 ml (2½ fl oz/⅓ cup) olive oil or 80 g (2¾ oz) unsalted butter,
   melted and cooled a little

Preheat the oven to 180°C (350°F/Gas 4). Place paper cases into a 12-hole muffin tin.

For the oven-dried tomatoes, place the cherry tomato halves, cut side up, on a baking tray and gently push a piece of basil leaf into each one. Sprinkle with salt and pepper and drizzle with the oil.

Roast for 30 minutes or until a little singed on the outside, but still soft in the middle. Remove from the oven and set aside to cool.

For the dry mix, place the flours, baking powder, salt, pepper and dulse flakes in a bowl and stir through with a whisk to lighten and break up the flours.

Grate the zucchini and place in a clean tea towel. Roll up the tea towel and wring as much liquid as you can from the zucchini. You should have 1 packed cup of zucchini. Add this to the dry mix with the basil, parmesan and olives and stir through to evenly distribute.

For the wet mix, place the milks, egg and oil into a bowl and whisk together.

Add the wet mix to the dry mix and gently mix together taking great care not to overmix and work the batter. Add the extra buttermilk as needed, and gently fold through the feta and oven-dried tomatoes.

Spoon the batter into the muffin tin and sprinkle with cheddar and pine nuts. Bake for 35–45 minutes or until lightly golden. Remove from the oven, cool in the tin for 10 minutes, then turn out and move to wire racks.

Dairy free

Replace the cheeses with ¼–⅓ cup of homemade dairy-free pesto (refer to *Coming Home to Eat* or *Wholefood For Children*), ½ cup roasted vegetables (such as eggplant/aubergine), and omit the roughly chopped basil (or replace with flat-leaf/Italian parsley if you have some on hand). The roasted vegetables will provide delicious flavour, moisture and texture to the muffin.

Replace the milk and cultured buttermilk with:

2 teaspoons apple cider vinegar

125 ml (4 fl oz/½ cup) rice milk

125 ml (4 fl oz/½ cup) coconut milk, plus 1 tablespoon extra,
as needed for spelt and extra for wheat

Add the vinegar to the wet mix ingredients in the jug.

Classic gluten-free muffins

GLUTEN FREE / CAN BE DAIRY FREE
MAKES 9–10 GOOD-SIZED MUFFINS

This is a lovely, all-purpose mix for gluten-free baking. You can replace the coconut with ground nuts if desired. As discussed, I prefer not to use gums in gluten-free baking, thus the increase in the amount of egg required for binding. You can expect to use 185 ml (6 fl oz/ ¾ cup) of milk, increasing it as you remove the egg.

1 quantity cinnamon and nut topping, or macadamia nut,
    coconut and palm sugar topping (see page 110)
400 g (14 oz) fruit (weighed whole), prepared

Dry mix
200 g (7 oz/1¼ cups) brown rice flour
30 g (1 oz/¼ cup) quinoa flour
30 g (1 oz/¼ cup) true arrowroot
25 g (1 oz/¼ cup) desiccated coconut
2½ teaspoons baking powder
75 g (2½ oz/½ cup) rapadura sugar

Wet mix
125 ml (4 fl oz/½ cup) milk
125 ml (4 fl oz/½ cup) cultured buttermilk, kefir milk
    (see page 276) or yoghurt
2 eggs, at room temperature
1 teaspoon natural vanilla extract
80 g (2¾ oz) unsalted butter, melted and cooled a little,
    or 80 ml (2½ fl oz/⅓ cup) macadamia nut or almond oil

DAIRY FREE

Replace the milk and cultured buttermilk with:
2 teaspoons apple cider vinegar
125 ml (4 fl oz/½ cup) rice milk
125 ml (4 fl oz/½ cup) coconut milk, plus 1 tablespoon extra, as needed

Add the vinegar to the wet mix ingredients in the jug.

Preheat the oven to 180°C (350°F/Gas 4). Place paper cases into a 12-hole muffin tin and have your topping prepared too.

For the dry mix, place the flours, arrowroot, coconut, baking powder and sugar in a bowl and stir through with a whisk to lighten and break up the flours and sugar clumps. Add the fruit (except if using berries) and stir gently to distribute evenly.

For the wet mix, place equal amounts of the two milks in a measuring cup to make 185 ml (6 fl oz/¾ cup). Add this to the eggs, vanilla extract and butter and whisk together in a small bowl.

Add the wet mix to the dry mix and gently mix together. Add the remaining mixed milks as needed — gluten-free batters should be slightly wetter than those made with spelt or wheat. (Gently fold through berries if using.)

Spoon the batter into the prepared muffin tin and generously sprinkle with the topping. Bake for 30–40 minutes or until golden. Remove from the oven, cool in the tin for 10 minutes, then turn out and move to wire racks.

Classic gluten-free muffins, egg free

GLUTEN FREE / EGG FREE
MAKES 9–10 GOOD-SIZED MUFFINS

It's always tricky to remove egg from gluten-free baking, as eggs help to bind and lighten the crumb, but it can be done — and without relying on gums. Again, chia seed is my favourite as it really helps to moisten, enrich and bind. Butter is also increased to provide extra richness and fat, but if using oil, keep it to 80 ml (2½ fl oz/⅓ cup). You can expect to use 185 ml (6 fl oz/¾ cup) milk plus 2 tablespoons.

1 quantity cinnamon and nut topping or macadamia nut,
    coconut and palm sugar topping (see page 110)
1 teaspoon ground chia seeds
400 g (14 oz) fruit (weighed whole), prepared

Dry mix
200 g (7 oz/1¼ cups) brown rice flour
30 g (1 oz/¼ cup) quinoa flour
30 g (1 oz/¼ cup) true arrowroot
25 g (1 oz/¼ cup) desiccated coconut
2½ teaspoons baking powder
75 g (2½ oz/½ cup) rapadura sugar

Wet mix
125 ml (4 fl oz/½ cup) milk
125 ml (4 fl oz/½ cup) cultured buttermilk, kefir milk
    (see page 276) or yoghurt
1 teaspoon natural vanilla extract
100 g (3½ oz) unsalted butter, melted and cooled a little
    or 80 ml (2½ fl oz/⅓ cup) macadamia nut or almond oil

Preheat the oven to 180°C (350°F/Gas 4). Place paper cases into a 12-hole muffin tin and have your topping prepared too.

Mix the ground chia seeds with 45 ml (1½ fl oz) warm water, stir and leave to thicken.

For the dry mix, place the flours, arrowroot, coconut, baking powder and sugar into a bowl and stir through with a whisk to lighten and break up the flours and sugar clumps. Add the fruit (except if using berries) and stir gently to distribute evenly.

For the wet mix, place equal amounts of the two milks in a measuring cup to make 185 ml (6 fl oz/¾ cup). Add this to the chia, vanilla extract and butter and whisk together in a small bowl.

Add the wet mix to the dry mix and gently mix together. Add the remaining mixed milks as needed — this should be a very moist, wet, but not runny mix. (Gently fold through berries if using.) Spoon the batter into the muffin tin and generously sprinkle with the topping. Bake for 30–40 minutes or until golden. Remove from the oven, cool in the tin for 10 minutes, then turn out and move to wire racks.

Classic gluten-free muffins, egg and dairy free

GLUTEN FREE / EGG FREE / DAIRY FREE
MAKES 9–10 GOOD-SIZED MUFFINS

Slightly denser than the Classic Gluten-Free Muffins, but quite respectable and delicious nonetheless. If you want a fluffier result, using an egg replacer (see page 34) will do the best job. As there is no butter in these muffins, you may find you'll need to use slightly more milk than usual to make up for the water in the butter.

1 quantity cinnamon and nut topping or macadamia nut,
    coconut and palm sugar topping (see page 110)
1 teaspoon ground chia seeds
400 g (14 oz) fruit (weighed whole), prepared

Dry mix
200 g (7 oz/1¼ cups) brown rice flour
30 g (1 oz/¼ cup) quinoa flour
30 g (1 oz/¼ cup) true arrowroot
25 g (1 oz/¼ cup) desiccated coconut
2½ teaspoons baking powder
75 g (2½ oz/½ cup) rapadura sugar

Wet mix
125 ml (4 fl oz/½ cup) rice milk
125 ml (4 fl oz/½ cup) coconut milk
1 teaspoon natural vanilla extract
2 teaspoons apple cider vinegar
80 ml (2½ fl oz/⅓ cup) macadamia nut or almond oil

Preheat the oven to 180°C (350°F/Gas 4). Place paper cases into a 12-hole muffin tin. Have your topping prepared and ready.

Mix the ground chia seeds with 45 ml (1½ fl oz) of warm water, stir and leave to thicken.

For the dry mix, place the flours, arrowroot, coconut, baking powder and sugar in a bowl and stir through with a whisk to lighten and break up the flours and sugar clumps. Add the fruit (except berries if using) and stir gently to distribute evenly.

For the wet mix, place equal amounts of the two milks in a measuring cup to make 185 ml (6 fl oz/¾ cup). Add this to the chia, vanilla extract, vinegar and oil and whisk together in a small bowl.

Add the wet mix to the dry mix and gently mix together. Add the remaining mixed milks as needed — this should be a very moist, wet, but not runny mix. (Gently fold through berries if using.)

Spoon the batter into the prepared muffin tin and generously sprinkle with the topping. Bake for 30–40 minutes or until golden. Cool in the tin for 10 minutes, then turn out and move to wire racks.

Cakes

Where would we be without cake? I cannot imagine my life without the memories of my daughter poring over the Women's Weekly birthday cake book all year trying to choose her favourite, the glow in her eyes when it actually came to be, or the warm delight when Mum would cook an apple cake for afternoon tea on the weekend. Neither can I imagine a special occasion without one — birthdays, naming days and weddings all centred around a cake — nor an afternoon tea without a simple comforting wedge of cake, or a lunchbox without a slice of pumpkin loaf nestled within it. This is not unhealthy, this is not excessive — this is celebrating special moments and tucking a bit of delicious comfort into an everyday life. A cake is powerful love medicine.

Cakes for every day and special occasions

Everyday cakes (see pages 139–150) are something we can easily and quickly put together, and we are accepting that we may not end up with a perfect crumb. Fruit or vegetables are very often used, and it doesn't really matter if the molasses from a rapadura sugar colours or flavours the result. Butter and sugar may not be creamed quite as perfectly (if used at all), air may not be fully realised, fat may or may not be reduced, but nonetheless the result will be something delicious that all will love and enjoy.

A plain crumb cake (see pages 151–167), however, stands alone — that crumb is the only show in town so to speak, and more work is needed to help it become all it can be, and its potential fully realised.

The more special the occasion, the more we need to address and take care with basic techniques, such as creaming butter and sugar, and adding eggs or whipping eggs and sugar to the ribbon. As we reduce fat and/or egg, more thought to technique is required, and drawing on our Box of Tricks (see page 59) can ensure a delicious result.

For myself, as a general rule, I prefer lighter cakes in summer, favouring a simple Génoise Sponge Cake (see page 151) or buttermilk cake (see pages 169–182), layered or topped with whipped cream and an abundance of fresh fruit or high-quality jam. In winter, cakes with a layer of rich frosting are what I'm attracted to — especially the Coffee and Walnut Cake (see page 154)! In this chapter you will find a range of cakes for all occasions, and a broad range of techniques put to use.

Teacakes, coffee cakes, quick breads and loaves

The cakes in this section are delicious and simple cakes to make, perfect to serve with tea or coffee. These are best eaten warm or at the least, very fresh. Mine is a little denser and darker than the cinnamon teacake my mum used to make on a weekend afternoon (most likely a Golden Wattle or CWA recipe) but it's just as good. These types of cakes are often less rich in oil or butter and sugar and thus the crumb will not be as delicious the second day.

Quick breads and loaves are very closely related to a teacake and coffee cake, but with more staying power. Simple to put together, I prefer mine generously studded with flavour and fruit or vegetable. With slightly more fat, these are sturdy workers for morning and afternoon tea and great additions to lunchboxes throughout the week.

Blueberry boy bait

WHEAT FREE
SERVES 6–8

As I was reading a very old collection of recipes from the American South, I was struck by the title of Blueberry Boy Bait — apparently it won boys over from far and wide. And true to form, when I presented tastings of the teacakes to the workers next door, a young man zeroed in immediately on the Boy Bait. 'Oooh, I'll start with this one,' he said. I stood amazed. Such is the power of the Boy Bait, dear reader. This should be a plain and simple cake, and a rapadura sugar overwhelms the pure and delicious flavours that come from the berry, butter and flour. Raw or demerara sugar sweetens, but allows that flavour to be fully available. Make sure to bake this in a large tin so you do get a shallow cake.

130 g (4½ oz/1 cup) unbleached white spelt flour
145 g (5¼ oz/1 cup) wholemeal spelt flour
2 teaspoons baking powder
1 teaspoon ground cinnamon
125 ml (4 fl oz/½ cup) milk
130 g (4½ oz/½ cup) yoghurt
125 g (4½ oz) unsalted butter, softened
105 g (3½ oz/½ cup) demerara sugar
2 eggs, at room temperature
1 teaspoon natural vanilla extract
155 g (5½ oz/1 cup) fresh blueberries

Topping
2 tablespoons rapadura sugar
1 teaspoon ground cinnamon
80 g (2¾ oz/½ cup) fresh blueberries

Preheat the oven to 180°C (350°F/Gas 4) or 165°C (320°F/Gas 2–3) if fan-forced. Grease a 30 cm x 20 cm (12 x 8 inch) baking tray and line the base with baking paper.

Place the topping ingredients in a small bowl and toss together. Set aside.

Place the flours, baking powder and cinnamon in a bowl and whisk through to break up any clumps. Whisk the milk and yoghurt together in a small bowl.

Using a stand mixer fitted with the paddle attachment, beat the butter and sugar until light and fluffy, scraping down the sides from time to time. Add the eggs, one at a time, beating well after each addition, and then the vanilla extract. Air is important in this recipe for a lovely crumb, so if the mix looks a bit curdled (read more about this in Air and Crumb on page 52), add half the flour mixture and half the milk mixture and beat gently until just combined, then add the remaining flour mixture and milk mixture and beat gently until just combined. Gently fold in the blueberries. Turn into the tray and evenly sprinkle over the topping. Bake for 35–40 minutes or until a skewer inserted in the middle comes out clean. Remove from the oven and cool in the tray for 10 minutes before serving.

HOW TO STORE

This cake is best served on the day of baking, but it will keep in an airtight container in a cool, dark place for up to 2 days, or it can be frozen in portions, thawed, then warmed in the oven.

Date and pecan streusel cake

WHEAT FREE / DAIRY FREE / EGG FREE
SERVES 8–10

A hearty and wonderful cake to have for morning tea, this is my interpretation of a cake by cookbook author Myra Kornfeld. I can't see any reason why this wouldn't make a fine and wholesome breakfast every now and then either — really you could take many of the ingredients and have porridge of sorts in another world.

145 g (5¼ oz/1 cup) wholemeal spelt flour
130 g (4½ oz/1 cup) unbleached white spelt flour
2½ teaspoons baking powder
80 ml (2½ fl oz/⅓ cup) macadamia nut or almond oil
75 g (2½ oz/½ cup) rapadura sugar
125 ml (4 fl oz/½ cup) apple juice
3 teaspoons apple cider vinegar
2 teaspoons natural vanilla extract
60 ml (2 fl oz/¼ cup) combined rice milk and coconut milk

Filling
100 g (3½ oz/1 cup) pecan halves
2 teaspoons brown rice syrup
2 teaspoons rapadura sugar
6 dates, pitted and cut into 1 cm (½ inch) pieces
1 teaspoon ground cinnamon
60 ml (2 fl oz/¼ cup) apple juice

Streusel
34 g (1¼ oz/¼ cup) oatmeal
50 g (1¾ oz/½ cup) pecan halves, roughly chopped
37 g (1¼ oz/¼ cup) rapadura sugar
1 teaspoon ground cinnamon
¼ teaspoon baking powder
60 ml (2 fl oz/¼ cup) macadamia nut or almond oil

Preheat the oven to 180°C (350°F/Gas 4). Line a 20 cm (8 inch) square cake tin with baking paper.

For the filling, toss the pecans with the syrup and sugar and place on a baking tray. Bake for 10 minutes or until fragrant and the sugars are caramelised but not burnt. Remove from the oven and cool, then chop into small pieces and place in a small bowl. Add the dates, cinnamon and apple juice and mix together, pressing down on the dates until they have absorbed the juice and you have a thick mix. Set aside.

For the streusel, place the oatmeal, pecans, sugar, cinnamon and baking powder in a small bowl. Drizzle over the oil and stir through — the mixture will be quite moist. Set aside.

Place the flours and baking powder in a bowl and whisk through.

In a separate bowl, whisk together the macadamia nut oil, sugar, apple juice, vinegar, vanilla extract and 2 tablespoons of the combined milks.

Add the wet ingredients to the dry ingredients and stir through to incorporate all of the flour — this should be a loose, moist mix and move very freely over the spoon, but it should not be at all runny. Add the remaining combined milk if necessary.

Gently spread half of the batter over the base of the tin, then gently spread the filling over this, ensuring it is even. Gently spread the remaining batter on top, then evenly drop little bits of streusel all over.

Bake for about 40 minutes or until a skewer inserted into the middle comes out clean. Check the cake after 20 minutes, reducing the oven temperature if needed. Remove from the oven and cool in the tin for 10 minutes before serving.

This cake is best served warm and fresh on the day of baking, but it will keep in an airtight container in a cool, dark place for up to 3 days, or it can be frozen in portions, thawed, then warmed in the oven.

Buckwheat, hazelnut and plum kuchen

GLUTEN FREE / DAIRY FREE
SERVES 8–10

This is a sturdy gluten-free batter that can handle a topping of moist fruits, which tend to ooze a lot of juice as they cook. Earthy hazelnuts tame the strong perfume of the buckwheat, and are a beautiful match for a santa rosa plum. Eggs provide a protein structure for the gluten-free buckwheat, but also do double duty by trapping air within the batter when beaten with the sugar.

1 apple, peeled, cored and cut into 1 cm (½ inch) pieces
135 g (4¾ oz/1 cup) raw hazelnuts
140 g (5 oz/1 cup) buckwheat flour
½ teaspoon baking powder
1 teaspoon ground cinnamon
1 tablespoon rapadura sugar, plus 113 g (4 oz/¾ cup) extra
3 eggs, at room temperature
1 teaspoon natural vanilla extract
6–8 plums (600 g/1 lb 5 oz), halved or quartered, stones removed

Preheat the oven to 180°C (350°F/Gas 4). Line a 27 cm x 18 cm (10¾ x 7 inch) rectangular cake tin with baking paper.

Place the apple in a very small saucepan with 60 ml (2 fl oz/¼ cup) of water. Cover and cook over medium heat for 10 minutes or until soft — if any water remains, remove the lid and reduce until the liquid has evaporated. Mash to a smooth mix and set aside.

Meanwhile, place the hazelnuts on a baking tray and roast for 10 minutes or until lightly coloured, fragrant and the skin is splitting. Pour the hot nuts onto a clean tea towel and rub the nuts together to loosen the skins. Pick out the nuts (you won't get all of the skin off — don't worry about that) and leave them to cool a little before finely grinding. Measure out 1 cup of ground hazelnuts and place in a bowl with the buckwheat flour, baking powder and half of the cinnamon. Whisk through to distribute the ingredients and break up any lumps.

Place the remaining ground hazelnuts in another bowl with the remaining cinnamon and the 1 tablespoon of rapadura. Set aside to sprinkle over the cake before baking.

Using hand-held electric beaters, whisk the 113 g of sugar and the eggs until thick and creamy and tripled in volume. The mixture is ready when you can lift the beaters and the mixture falls back into the bowl in a ribbon that rests on the surface for about 10 seconds. This should take about 5 minutes.

Gently whisk in half of the flour mixture, the apple purée and the vanilla extract, then add the remaining flour mixture. The mixture will most likely collapse a good deal — this is fine. Turn into the tin, then press the plums, cut side down, into the batter and sprinkle the topping evenly over. Bake for 45–50 minutes or until a skewer inserted into the middle comes out clean. Remove from the oven and cool in the tin for 10 minutes before serving directly from the tin.

BAKING NOTES

• I like to use a fragrant apple that cooks down well, such as the mutsu, but granny smiths (green) work just as well.
• You could use this recipe as a base for a gluten-free apple cake too: slice 3 large apples (with or without skin) into 3 mm (⅛ inch) thick slices, and press the slices into the cake before baking.

HOW TO STORE

This cake is best served warm and fresh on the day of baking, but it will keep in an airtight container in a cool, dark place for up to 2 days, or in the fridge if the weather is hot.

Oat and barley pumpkin gingerbread

WHEAT FREE / LOW GLUTEN
SERVES 8–10

Dark and secretive, this is a deeply flavoured and gorgeous gingerbread. Because both oat and barley are very low in gluten, you won't get a very high rise in this bread, and though it doesn't look quite as sexy as some, once you taste it, you are done for (that's the secret). This would also make a delicious dessert served with poached or baked pears.

Dry mix

75 g (2½ oz/¾ cup) rolled oats

82 g (2¾ oz/¾ cup) barley flour

65 g (2¼ oz/½ cup) unbleached white spelt flour

2 teaspoons baking powder

1 teaspoon ground cinnamon

2 teaspoons ground ginger

¼ teaspoon freshly grated nutmeg

75 g (2½ oz/½ cup) rapadura sugar

110 g (3¾ oz/½ cup) glacé ginger, finely chopped

Wet mix

2 eggs, at room temperature

80 ml (2½ fl oz/⅓ cup) macadamia nut oil

90 g (¼ oz/¼ cup) unsulphured blackstrap molasses

1 teaspoon natural vanilla extract

250 g (9 oz/1 cup, firmly packed) roasted or steamed mashed
   pumpkin (winter squash) (drained of water if steamed)

70 g (2½ oz/¼ cup) yoghurt or cultured buttermilk

60 ml (2 fl oz/¼ cup) milk

Preheat the oven to 175°C (340°F/Gas 3–4). Line a 1 litre (35 fl oz/4 cup) capacity loaf (bar) tin with baking paper.

For the dry mix, place all of the dry ingredients, except the ginger, in a bowl and stir through with a whisk to break up the flours and evenly distribute. Add the ginger and toss through. Set aside.

For the wet mix, place the eggs, oil, molasses, vanilla extract, pumpkin and 1½ tablespoons each of the yoghurt and milk in a bowl and whisk together.

Add the wet mix to the dry mix, stirring gently to combine. Add a little of the remaining milk and yoghurt as needed to only just loosen the batter — it should move smoothly and freely over the spoon as you mix, but it should not be at all runny. Turn into the tin.

Bake for 65 minutes or until a skewer inserted into the middle comes out clean. Remove from the oven and cool in the tin for 15 minutes, then move to a wire rack.

Store in an airtight container in a cool, dark place for up to 5 days, or in the fridge if the weather is hot.

BAKING NOTE

Don't worry if this batter looks quite stiff — the oats will provide the moistness it needs.

Banana and coconut bread with passionfruit icing

GLUTEN FREE / DAIRY FREE
SERVES 8–10

The recipe from Wholefood: Heal, Nourish, Delight *for banana bread remains my favourite — generous of fruit with sweetness coming only from banana, sultanas and dates. But, I had long wanted to achieve a light, delicious gluten-free loaf that was also dairy free as I have many clients in this situation. This recipe is a good example of using technique to help solve some of the problems that arise when baking gluten free without the aid of xanthan gum — namely, you need to get air and lift (read more about this in* Factors That Affect Crumb *on page 52). I've chosen to cream the sugar and eggs, knowing also that those eggs will help to bind the batter.*

If you are one who enjoys chocolate in your banana bread, this is a perfect recipe for it.

37 g (1¼ oz/¼ cup) rapadura or 46 g (1½ oz/⅓ cup) granulated
   coconut palm sugar
2 eggs, at room temperature
2 extra-ripe bananas, cut into 1–2 cm (½–¾ inch) slices

Dry mix
120 g (4¼ oz/¾ cup) brown rice flour
30 g (1 oz/¼ cup) quinoa flour
70 g (2½ oz/½ cup) teff flour
30 g (1 oz/¼ cup) true arrowroot
25 g (1 oz/¼ cup) desiccated coconut
2½ teaspoons baking powder
½–1 teaspoon ground cinnamon
40 g (1½ oz/¼ cup) lightly roasted macadamia nuts,
   roughly chopped

Wet mix
80 ml (2½ fl oz/⅓ cup) macadamia nut or almond oil
3–4 medium bananas (about 400 g/14 oz unpeeled),
   roughly mashed
125 ml (4 fl oz/½ cup) coconut milk
2 teaspoons apple cider vinegar
1 teaspoon natural vanilla extract

Icing
150 g (5½ oz/1 cup) golden icing (confectioners') sugar
20 g (¾ oz) coconut oil, softened
2 tablespoons passionfruit pulp

BAKING NOTE
Coconut palm sugar will give a darker flavour, less sweetness and a denser crumb than rapadura.

Preheat the oven to 180°C (350°F/Gas 4). Line a 1 litre (35 fl oz/4 cup) capacity loaf (bar) tin with baking paper.

For the dry mix, place all of the ingredients in a large bowl and stir through with a whisk to break up the flours and evenly distribute the nuts. Set aside.

For the wet mix, place all of the ingredients in a bowl and whisk until well combined.

Add the wet mix to the dry mix and stir until combined as best you can — it will be too thick to combine completely.

Using hand-held electric beaters, whisk the sugar and eggs until thick and creamy and tripled in volume. The mixture is ready when you can lift the beaters and the mixture falls back into the bowl in a ribbon that rests on the surface for about 10 seconds. This should take about 5 minutes. As gently as possible, fold one-third of the creamed sugar and egg mixture into the banana mixture, loosening the mix. Fold in another third, trying to deflate it as little as possible, then add the final third. Add the sliced banana and gently fold through. Gently turn the mix into the tin.

Bake for 50–70 minutes or until golden and a skewer inserted in the middle comes out clean.

While the cake is cooking, make the icing. Sieve the icing sugar into a small bowl, add the coconut oil and passionfruit pulp and mix with a wooden spoon until very smooth. Set aside.

Remove the cake from the oven and cool in the tin for 15 minutes, then move to a wire rack. When the cake is completely cool, pour over the icing.

This cake will keep in an airtight container in a cool, dark place for up to 3 days, or in the fridge if the weather is hot.

Pumpkin bread

WHEAT FREE / DAIRY FREE
SERVES 8–10

Not too dense or too sweet and deliciously chewy thanks to the oats and pumpkin that fleck this bread, this pumpkin bread is a keeper.

255 g (9 oz/2 cups) grated raw pumpkin (winter squash)

Topping
1 tablespoon rapadura sugar
1½ tablespoons pumpkin seeds (pepitas)
1½ tablespoons roughly chopped walnuts or pecans

Dry mix
145 g (5¼ oz/1 cup) wholemeal spelt flour
98 g (3½ oz/¾ cup) unbleached white spelt flour
25 g (1 oz/¼ cup) rolled oats
2½ teaspoons baking powder
1 teaspoon ground cinnamon
¼ teaspoon ground mace or freshly grated nutmeg
113 g (4 oz/¾ cup) rapadura sugar
40 g (1½ oz/¼ cup) pumpkin seeds (pepitas), roughly ground
30 g (1 oz/¼ cup) roasted walnuts or pecans, roughly chopped
85 g (3 oz/½ cup) sultanas

Wet mix
2 eggs, at room temperature
125 ml (4 fl oz/½ cup) macadamia nut or almond oil
1 teaspoon natural vanilla extract
2 teaspoons apple cider vinegar
125 ml (4 fl oz/½ cup) coconut milk

BAKING NOTES

• You will need to start with about 300 g (10½ oz) jap or butternut pumpkin, peeled and seeds removed.

• Mace is a spice made from the fine membrane that covers nutmeg. Bright orange in colour, with strong overtones of citrus orange, it's wonderful.

HOW TO STORE

Store in an airtight container in a cool, dark place for up to 5 days, or it can be frozen in portions, thawed, then warmed in the oven.

Preheat the oven to 175°C (340°F/Gas 3–4). Line a 1 litre (35 fl oz/4 cup) capacity loaf (bar) tin with baking paper.

For the topping, combine all of the ingredients in a small bowl and toss together. Set aside.

For the dry mix, place all of the ingredients in a bowl and stir through with a whisk to break up the flours and evenly distribute. Add the grated pumpkin and use your fingers to gently toss it through the flour mix. Set aside.

For the wet mix, place all of the ingredients, except half of the coconut milk, into a bowl and whisk together.

Add the wet mix to the dry mix, stirring gently to combine. Add the remaining milk as needed — the batter should be moist enough to hold together. Turn into the tin and sprinkle with the topping. Bake for 70 minutes or until a skewer inserted in the middle comes out clean. Remove from the oven and cool in the tin for 15 minutes, then move to a wire rack.

Everyday cakes

With a bit more attention to detail, a frosting or syrup, the following cakes still make use of fruit, vegetables and nuts, but are dressed up for something a little more special than a lunchbox.

Bittersweet banana, chocolate and quinoa cake

WHEAT FREE
SERVES 10–12

This is a rich cake with the bitterness of quinoa and dark chocolate set against the sweetness of banana — a very adult cake. I suspect quinoa, chocolate and banana really are the original ménage à trois — they are truly glorious in combination.

145 g (5¼ oz/1 cup) wholemeal spelt flour
120 g (4¼ oz/1 cup) quinoa flour
2½ teaspoons baking powder
4 small bananas, mashed (about ¾ cup)
200 g (7 oz/¾ cup) yoghurt, plus 2 tablespoons extra, if needed
1 teaspoon natural vanilla extract
125 ml (4 fl oz/½ cup) coconut oil
113 g (4 oz/¾ cup) rapadura sugar
2 eggs, at room temperature
100 g (3½ oz) dark chocolate (70%), chopped
140 g (5 oz/1 cup) roasted walnuts or pecans, roughly chopped
1 quantity dark chocolate and coconut ganache (see page 265)

Preheat the oven to 180°C (350°F/Gas 4). Line a 22 cm (8½ inch) springform cake tin with baking paper.

Place the flours and baking powder in a mixing bowl and whisk through to evenly distribute the ingredients. Set aside.

Combine the mashed banana with the yoghurt and vanilla extract. Set aside.

Using a stand mixer fitted with the paddle attachment, beat the coconut oil and sugar until light and fluffy, scraping down the sides from time to time. Add the eggs, one at a time, beating well after each addition. Add the flour mixture and the banana mixture, and beat very slowly until it has just come together. Remove the bowl from the mixer and fold through the chocolate and nuts. Turn into the tin. Bake for 50–60 minutes or until a skewer inserted into the middle comes out clean. Remove from the oven and cool in the tin for 30 minutes, then release the springform side of the cake tin. Slide onto a wire rack (still in the paper) and leave to completely cool before icing.

BAKING NOTE

Starting with the right texture of coconut oil is important when creaming it. It is best for creaming when it is a soft, not quite set hard or a gooey consistency, and it should be a cloudy white colour (read more about this in Air and Crumb on page 52).

HOW TO STORE

Store in an airtight container in a cool, dark place for up to 4 days, or in the fridge if the weather is hot.

Walnut and yoghurt cake for Easter

WHEAT FREE
SERVES 8–10

With the cooler days of autumn come walnuts and Easter. And some time over the Easter weekend (or any weekend really) you are going to want a piece of cake with a cup of tea or coffee — nothing too rich or time consuming to make, but wholesome, simple and quick. It's not too sweet and keeps very well — in fact, it just gets better. This is a beautiful place to use aged honey if you can find it (I am lucky enough to do so) and you will be rewarded with a stunning depth of flavour.

It's also the perfect recipe to use 100 per cent wholemeal spelt flour. This is a good cake for wheat as the syrup softens up everything, just in case it may be a little dry. This cake is very versatile and you might like to ice it with the Honey and Cream Cheese Icing (see page 263) or serve it with a Honey and Cinnamon Labne (see page 249) and Honey-roasted Figs (see page 275) — and if you happen to have some thyme blossom, sprinkle a little over the cake, labne and figs before serving.

Dry mix
110 g (3¾ oz/1 cup) lightly roasted walnuts, roughly chopped
145 g (5¼ oz/1 cup) wholemeal spelt flour
1½ teaspoons baking powder
1 teaspoon ground cinnamon
finely grated zest of ½ lemon and 1 small orange

Wet mix
2 eggs, at room temperature
80 ml (2½ fl oz/⅓ cup) good-quality extra virgin olive oil
200 g (7 oz/¾ cup) labne (see page 249)
75 g (2½ oz/½ cup) rapadura sugar

Syrup
185 ml (6 fl oz/¾ cup) freshly squeezed orange juice
60 ml (2 fl oz/¼ cup) freshly squeezed lemon juice (or more if the
    lemon is not very acidic, such as meyer)
1 cinnamon quill
90–175 g (3¼–6 oz/¼–½ cup) raw honey

BAKING NOTE

Choose an olive oil with a full and fragrant flavour and make extra sure your walnuts are not rancid.

Preheat the oven to 180°C (350°F/Gas 4). Line the base and sides of a 20 cm (8 inch) square cake tin with one piece of baking paper — do not cut the paper to fit the tin, but rather fold it, so the syrup that is poured on later can't seep through.

For the dry mix, place all of the ingredients in a mixing bowl and whisk through to evenly distribute.

For the wet mix, place all of the ingredients in a small bowl and whisk together.

Add the wet mix to the dry mix and stir through until just combined. Turn into the tin.

Bake for 30–35 minutes or until a skewer inserted into the middle comes out clean.

While the cake is cooking, make the syrup. Place the orange and lemon juices and cinnamon quill in a small saucepan and simmer over medium heat for 10 minutes or until reduced by three-quarters, to about 185 ml (6 fl oz/¾ cup). Remove from the heat and add ¼ cup of the honey, stirring to dissolve. Taste and add more honey as desired.

Remove the cake from the oven, use the skewer to poke a few holes in the cake, and immediately pour the syrup over the cake — it may look like a lot of syrup, but the cake will absorb it. Leave to sit for 15–30 minutes to soak through.

Leftovers will keep in an airtight container in a cool, dark place for up to 5 days, or if the weather is hot, refrigerate due to its high moisture content. It also freezes well, but it does lose some of its syrupy deliciousness.

Meyer lemon, barley and olive oil cake

WHEAT FREE / LOW GLUTEN
SERVES 8–10

This is my interpretation of my dear friend Jeanie's meyer lemon, almond and olive oil cake, and it's my favourite cake in the book. I've replaced wheat flour with barley flour (knowing that there is enough air and support for such a low-gluten flour with egg) and raw sugar with rapadura for goodness — the lemon, barley and rapadura combination is glorious. This is an honest and deliciously textured and flavoured cake. I hope you love it as much as I do.

3 meyer lemons
110 g (3¾ oz/1 cup) barley flour
2 teaspoons baking powder
85 g (3 oz) almond meal (ground almonds)
a pinch of sea salt
80 ml (2½ fl oz/⅓ cup) extra virgin olive oil
95 g (3¼ oz/⅓ cup) yoghurt
2 eggs, at room temperature
113 g (4 oz/¾ cup) rapadura sugar

BAKING NOTE

Meyer lemons are thin skinned, less acidic and sweeter than a traditional lemon. You can't replace them in this recipe with the traditional lemon.

Place the whole lemons in a medium saucepan, cover with water, then a lid, bring to the boil and simmer for 25 minutes. Drain and set the lemons aside to cool.

Preheat the oven to 170°C (325°F/Gas 3). Grease and line the base and side of a 20 cm (8 inch) springform cake tin with baking paper.

Place the flour, baking powder, almond meal and salt in a medium bowl (you will need some room for folding a bit later) and whisk through to evenly distribute the ingredients.

When the lemons are cool, cut them in half and scoop out the flesh — it will separate from the skin and be very easy to remove. Place the lemon skins in a food processor or blender. Pick through the lemon flesh so you have ¼ cup — it's easier than it sounds as the fleshy segment separates from the pithy membrane during cooking. Some of the juice mixed in with the flesh is fine. (Don't throw away the remainder as you can strain it, discard the solids, and use the liquid to flavour yoghurt — and it's great for a cold or sore throat.) Add the ¼ cup of lemon flesh, oil and yoghurt to the food processor and process very well until the lemon skin is as fine as possible.

Using a stand mixer fitted with the whisk attachment, whisk the eggs and sugar until they have at least doubled in volume and are as much to the ribbon as possible.

Add the yoghurt and lemon mixture and two-thirds of the egg mixture to the flour mixture and, using a spatula, fold through as gently as possible. When just combined, add the remaining egg mixture and fold through lightly. Turn the mix into the tin.

Bake for 40–50 minutes or until the cake is golden and the middle of the cake is firm to the touch. At this point, turn off the oven, open the door and leave the cake in the warm oven for 15 minutes before removing. Completely cool in the tin before removing.

This cake is lovely served with yoghurt that has had some of the strained lemon and a small amount of finely grated lemon zest stirred through, and fresh blueberries.

Store in an airtight container in a cool, dark place for up to 1 week.

Apple cake

WHEAT FREE
SERVES 8–10

I have many a memory of Mum's cinnamon apple teacake on a weekend afternoon, and this is my attempt to replicate that cake using the more wholesome ingredients I love. But as soon as a less-refined flour and whole sugar are introduced, the cake crumb is going to get dense, and this is why I've cooked the apples first, so they are moist, delicious and caramelised. The best apples to use in this recipe are ones that hold their shape — golden delicious, pink lady and gala are all good. Serve warm from the oven as it is or with sweetened labne (see page 249) or Kefir Cream (see page 251).

Apples
6 apples (about 700 g/1 lb 9 oz)
30 g (1 oz) unsalted butter
2–3 teaspoons rapadura sugar
60 ml (2 fl oz/¼ cup) brandy, Calvados or cider
finely grated zest of 1 lemon

Topping
1 teaspoon ground cinnamon
30 g (1 oz/¼ cup) chopped pecans, walnuts or almonds

Dry mix
135 g (4¾ oz/1 cup) oatmeal
130 g (4½ oz/1 cup) unbleached white spelt flour
150 g (5½ oz/1 cup) rapadura sugar (with 1 tablespoon
    taken out for the topping)
2 teaspoons baking powder
½ teaspoon ground cinnamon
½ teaspoon freshly grated nutmeg
a pinch of ground cloves

Wet mix
100 g (3½ oz) unsalted butter, melted and cooled
1 egg, at room temperature
1 teaspoon natural vanilla extract
125 ml (4 fl oz/½ cup) milk (I like to use half milk, half cultured
    buttermilk or yoghurt)

BAKING NOTE

I like the lightness that comes from using a white spelt flour, but this is an easy cake to swap the white spelt flour for wholemeal spelt flour. You will need to increase the milk (or cultured buttermilk or yoghurt) by 1–2 tablespoons more to loosen the mix a little.

Preheat the oven to 180°C (350°F/Gas 4). Line the base and sides of a 20 cm (8 inch) square cake tin with baking paper.

For the apples, peel the apples and cut into quarters. Cut out the core, and depending on the size of the apples, cut each quarter into two or three wedges or four or five if large. Melt the butter and sugar in a 24 cm (9½ inch) frying pan over medium heat. Add the apples, toss to coat, and cook (not too gently or you won't get any caramelisation) for 10 minutes, shaking the pan frequently to stop the apples from burning. Add the brandy — it should sizzle and reduce rapidly when it hits the pan. Continue to cook for 10 minutes or until the apples are just about cooked and ever so lightly golden in places, and the brandy has reduced to almost nothing. Remember to keep shaking the pan frequently. When ready, stir in the lemon zest.

For the topping, place the cinnamon, nuts and the 1 tablespoon of sugar from the dry mix in a small bowl. Mix together and set aside.

For the dry mix, place all of the ingredients in a bowl and whisk through to evenly distribute.

For the wet mix, place all of the ingredients in a small bowl and whisk together.

Add the wet mix to the dry mix and gently stir until just combined. (If using wholemeal flour, you may need to add a little more milk.) Turn into the tin and gently spread the mix. Pour the apples over the top — I like to press some deep into the batter, and make sure some pieces are on the sides as they caramelise even more during the baking process.

Bake for 45 minutes or until a skewer inserted into the middle comes out clean. Remove from the oven, cool in the tin for about 15 minutes, before removing from the tin, using the paper to lift it out and placing on a wire rack (still with the paper underneath). At this stage it is easy to slide onto a plate.

Rhubarb, candied hazelnut and buckwheat cake

GLUTEN FREE
SERVES 10–12

This is a very light and fragrant cake made with a very deliberate use of ingredients and technique. I love rhubarb but wanted something other than the usual almond meal–rhubarb cake. I thought it would look wonderful against the soft buff of buckwheat, and it does, but it was really the maple syrup that brought it all together. Maple syrup is a highly fragrant and generous sweetener — full and luscious, and this softens an assertive buckwheat and bitter rhubarb, as does the vanilla. Air has been achieved by creaming butter and syrup, with the addition of eggs to help bind. With a soft, almost sponge-like, crumb, this is a cake all dressed up and ready to go out somewhere special.

80 g (2¾ oz) unsalted butter, softened
125 ml (4 fl oz/½ cup) maple syrup
2 eggs, at room temperature
1 teaspoon natural vanilla extract
60 ml (2 fl oz/¼ cup) milk
60 ml (2 fl oz/¼ cup) cultured buttermilk or yoghurt

Rhubarb
8 stalks trimmed rhubarb (about 400 g/14 oz), washed and
    cut into 1–1.5 cm (½–⅝ inch) pieces
1 tablespoon maple syrup
1 teaspoon natural vanilla extract

Nut topping
75 g (2½ oz/½ cup) lightly roasted hazelnuts (skins removed),
    roughly chopped (see Baking Note)
2–3 teaspoons maple syrup
1 teaspoon natural vanilla extract

Dry mix
160 g (5¾ oz/1 cup) brown rice flour
35 g (1¼ oz/¼ cup) buckwheat flour
75 g (2½ oz/½ cup) roasted hazelnuts (skins removed),
    roughly ground (see Baking Note)
2 teaspoons baking powder

Preheat the oven to 180°C (350°F/Gas 4). Line a 24 cm (9½ inch) springform cake tin with baking paper.

For the rhubarb, combine all of the ingredients in a bowl and set aside.

For the nut topping, combine all of the ingredients in a small bowl and set aside.

For the dry mix, place all of the ingredients in a small bowl and whisk through to evenly distribute the ingredients and break up any clumps.

Place the butter and maple syrup in the bowl of a stand mixer fitted with the whisk attachment and beat until creamy, scraping down the sides from time to time. Add the eggs, one at a time, beating well after each addition, then add the vanilla extract. Add the dry mix, milk and buttermilk and fold together with a spatula. It will look quite moist, which is as it should be. Leave to sit for 1–2 minutes and you will notice it will thicken up. Turn the mix into the tin, top with the rhubarb — I like to press some deep into the batter, and make sure some pieces are on the sides as they caramelise even more during the baking process — and sprinkle all over with nut topping.

Bake for 50 minutes or until a skewer inserted into the middle comes out clean.

Remove from the oven and cool in the tin for 30 minutes, then release the springform side of the cake tin. Slide onto a wire rack (still in the paper) and leave to completely cool before cutting.

Store in an airtight container in a cool, dark place for up to 4 days, or in the fridge if the weather is hot.

BAKING NOTE

To roast the nuts for both the topping and the cake, place all the hazelnuts on a baking tray and place in a 180°C (350°F/Gas 4) oven. The ½ cup for the topping will only need a few minutes, keep an eye on them and remove that ½ cup as soon as you see the skins loosening. Leave the other ½ cup until the skin is well cracked and they are lightly golden, about another 5–6 minutes. When both are cool enough to handle, rub each batch separately (this way you won't get them mixed up). Those that are very lightly roasted can be roughly chopped in half and mixed with the maple syrup and vanilla in a small bowl and set aside for the topping, and the well roasted ones can be ground to a rough meal and set aside to add to the cake. Don't grind the hazelnuts for the cake too finely, as a rough meal gives a lovely texture to the cake.

Carrot, pistachio and amaranth cake

GLUTEN FREE / WHEAT FREE / DAIRY FREE
SERVES 10–12

When it comes to gluten-free, I'm over the ubiquitous orange and almond cake, and this is my alternative. It's the result of my quest for a lighter carrot cake. The carrot and pistachio here are a wonderful match for amaranth, while the orange and cardamom keep the grassy, beetroot flavours of amaranth at bay. It is incredibly moist and keeps exceptionally well. I think this cake is best without icing, but should you prefer it, top it with the suggested icing. If you don't mind dairy, a thin layer of Honey and Cream Cheese Icing (see page 262), with finely grated orange zest added to it, would be delicious too, but keep it light as too much of this topping will weigh this fragile cake down.

113 g (4 oz/¾ cup) rapadura sugar
3 eggs, at room temperature
63 g (2¼ oz/½ cup) amaranth flour
¼ teaspoon baking powder
finely grated zest of 2 oranges
½ teaspoon freshly ground cardamom
100 g (3½ oz) lightly roasted pistachios, ground neither
    too fine nor too coarse
180 g (6¼ oz) finely grated carrot (about 1 carrot)
80 ml (2½ fl oz/⅓ cup) macadamia nut oil

Glazed orange icing
150 g (5½ oz/1 cup) golden icing (confectioners') sugar
2 teaspoons freshly squeezed orange juice
2 drops of orange oil
1–2 drops of natural orange food colour
35 g (1¼ oz/¼ cup) lightly roasted pistachios, finely chopped
orange-coloured edible flower petals, such as calendula,
    to decorate (optional)

Preheat the oven to 180°C (350°F/Gas 4). Line the base and side of an 18 cm (7 inch) springform cake tin with baking paper.

Using a stand mixer fitted with the whisk attachment, whisk the sugar and eggs until thick and creamy and tripled in volume. The mixture is ready when you can lift the beaters and the mixture falls back into the bowl in a ribbon that rests on the surface for about 10 seconds. This should take about 5 minutes.

While they are beating, place the amaranth flour, baking powder, orange zest, cardamom and pistachios in a mixing bowl large enough for folding ingredients. Whisk through to evenly distribute the ingredients. Add the carrot and use your fingers to very lightly mix it with the dry flour mix. Add the oil and, again, use your fingers to very gently distribute it.

Add half of the egg mixture to the flour mixture and very gently fold through, doing your best to make sure the carrot is evenly distributed without over-folding the egg mixture and collapsing the air. Add the remaining egg mixture and fold through gently with a light, long sweeping movement. Turn the mix into the tin.

Bake for 50–60 minutes or until the mixture feels firm and set in the middle when you touch it. If you have trouble discerning this, feel the sides and then the middle — the sides will be quite firm and sturdy, and the middle firm, but less so.

When cooked, turn the oven off, open the door and leave the cake to sit until warm to cool, then remove from the oven and completely cool in the tin before moving to a wire rack and icing, if desired.

For the glazed orange icing, sieve the icing sugar into a small bowl and add the juice, oil and food colouring and stir until smooth — if it feels as if there is not enough liquid, be patient as too much juice will simply make the icing dissolve into the cake, rather than sit on top of it, and this cake is too moist to handle this. Spread the icing on the cooled cake and leave to set, then sprinkle with pistachios and the flower petals (if using).

Un-iced, the cake will keep in an airtight container in a cool, dark place for 4–6 days, or in the fridge if the weather is hot. When iced, the cake will keep under a cake dome in a cool, dark place for up to 2 days.

Holiday fruit cake

WHEAT FREE / LOW GLUTEN
SERVES 10–12

No, not a Christmas cake, but a lighter fruit cake to have around the house — very reminiscent of a light golden fruit cake. I've called it Holiday Fruit Cake because this is what I like to bake when we travel down south (to the bush) for holidays. Use the best-quality raisins (sun muscatels are gorgeous and deeply flavoured) and only the best-quality dry fruit. Fruit brings out the best in barley, and while it's low gluten and does make the cake marginally more crumbly, it's worth it. You'll see I've broken my own rule of not using honey in baking, but it adds divine flavour and gives the slightly chewy consistency that I love. If you prefer not to use it, replace it with brown rice syrup or golden syrup.

145 g (5¼ oz/1 cup) wholemeal spelt flour
55 g (2 oz/½ cup) barley flour
1 teaspoon baking powder
½–1 teaspoon ground cinnamon
¼ teaspoon freshly grated nutmeg
180 g (6¼ oz) unsalted butter, softened
75 g (2½ oz/½ cup) rapadura sugar
2 tablespoons raw honey

3 eggs, at room temperature

85 g (2¾ oz/¼ cup) nice, bittersweet marmalade (I use cumquat jam) (to make it yourself, see page 271)

1 teaspoon natural vanilla extract

80 g (2¾ oz/½ cup) blanched almonds, roughly chopped

Fruit mix

80 g (2¾ oz) dried figs

150 g (5½ oz) dried apricots

70 g (2½ oz) glacé ginger, roughly chopped

150 g (5½ oz) seedless raisins, roughly chopped

60 ml (2 fl oz/¼ cup) Pedro Ximénez or equivalent

60 ml (2 fl oz/¼ cup) vincotto

125 ml (4 fl oz/½ cup) freshly squeezed orange juice

Preheat the oven to 180°C (350°F/Gas 4). Line the base and sides of a 20 cm (8 inch) square cake tin with baking paper.

For the fruit mix, roughly cut the figs and apricots into small pieces with scissors, then add them to a small saucepan with the remaining ingredients. Leave to soak overnight, or bring to the boil, then immediately remove from the heat and leave to soak for 1 hour or until the dried fruit has absorbed 90% of the liquid — make sure the fruit is covered by or at the same level as the liquid and press or weigh down if necessary.

Place the flours, baking powder and spices in a mixing bowl and whisk through to distribute the ingredients evenly and break up any clumps.

Using a stand mixer fitted with the paddle attachment, beat the butter, sugar and honey until creamy and light in colour, scraping down the sides from time to time. Add the eggs, one at a time, beating well after each addition. If it starts to look curdled, you may need to wrap the bowl with a warm cloth or place the bowl in hot water for a few seconds to soften the butter, and add 1 tablespoon of the flour mixture.

Add the flour mixture, fruit mixture, marmalade, vanilla extract and almonds and mix on the lowest speed or until the ingredients are just combined. Turn into the tin.

Bake for 1½ hours or until a skewer inserted into the middle comes out clean and very fine cracks should be evident over the entire surface of the cake when it is ready. Remove from the oven and completely cool in the tin.

Store in an airtight container in a cool, dark place — I've had mine in the pantry for up to 4 weeks and, while it's not quite as wonderful, it's still mighty fine.

BAKING NOTES

• This is a tricky cake to bake. Using honey will encourage the top to brown more easily, but this cake is better with a very brown top and sides. If you feel the colour is getting too dark after 1 hour, place a piece of foil on the cake and continue baking.

• You can make a mix of 250 ml (9 fl oz/1 cup) liquid to soak the fruit mix in as desired, but choose at least 60 ml (2 fl oz/¼ cup) of a deep or well-flavoured alcoholic option (such as a late-harvest riesling, plum wine, port or Calvados) and 60 ml (2 fl oz/¼ cup) of a deep or well-flavoured non-alcoholic option such as fruit juice concentrate — cherry, apple or pear.

Apple and pecan cake with honey and cream cheese icing

WHEAT FREE / CAKE IS DAIRY FREE
SERVES 10–12 GENEROUSLY

This makes a hearty alternative to carrot cake, and even with 100 per cent wholemeal flour it is exceptionally moist. This cake still tastes just as moist and wonderful after a couple of days.

290 g (10¼ oz/2 cups) wholemeal spelt flour
2½ teaspoons baking powder
150 g (5½ oz/1 cup) rapadura sugar
100 g (3½ oz/1 cup) lightly roasted pecans, roughly chopped
130 g (4½ oz/¾ cup) sultanas
1 teaspoon ground cinnamon
¼ teaspoon freshly grated nutmeg
finely grated zest of 1 lemon
3 good-sized apples, peeled, cored and cut into 1 cm (½ inch)
    pieces
185 ml (6 fl oz/¾ cup) macadamia nut or almond oil
3 eggs, at room temperature
1 teaspoon natural vanilla extract
1½ tablespoons brandy or whisky
70 g (2½ oz/¼ cup) yoghurt
1 quantity honey and cream cheese icing (see page 263)

Preheat the oven to 180°C (350°F/Gas 4). Grease and line the base and side of a 24 cm (9½ inch) springform cake tin with baking paper.

Place the flour, baking powder, sugar, pecans, sultanas, cinnamon, nutmeg and lemon zest in a mixing bowl and whisk through to evenly distribute the ingredients. Add the apples and mix through.

Place the oil, eggs, vanilla extract, brandy and yoghurt in another bowl and whisk together until combined. Add to the dry mix and stir until just combined. Turn into the tin.

Bake for about 1 hour or until a skewer inserted into the middle comes out clean. Remove from the oven and cool in the tin for 15 minutes, then move to a wire rack and completely cool before icing.

Store under a cake dome or in an airtight container in a cool, dark place for up to 5 days.

Plain crumb cakes

A cake with a plain crumb is not the easiest of things to make using whole and semi-refined grains and sweeteners. That lovely looking organic, unbleached white spelt or wheat flour is a very different thing from the generic packets of white plain (all-purpose) and self-raising baking flour many of us have grown up with. Here there is no fruit or vegetable to help lift the batter and disguise any failings. The prime consideration in a plain crumb cake is how to achieve air — we simply cannot keep adding leavening — and there are no other ingredients to soften assertive flavours. (You can read more about this in Air and Crumb on page 52.) In the following recipes you will find a broad range of approaches to achieving this. I'm sure you'll notice that many have an icing — this is a wonderful way to provide a more delicious mouthfeel. It's especially important to assess your white spelt flour before baking (see White Spelt on page 14).

Génoise sponge cake

WHEAT FREE / CAN BE GLUTEN FREE
SERVES 8–12

This basic cake is well worth perfecting and is best described as a sturdy sponge and it is also the base of many a wonderful cake or dessert. It keeps and freezes exceptionally well if protected from the air — because it has so little fat, it will become stale quickly. If making the day before using or freezing, wrap it well in plastic wrap and store it in the fridge (or freezer) or in an airtight container.

I use this basic cake in a variety of ways — simply served with whipped cream and topped with fresh seasonal fruits, such as banana, and passionfruit, being the favourite. Two cakes filled and iced with the Quick and Simple Butter Icing (see page 257), makes a wonderful showpiece for a dressier occasion. It's also the base of the Blackberry and Cocoa Nib Panna Cotta Trifle (see page 158), the Summer Strawberry and Peach Trifle (see page 160) and the Bûche de Noël (see page 156), or you can use it to make Jelly Cakes from Wholefood for Children. Master this recipe, and you'll have many a delicious option up your sleeve.

4 eggs, at room temperature
105 g (3½ oz/½ cup) golden caster (superfine) sugar or
    75 g (2½ oz/½ cup) rapadura sugar
1 teaspoon natural vanilla extract
120 g (4¼ oz) unbleached white spelt flour (this is 1 cup minus
    1 tablespoon)
40 g (1½ oz) unsalted butter, melted and cooled

Preheat the oven to 180°C (350°F/Gas 4). Grease and line the base and sides of a 22 cm (8½ inch) springform cake tin with baking paper.

Using a stand mixer fitted with the whisk attachment, whisk the eggs and sugar until thick and creamy and tripled in volume. The mixture is ready when you can lift the beaters and the mixture falls back into the bowl in a ribbon that rests on the surface for about 10 seconds. Add the vanilla extract during the last moments of whisking.

Remove the bowl from the mixer. Sieve one-third of the flour onto the mixture and gently fold through — I like to use a whisk. Stop as soon as the flour looks incorporated. Fold in the remaining flour in two more additions. Place the melted butter in a small bowl, then gently fold in 1 cup of the batter through the butter. Add this back to the egg mixture and gently fold through. Take care not to overmix. Turn into the tin.

Bake for 20–25 minutes or until the centre springs back when lightly touched, and the cake is coming away from the side. If the cake is browning too quickly and is not ready, reduce the oven temperature and continue cooking. When the cake is cooked, turn off the oven and leave the door ajar until the cake is cool. Remove from the oven and completely cool in the tin.

BAKING NOTES

- I achieve the best results with my génoise when I leave it to cool in the oven instead of shocking it with cold, which can immediately shrink the cake. When cooked, turn the oven off and leave the door open or ajar until the cake is absolutely cool. Alternatively, remove it from the oven and immediately cover with a lightweight tea towel until cool. Cupcakes and patty cakes also need to completely cool in the tins before moving to a wire rack.

- If you use rapadura sugar instead of golden caster (superfine) sugar, the result will not be quite as light, but it will still be a beautiful cake.

- This recipe makes one 22 cm (8½ inch) round cake, which will relax to a depth of 3.5 cm (1¼ inch) when cool. Cut in half horizontally, this is a good depth for a cake, especially when filled with whipped cream, jam and fruit.

- This recipe makes one 20 cm (8 inch) round cake, which will relax to a depth of 5 cm (2 inches) when cooled. It will take 30–35 minutes to cook.

- This recipe makes one 18 cm (7 inch) round cake, which will relax to a depth of 5.5–6 cm (2¼–2½ inches) when cooked. It takes about 45–50 minutes to cook (see baking notes, page 156). I use this size for the Bûche de Noël (see page 156).

- This recipe makes one 30 cm x 20 cm (12 x 8 inch) rectangular cake as for a Swiss roll (jelly roll). It will take 20–25 minutes to cook.

- This recipe makes one 27 cm x 18 cm x 4 cm (10¾ x 7 x 1½ inch) rectangular cake, which will relax to a depth of about 3 cm (1¼ inches) when cooled and is good for layering.

- To make a three-tiered 22 cm (8½ inch) round cake you will need to double the mixture and divide the batter between three 22 cm sponge cake tins.

- This recipe makes 10–12 cupcakes. These will take 25–30 minutes to cook.

Chocolate

Reduce the white spelt flour to 92 g (3¼ oz) and add 30 g (1 oz/¼ cup) unsweetened dutched cocoa powder. Sieve the flour and cocoa together.

Nut

Reduce the white spelt flour to 92 g (3¼ oz) and add 25 g (¾ oz/¼ cup) ground roasted pecans or other nut. Sieve the flour, then add the nuts and whisk through to make sure the ingredients are evenly distributed.

Gluten free

Replace the white spelt flour with 80 g (2¾ oz/½ cup) brown rice flour, 30 g (1 oz/¼ cup) true arrowroot and 25 g (1 oz/¼ cup) almond meal (ground almonds). Place in a bowl and whisk through to distribute the ingredients evenly.

Coffee and walnut cake

WHEAT FREE
SERVES 10–12

Along with the Oat and Barley Fig Pillows (see page 84), this is the other recipe I knew I wanted to include when this book was just a dream in my heart. It's seriously old-fashioned, so imagine how surprised I was not only to see Nigella making her version of this cake at the Melbourne Food and Wine Festival, but also to see a version on MasterChef! Another impeccable reference comes from Nigel Slater — this is his last supper meal. Yes, just the cake. It's that good a combination. Mine, as you can imagine, is a slightly denser one than Nigel's (please read the Baking Notes), but honestly, I love that and it's less sweet also. It's my favourite way to have coffee.

10–12 lightly roasted walnut halves, to decorate

Cake
195 g (6¾ oz/1½ cups) unbleached white spelt flour
2¼ teaspoons baking powder
2 teaspoons instant coffee granules
195 g (6¾ oz) unsalted butter, softened
113 g (4 oz/¾ cup) rapadura sugar
4 eggs, at room temperature
60 g (2¼ oz) walnuts, finely chopped but not too fine
2 teaspoons natural vanilla extract
1 tablespoon milk

Icing
1 teaspoon instant coffee granules
100 g (3½ oz) unsalted butter, softened
200 g (7 oz) golden icing (confectioners') sugar
1 teaspoon natural vanilla extract

BAKING NOTES

• Four eggs is a lot to get into this amount of butter, and I find I need to pick up the bowl every now and then and pop it in a little hot water to soften the butter up to ensure that the egg emulsifies well.

• Using rapadura sugar results in a denser crumb, but a deeper flavour. If you prefer a much lighter texture, replace the rapadura sugar with golden caster (superfine) sugar, reduce the baking powder to 2 teaspoons and omit the milk.

Preheat the oven to 180°C (350°F/Gas 4). Grease and line the base and sides of two 20 cm (8 inch) sandwich cake tins with baking paper.

For the cake, sieve the flour and baking powder into a mixing bowl and set aside.

Combine the coffee granules and 25 ml (¾ fl oz) of water and set aside.

Using a stand mixer fitted with the paddle attachment, beat the butter and sugar until light and creamy, scraping down the sides from time to time. Add the eggs, one at a time, beating very well after each addition. The first two will probably go fine, after that it gets a bit tricky and before you add the third egg, you may like to place the bowl in a little hot water to soften the mix — not melt it, just soften it a little. When you add the fourth egg, add 1 tablespoon of the flour mixture to help stop the curdling. You will need to stop and scrape down the sides from time to time throughout the process. When the mix is pale, thick and creamy, add the remaining flour mixture, the nuts, vanilla extract, milk and coffee, and on the lowest speed, beat until the flour is well combined. Spoon half of the mix into each tin, and gently spread and even out.

Bake for 20–25 minutes or until a skewer inserted into the middle comes out clean. Take care not to overcook this cake. Remove from the oven and completely cool in the tins before moving onto wire racks.

For the icing, place the coffee granules and 1½ tablespoons of water in a small bowl and mix through to dissolve. Using a stand mixer fitted with the paddle attachment, beat the butter and icing sugar until light and fluffy, scraping down the sides from time to time. Add the coffee and vanilla extract and beat in, starting on low speed so the coffee doesn't splash everywhere and gradually increasing to medium–high speed. Beat until the icing is soft, pale and creamy, adding a tiny bit more water if you feel it needs it. You will need to stop and scrape down the sides from time to time.

To put together the cake, place one cake on a cardboard round or serving platter. Using a palette knife, spread half of the icing evenly over the cake just to the edge. Place the remaining cake onto the icing. Spread the remaining icing over the top. The weight of the top layer will push the filling out a little making it look delicious. Place the walnut halves at even intervals on top.

This cake can be made 3–5 hours ahead of serving time and is best kept under a cake dome at room temperature. If the ambient room temperature is very hot, you can refrigerate it, but remove the cake 1 hour before serving.

Bûche de Noël

WHEAT FREE / CAN BE GLUTEN FREE
SERVES 10–12

This is pure whimsy, but I am all for that — we need more of it. After seeing the classic Christmas Bûche de Noël made as a stump de Noël, I've heartily taken it on, as it's far easier to make and put together. It is a little bit of a production, but both cake and buttercream can be made ahead (frozen, even, then thawed) and brought to room temperature before using. The mushrooms need to be made closer to the time, but I love the touch they add.

Chocolate ganache
100 g (3½ oz) dark chocolate (55%), roughly chopped into very
   small pieces
155 ml (5 fl oz) thin (pouring) cream
60 g (2¼ oz) unsalted butter, cut into small pieces and softened

Pecan meringue mushrooms
2 egg whites, at room temperature
105 g (3½ oz/½ cup) golden caster (superfine) sugar
½ teaspoon natural vanilla extract
25 g (1 oz/¼ cup) finely ground lightly roasted pecans
unsweetened dutched cocoa powder, for dusting

To put together
1 x 18 cm (7 inch) round pecan génoise sponge cake
   (see pages 151–153)
1 quantity maple syrup meringue buttercream (see page 261)
250 g (9 oz) dark berries (I like blackberries or youngberries)

BAKING NOTES

• The ganache does make more than you need, but it is simple to make and will keep for about 2 weeks, covered, in an airtight container in the fridge, and it freezes well too. Bring to room temperature before using, and if stiff, you can ever so slightly warm it and give it a little stir.

• The recipe for the pecan meringue mushrooms makes far more than you will need, but it's easier to work with two egg whites than one. Once you've piped the number of mushrooms you need, simply pipe the remaining mixture into a simple meringue shape and bake — they will keep in an airtight container at room temperature for up to 2 weeks.

• Because the cake is deeper, it is best baked in a preheated 175°C (340°F/Gas 3–4) oven for 45–50 minutes.

For the chocolate ganache, place the chocolate in a heatproof bowl. Bring the cream to just below boiling point and pour over the chocolate, stirring until the chocolate has completely melted. Add the butter, a piece at a time, and stir until it has completely melted into the chocolate and cream and is combined. Leave to cool but not set, or refrigerate in an airtight container if not using on the day. When ready to use, if it is too firm or has been refrigerated, bring it to a spreadable room temperature before using.

For the pecan meringue mushrooms, preheat the oven to 150°C (300°F/Gas 2) or 130°C (250°F/Gas 1) if fan-forced, and line a baking tray with baking paper.

Bring a saucepan half-filled with water to a simmer. Place the egg whites and sugar in a heatproof bowl that can sit on the saucepan without its base touching the water. Place the bowl over the simmering water and whisk until the sugar has completely dissolved and the mixture is warm. Take care not to let the bowl get too hot as the egg white will begin to cook. Turn the egg white mixture into the bowl of a stand mixer fitted with the whisk attachment and beat until very dense and shiny, about 5 minutes.

Remove the bowl from the stand and gently fold in the vanilla extract and pecans with a spatula. Scoop the meringue into a piping (icing) bag fitted with a 1 cm (½ inch) plain nozzle.

Pipe out small tube shapes, to make mushroom stalks of varying heights ranging up to 2.5 cm (1 inch). Also pipe small circular tops onto the prepared tray. I like to make different shapes and different sizes for my mushrooms. You will need about 5–6 mushrooms.

Bake the meringues until they are firm to the touch and dry (you can break one open to look inside), about 30 minutes. If they are not dry, reduce the oven temperature to 120°C (235°F/Gas ½) and cook for a further 10 minutes. Remove from the oven and leave to completely cool.

Use a small amount of chocolate ganache to glue the mushroom tops to the stalks. If you want to go all out, you can pipe very fine lines of ganache on the underside of the tops.

To assemble the bûche de Noël, cut the sponge cake horizontally into thirds. Place the bottom layer on a large serving plate or wooden board, and spread with a thin layer of ganache and then gently spread with ½ cup of the buttercream. Top with half of the berries. Place another layer of cake on top, gently spread a thin layer of ganache and then gently spread with another ½ cup of the remaining buttercream and top with the remaining berries. Place the final layer on top. At this point, if the weather is hot, you may need to put the cake in the fridge to firm up a little. Using a palette knife in an upward motion, spread enough of the remaining buttercream (you should have 1 cup still) to cover the sides. Spread the remaining buttercream over the top of the cake in circular motions — it shouldn't be smooth as you want it to be textured like bark. Place the cake in the fridge to chill.

To finish decorating the bûche de Noël, use the chocolate ganache to define a wood-like pattern (a very loose interpretation) on the cake. Make sure the ganache is at a soft but not hot consistency before using. Use a palette knife to decorate the sides of the cake with an upward motion, and circular motions on the top of the cake.

You can store the cake in the fridge for up to 5 hours before serving — any longer and the berries will bleed. Make sure to bring it out of the fridge to sit for 1 hour, or 30 minutes if the ambient temperature is hot, before serving, so the buttercream can soften and become luscious.

Just before serving, dust the mushrooms with cocoa and arrange, as desired, on or next to the cake. I also like to add a couple of pieces of our Christmas pine tree to the plate or board for greenery.

I store leftovers under a cake dome, as I find they are eaten very quickly, but if the weather is hot, store in an airtight container in the fridge for up to 2 days. The iced cake also freezes exceptionally well.

Blackberry and cocoa nib panna cotta trifle

WHEAT FREE / CAN BE GLUTEN FREE / CAN BE VEGETARIAN
SERVES 10–12

We are big into trifle in my house — you can make it as simple or as complex as desired. This is a very grown-up version and came about a couple of summers ago when my love affair with cookbook author Alice Medrich's cocoa nib panna cotta from Bittersweet, Tales of a Life in Chocolate was at its height and Australian Gourmet Traveller ran a dark berry trifle in their Christmas issue. Cocoa nib panna cotta and blackberries are a match made in heaven, but when made with less-refined ingredients, deeper flavour is the result. You can use frozen berries for this, but when they are fresh and organic (which is usually at Christmas time), it's about as good as it gets. Yes, this is a bit of a labour of love, but oh my, it's worth it.

1 x 20 cm (8 inch) round chocolate génoise sponge cake
    (see pages 151–153)
piece of dark chocolate, for grating

Jelly
1.25 kg (2 lb 12 oz) fresh blackberries (or other dark berries
    such as youngberries)
160 g (5¾ oz) golden caster (superfine) sugar
2 tablespoons high-quality powdered gelatine
250 ml (9 fl oz/1 cup) moscato or fruity dessert wine

Panna cotta
750 ml (26 fl oz/3 cups) thin (pouring) cream, plus 1 tablespoon
75 g (2½ oz/½ cup) cocoa nibs, if whole, coarsely chopped into
    very small pieces
1 vanilla bean, halved lengthways and seeds scraped
2¾ teaspoons high-quality powdered gelatine
250 ml (9 fl oz/1 cup) milk
52 g (1¾ oz/¼ cup) golden caster (superfine) sugar, or to taste
a pinch of sea salt

BAKING NOTES

• You will need a 3–3.5 litre (105–122 fl oz) capacity trifle bowl (mine has a diameter of 20 cm/ 8 inches).

• When made with gelatine, the trifle will take you a whole day and possibly some of the evening to put together — not actual manhours, but for each layer of jelly and panna cotta to set. You can save time by making the génoise sponge cake earlier and freezing it.

• I prefer a soft-set jelly, but when the weather is hot (as it is wont to be at Christmas in Australia) it will melt rapidly when out of the fridge. If you prefer a sturdier set, increase the gelatine to 2½ tablespoons.

• I've made this trifle with a couple of alcohol options in the jelly — moscato and a sweet boysenberry dessert wine, which both were wonderful.

Begin by making the jelly. Do not start on the panna cotta until the first layer of jelly is almost set. Place 800 g (1 lb 12 oz) of the berries, the sugar and 750 ml (26 fl oz/3 cups) of water in a saucepan. Stir through and bring to a gentle boil over medium heat. Continue to simmer over low heat (not too rapid a boil or you will evaporate off too much liquid) for 50 minutes. Strain the mixture through a fine sieve, pressing lightly on the solids to extract as much juice as possible. You should have 1 litre (35 fl oz/4 cups) of liquid; if you have less, you will need to make this up with water; if you have more, set the excess aside for another use. Return the 1 litre of liquid to the pan and bring to the boil. Immediately turn off the heat, sprinkle the gelatine over the juice and whisk through for about 1 minute or until it is well dissolved. Add the moscato and stir through.

Pour half of the jelly into your trifle bowl and add half of the remaining berries (if frozen, they will need to be thawed, with any juice discarded). Place in the fridge to set — this will take 3–4 hours. Leave the remaining jelly in the pan at room temperature so it does not set.

While the jelly in the fridge is setting, make the génoise sponge cake (if you have not already made it ahead of time).

When the jelly has nearly set, begin making the panna cotta. Place the cream, cocoa nibs, vanilla bean seeds and bean in a saucepan over medium heat and bring just to the boil, then immediately remove from the heat. Press a piece of baking paper gently onto the surface so a skin doesn't form and set aside for 20 minutes to infuse.

Meanwhile, sprinkle the gelatine over the cold milk in a small bowl and set aside to let the gelatine soften.

Strain the cream through a fine mesh sieve, pressing on the nibs to extract all the liquid. Discard the nibs and bean. Return the cream to the pan, add the sugar and bring to a gentle simmer. Immediately turn off the heat and whisk in the milk mixture and salt, gently stirring for 1 minute or until the gelatine is completely dissolved. Set aside to cool.

Carefully ladle half of the panna cotta over the set jelly (if you pour it, it may well break into the jelly) and return to the fridge for 1–2 hours or until the panna cotta is set. Press a piece of baking paper onto the surface of the remaining panna cotta in the pan to stop a skin from forming and leave at room temperature so it does not set.

When the panna cotta in the bowl has set, cut the génoise in half horizontally, and place one half carefully onto the set panna cotta. If your cake is smaller than the bowl and does not come right to the edges, it is fine to just break it up into pieces and scatter evenly over the top. Pour the remaining blackberry jelly onto the cake — some of it will seep into the cake, which is fine. Place in the fridge for 2–4 hours or until the jelly is just about set (you don't want to wait for a full set as you need to use the remaining panna cotta that has been sitting out as soon as possible).

Gently place the remaining cake half on top of the jelly. Scatter over the remaining berries and very gently ladle over the remaining panna cotta. Place in the fridge for 1–2 hours or until the panna cotta has set.

Just before serving, grate the chocolate as desired over the trifle.

Vegetarian

I would make the jelly first (see below), get the first layer setting in the fridge, then make the panna cotta (see below) and set each layer in the fridge, keeping the remaining jelly and panna cotta out of the fridge, so they don't set. It will take about 2 hours to put together.

For the vegetarian jelly, replace the gelatine with 2½ teaspoons agar powder and 2 teaspoons kudzu (kuzu).

Place the 1 litre of strained berry juice in a saucepan and whisk in the agar. Return to the heat and bring to a gentle simmer, whisking frequently because as the agar dissolves it likes to sink to the bottom and stick to the base. Gently simmer for 6 minutes from the time it comes to the boil, whisking frequently.

Meanwhile, combine the kudzu with 1 tablespoon of the moscato and mix to a smooth slurry.

When the agar mixture is ready, remove from the heat and whisk in the kudzu mixture.

Return to the heat and bring to the boil, whisking constantly. Remove from the heat and whisk in the remaining moscato.

For the vegetarian panna cotta, replace the gelatine with 1 teaspoon agar powder and 1 teaspoon kudzu (kuzu).

Return the hot strained cream to the pan, add the sugar and whisk in the agar powder. Bring to a gentle simmer, whisking frequently because as the agar dissolves it likes to sink to the bottom and stick to the base. Simmer gently for 6 minutes from the time it comes to the boil, stirring frequently with a flat-edged spoon.

Meanwhile, combine the kudzu with a small amount of the milk and mix to a smooth slurry before adding the remaining milk.

When the agar mixture is ready, remove from the heat and whisk in the kudzu mixture. Return to a medium heat and bring to the boil, stirring constantly with a flat-edged spoon, then whisk in the salt, remove from the heat and set aside to cool.

Summer strawberry and peach trifle

WHEAT FREE / CAN BE GLUTEN FREE / CAN BE VEGAN
SERVES 10–12

I think this is one of the best desserts, using lots of seasonal, ripe, glorious fruit with a light, dairy-free vanilla bean–flecked almond custard cream. This trifle is a bit more old-fashioned than the Blackberry and Cocoa Nib Panna Cotta Trifle (see page 158) — and quicker to make. I've been known to have leftovers for breakfast, and on a hot summer morning, I can't think of anything better.

250 g (9 oz) very fresh ripe strawberries
250 g (9 oz) very fresh, very ripe raspberries
1 x 20 cm (8 inch) round génoise sponge cake (see page 151) or
    vanilla and almond cake (for vegan; see page 163)
2 tablespoons sweet sherry or berry liqueur, such as
    crème de framboise, or to taste
2 very fresh ripe medium peaches
1 quantity vanilla bean almond custard cream (see pages 246–247)
35 g (1¼ oz/¼ cup) lightly roasted slivered almonds

Jelly
500 g (1 lb 2 oz) very fresh ripe strawberries
1¼ teaspoons agar powder
1½–2 tablespoons golden caster (superfine) or raw sugar,
    or to taste

BAKING NOTES
• You will need a 3–3.5 litre (105–122 fl oz) capacity trifle bowl (mine has a diameter of 20 cm/ 8 inches). I've also assembled this in one large baking tray, instead of a bowl, and it worked brilliantly.

• If making a vegan version using the vanilla and almond cake, because it is dairy free and egg free), the main thing to keep in mind is that the cake will be far more fragile than a regular sponge and it may be difficult to place in the trifle bowl as one whole piece, so it is better to cut it into fingers and arrange in the bowl.

Fruit purée

250 g (9 oz) very fresh ripe strawberries or raspberries

2–3 tablespoons sweet sherry or berry liqueur, such as crème de
    framboise, or to taste

For the jelly, first choose a dish to set the jelly in, about 20 cm (8 inches) square with a minimum depth of 3 cm (1¼ inches).

Wash and hull the strawberries, roughly chop and place in a small saucepan. Add 250 ml (9 fl oz/1 cup) of water and bring to a gentle simmer. Cover with a tight-fitting lid and cook over very low heat for 10–15 minutes or until well softened, taking care no steam is lost as they cook. Strain through a fine sieve into a bowl, gently pressing down on the solids with the back of a spoon or ladle to extract as much liquid as possible but without pressing the pulp into the juice. You will need 500 ml (17 fl oz/2 cups); if you have less, add a little water to the sieve and press out a little more juice; if you have more, set it aside. Return the 500 ml of juice to the pan and whisk in the agar and sugar. Bring to a gentle simmer, whisking frequently to stop the agar sinking to the bottom and sticking to the base. Once the mixture comes to the boil, simmer gently for 7 minutes. Test for sweetness and adjust as desired (remember that the almond custard cream is quite sweet). Pour into the dish, and refrigerate for 1 hour or until set.

For the fruit purée, wash and dry the berries, and hull the strawberries, if using. Place in a blender with 2 tablespoons of the sherry or liqueur and blend until smooth. Taste and add extra liqueur as desired. You don't have to strain the purée, but if you prefer it without the small pips, strain it through a fine sieve, making sure to press against the fruit and extract as much juice as possible.

To put together the trifle, first wash and dry the berries. Cut the génoise in half horizontally and place half at the base of the trifle bowl. Drizzle with half of the fruit purée and 1 tablespoon of sweet sherry or liqueur. Cut enough strawberries in half (lengthways) and stand the halves on the cake, pressing the cut sides to the glass — do this around the entire edge of the cake. Add the raspberries — you can use these to help keep the strawberries in place if needed — and any remaining strawberries. Using a vegetable peeler or small knife, peel and cut the peaches into thin slices over the bowl, so the juices and slices fall directly into the bowl. When finished, squeeze any remaining pulp that clings to the stones so the juices drip into the bowl. Pour half of the custard cream over the fruit. Top with the remaining génoise and drizzle with the remaining fruit purée and remaining sweet sherry or liqueur. Cut the jelly into small squares and place on top of the cake. Pour over the remaining custard cream. Place in the fridge for 1 hour.

Just before serving, sprinkle with the slivered almonds.

Vanilla and almond cake with rose almond cream and raspberry jam

WHEAT FREE / DAIRY FREE / EGG FREE
SERVES 8–10

A plain crumb, egg-free and dairy-free cake is one of the hardest cakes to do. This is a variation on my most trusted of cakes, which I turn to in this situation, the Dairy-free and Egg-free Vanilla and Coconut Cupcakes (see page 186). It keeps exceptionally well. You could also use the Creamy Chocolate and Coconut Fudge Frosting (see page 253) or Creamy Cocoa Butter and Vanilla Frosting (see page 254) and layer the cake.

50 g (1¾ oz/½ cup) flaked almonds
1 teaspoon golden caster (superfine) sugar
195 g (6¾ oz/1½ cups) unbleached white spelt flour
1 teaspoon baking powder
¾ teaspoon baking soda (bicarbonate of soda)
50 g (1¾ oz/½ cup) almond meal (ground almonds)
185 ml (6 fl oz/¾ cup) maple syrup
125 ml (4 fl oz/½ cup) coconut milk
80 ml (2½ fl oz/⅓ cup) macadamia or almond oil
2 teaspoons apple cider vinegar
1 teaspoon vanilla paste
1 teaspoon natural vanilla extract
165 g (2¼ oz/½ cup) raspberry jam (to make it yourself,
   see page 271)
1 quantity vanilla bean almond cream infused with rose geranium
   leaves (see Baking Notes, page 246)

Preheat the oven to 180°C (350°F/Gas 4). Line the base of a 20 cm (8 inch) springform sandwich cake tin with baking paper.

Mix the flaked almonds and caster sugar together and set aside.

Sieve the flour, baking powder and baking soda into a bowl, add the almond meal and whisk through.

Place the maple syrup, coconut milk, oil, vinegar and vanilla paste and extract in another bowl and mix together. Add to the dry ingredients and mix until just combined. Turn into the tin and sprinkle with the flaked almond mixture, taking care to make some end up right on the edges (and even down the side a little) of the batter.

Bake for 40–50 minutes or until a skewer inserted into the middle comes out clean. This cake is best well cooked, so the maple syrup has a chance to crisp on the skin of the cake where it is exposed to the heat of the oven.

Remove from the oven and cool in the tin on a wire rack until completely cooled before releasing the springform side (it will still have the tin base in place and be sitting on the wire rack). Place a baking tray lightly on top of the cooled cake and invert the cake and wire rack

BAKING NOTES

- This cake will be all the better for your own homemade almond meal, made from lightly roasted almonds. You will need 50 g (1¾ oz) blanched almonds, lightly roasted before grinding. If desired, you may like to add a tiny drop of natural almond extract — go carefully, as too much can be overwhelming. If preferred, you can swap the almonds for 45 g (1½ oz/½ cup) desiccated coconut.

- I would strongly encourage you to make this cake in a springform sandwich tin, which enables you to take it out of the tin without inverting it, and gives you more control when removing the paper.

- This cake is best put together as close as possible to the time of serving, but no longer than 1 hour as the filling can soften the cake and make it too fragile.

- To make a three-tiered 20 cm (8 inch) cake, you will need to double the mixture and divide it between three 20 cm (8 inch) sandwich cake tins.

- To make a 24 cm (9½ inch) round cake, you will need to double the mixture. Cut in half and filled, this will give you a lovely tall cake.

onto the tray. Quickly remove the wire rack, then the tin base and baking paper from the cake. Lightly place another baking tray on the cake and invert again so the cake is right side up.

Cut the cake in half horizontally. This cake will not have the same sturdiness as those made with egg, so rather than lifting the top half of the cake off and setting it aside, it is best to slide a flat baking tray, tart tin base or something thin and sturdy between the layers to support the top layer. Using the same technique or two large palette knives, move the base of the cake, cut side up, to a serving platter.

Spread the jam evenly over the cake base, leaving a 1.5 cm (⅝ inch) border. Gently spread the almond cream over the top, again taking care to leave a small border. Pick up the top of the cake (on its tray) and carefully slide it onto the almond cream.

This cake is best served straight away or within 2 hours as the filling can soften the cake, making the crumb more fragile. Without the almond cream and jam, the cake will keep in an airtight container for 4–6 days.

Nut free (but not dairy free)

Replace the almond meal with 45 g (1½ oz/½ cup) desiccated coconut, 80 g (2¾ oz) melted butter, and omit the sugared flaked almond topping. You can also use 80 g coconut oil, melted and cooled — the cake will be lovely while still fresh, but the crumb will toughen and constrict a little when it has sat for some time or been in the fridge.

Adding egg

This firms up the crumb and makes the cake more sturdy for building (but you don't need to add this to the cupcake version on page 186 as they are sturdy enough already). Add 1 egg and reduce the coconut milk to 60 ml (2 fl oz/¼ cup).

Classic butter cake

WHEAT FREE
SERVES 8–12

This is my version of a classic butter cake, using white spelt flour and a reduced amount of a semi-refined sugar. It's a very good cake and will give you a moist yet sturdy crumb, which will last very well. This is the kind of cake to keep in a tin, ready for lunches or afternoon teas. You could flavour the cake with citrus zest. Older, drier leftovers are delicious grilled or toasted and served with fruit (baked, grilled, fresh or stewed), or jam with cultured cream (see pages 250–251) or Honey and Cinnamon Labne (see page 249).

260 g (9¼ oz/2 cups) white spelt flour
1½ teaspoons baking powder
250 g (9 oz) unsalted butter, softened, plus extra, for greasing
170 g (6 oz) golden caster (superfine) or golden raw sugar
4 eggs, at room temperature
2 teaspoons natural vanilla extract
60–125 ml (2–4 fl oz/¼–½ cup) milk

Preheat the oven to 170°C (325°F/Gas 3). Grease the base and side of a 22 cm (8½ inch) round cake tin and line with baking paper.

Sift the flour and baking powder into a bowl and set aside.

Using electric beaters, beat the butter and sugar until pale, light and fluffy. Add the eggs, one at a time, beating well after each addition. If the mix begins to split and look curdled, it is because it has become too cold to incorporate the eggs. A good trick is to place the mixing bowl in a little warm water for a few minutes — this will soften the butter again and allow it to absorb the eggs. Add the vanilla extract and beat well.

Add the sifted flour mixture and 60 ml (2 fl oz/¼ cup) of milk and gently beat in — if using electric beaters, begin very slowly to prevent the flour going everywhere. Beat until smooth and the flour and milk are well incorporated. Only add the extra milk if the mix is very heavy (this will generally be because of the presence of bran and germ from the flour). Spoon into the tin.

Bake for 1 hour or until a skewer inserted into the middle comes out clean. Cool in the tin for 30 minutes, then transfer to a wire rack to cool completely. It will shrink a little and deflate which is normal.

Ice with your choice of icing or frosting, as desired (see pages 252–263).

The un-iced cake will keep in an airtight container for up to 5 days.

BAKING NOTES

- Even if you have a lovely white spelt flour with no bran and germ, weigh the amount of flour needed rather than relying on a cup measurement. This is because the weight of white spelt flours varies between brands — 1 cup could actually weigh 140 g (5 oz), which would be too heavy for this recipe.

- However, if your white spelt flour looks more like a light wholemeal, I recommend sifting 325 g (11½ oz/2½ cups) in a fine sieve. This will catch most of the germ and bran, which you can discard. Measure 260 g (9¼ oz/2 cups) from this sifted flour.

- It is very important that the butter is soft — the consistency should be similar to that of a face cream. The main technique used to raise the cake in this recipe is by beating air into the butter and sugar, and for this you need a soft (but not melted) butter.

- I use golden caster sugar for this cake, but you could also use the slightly larger grained unrefined golden raw sugar.

Gluten-free almond butter cake

GLUTEN FREE
SERVES 10–12

The recipe you see here is the result of a collaboration between myself, Angie Cowan and Leanne Coyte — students from the 2010 Whole and Natural Foods Chef Training Program. Their task was to take a traditional pound cake, and make it gluten free. As is normal, this took at least six attempts, working on one principle at a time. The recipe below is a beautiful — and you would hardly ever guess — gluten-free butter cake. Ultimately a successful conversion is a mixture of technique and ingredient — in this recipe baking powder is minimal. Rather, the eggs have been separated, allowing two opportunities for building air. It has a sturdy but moist crumb, and keeps (and freezes) stunningly well. Serve it with fresh fruit, cream, almond cream or your favourite icing.

100 g (3½ oz) brown rice flour
25 g (1 oz) coconut flour
80 g (2¾ oz) true arrowroot
½ teaspoon baking powder
60 g (2¼ oz) almond meal (ground almonds)
4 eggs, at room temperature, separated
2 egg yolks, at room temperature
200 g (7 oz) unsalted butter, softened
105 g (3½ oz/½ cup) golden caster (superfine) sugar
60 ml (2 fl oz/¼ cup) maple syrup
2 teaspoons natural vanilla extract
¼ teaspoon sea salt

BAKING NOTE

You can substitute any ground nuts – lightly roasted hazelnuts would be wonderful.

Preheat the oven to 180°C (350°F/Gas 4). Line the base and side of a 22 cm (8½ inch) springform cake tin with baking paper.

Sieve the flours, arrowroot and baking powder into a bowl and discard the rice bran/germ left in the sieve. Add the almond meal and whisk through to evenly distribute the ingredients.

Place all of the egg yolks in one bowl, and the 4 egg whites in another bowl that is a good size for beating. (Store the leftover eggwhites in an airtight glass jar in the fridge or freezer for another use.)

Using a stand mixer fitted with the paddle attachment, beat the butter and sugar until light and fluffy, scraping down the sides from time to time. Add the egg yolks one at a time, beating very well after each addition until the mix is pale in colour, fluffy and creamy, turning the machine off and scraping down frequently. Because you are not using the whites at this stage, the mixture shouldn't curdle, but if it does, wrap a warm cloth around the bowl or place the bowl in hot water for a few seconds.

Whisk the egg whites using hand-held electric beaters until soft peaks form — do not overbeat.

To the butter and sugar mixture add the flour mixture, the maple syrup, vanilla extract, salt and half of the egg whites and fold in using a spatula. It will be stiff, but just do the best you can. When just combined, gently fold in the remaining egg whites, again it will be fairly stiff — it is after all a pound cake — just do it as lightly as possible, using the spatula to cut through the mix and fold, rather than a straight folding motion. Turn into the tin.

Bake for 50 minutes or until the cake is lightly golden on top and a skewer inserted into the middle comes out clean. Remove from the oven and cool in the tin for 20 minutes, then move to a wire rack.

Store in an airtight container in a cool, dark place for 5–6 days (I have kept it up to 10 days but it depends on the weather), or in the fridge if the weather is hot.

The buttermilk cake

A butter cake (see page 165) is a classic plain crumb cake, with plenty of butter and eggs to ensure a soft and moist crumb and is a wonderful special occasion cake. However, I had long wanted to develop something a little lighter, more everyday, but still easily dressed up for a celebration. The solution I found was buttermilk. It makes a luscious, light crumb with a slight tang, and the resulting cake is the perfect summer cake layered, or cut and served, with cream and fresh fruit (or with jam in winter). A buttermilk cake lasts exceptionally well, developing in flavour, and when it begins to go stale, you can toast it and serve warm with delicious fruits.

The buttermilk family tree

The everyday buttermilk cake and the prettier buttermilk cake (made from wholemeal) have different crumbs that suit different uses; the pretty buttermilk cake has a lovelier and finer crumb perfect for dressing up.

CLASSIC BUTTER CAKE

EVERYDAY BUTTERMILK CAKE

* Raspberry and lemon buttermilk cake

* Summer fruit buttermilk slab

PRETTY BUTTERMILK CAKE

* Pretty buttermilk cake with ginger cream and peaches

* Raspberry and white chocolate layer buttermilk cake

* Upside-down jewelled pudding

* Sweet and sour dark chocolate buttermilk cake

Everyday buttermilk cake

WHEAT FREE
SERVES 8–10

This is a hardworking, everyday, not too rich buttermilk cake and it has some characteristics I'd like to point out. With only two eggs, this cake has a tweedy, sturdy but soft texture, which makes it exceptionally good for supporting fruit. I was very torn between giving you the two- or three-egg version, and as you can see I've settled on the two. Made with three, this cake will have more air pockets — at some time I recommend you making it with three eggs and see which one you prefer. Personally I felt the extra egg compromised the texture. My faithful team of testers (and tasters) over many a buttermilk cake were spreading a bit of jam on a slice and tucking it into their kids' lunchboxes with great success. You can easily add fruit and citrus zest to enrich the cake or lay the batter in a slab tin and press berries and/or summer stone fruits into it (opposite) — they are all very good.

260 g (9¼ oz/2 cups) unbleached white spelt flour
½ teaspoon baking powder
½ teaspoon baking soda (bicarbonate of soda)
a pinch of sea salt
2 teaspoons natural vanilla extract
185 ml (6 fl oz/¾ cup) cultured buttermilk
125 g (4½ oz) unsalted butter, softened
105 g (3½ oz/½ cup) golden caster (superfine) sugar
2 eggs, at room temperature

Preheat the oven to 180°C (350°F/Gas 4). Line the base and sides of a 20 cm (8 inch) springform cake tin with baking paper.

Sieve the flour, baking powder, baking soda and salt into a bowl and set aside.

Add the vanilla extract to the buttermilk and set aside.

Using a stand mixer fitted with the paddle attachment, beat the butter and sugar until light and fluffy, scraping down the sides from time to time. Add the eggs, one at a time, beating well after each addition. Add half of the flour mixture and half of the buttermilk and beat on the lowest speed until just mixed through. Add the remaining flour mixture and the buttermilk and beat on the lowest speed until just combined. Turn into the tin and gently smooth over the surface with an offset spatula.

Bake for 50 minutes or until a skewer inserted into the middle comes out clean.

Remove from the oven and cool in the tin for 30 minutes before releasing the springform side of the cake tin. Slide onto a wire rack (still in the paper) and leave to completely cool before icing, if desired.

Store in an airtight container at a moderate room temperature for up to 4 days. It freezes exceptionally well too.

Raspberry and lemon buttermilk cake

A perfect cake for a summer weekend, with any leftovers lasting very well for the week ahead. Add 2 tablespoons of finely grated lemon zest to the dry ingredients and fold 125 g (4½ oz/1 cup) fresh or frozen raspberries (if frozen, do not thaw) into the finished batter. This cake is best eaten on the day of making. Serves 8–10.

Summer fruit buttermilk slab

The Everyday Buttermilk Cake also makes a wonderful slab cake, baked in a 30 cm x 20 cm (12 x 8 inch) rectangular cake tin, which is perfect to stud with summer stone fruits as the mix is sturdy enough to cope with their lush juices. Lay the batter in the lined tin before pressing sliced, halved or quartered stone fruit (peaches need to be peeled first) and berries too, if desired, into the batter. Sprinkle with nuts if you like. Don't be afraid to use a large amount of fruit, as it will shrivel during cooking. I make this slab cake in late summer, studded with peeled figs, drizzle it with some raw honey as it comes out of the oven and serve it with Honey and Cinnamon Labne (see page 249). It's very good. Serves 8–10.

BAKING NOTES

- It can be tempting to think the mix needs a little extra milk, but don't do this as there is plenty of fat in this mix to give you a moist, lovely crumb — too much liquid will collapse the cake.
- If at all possible, make this cake with cultured butter for a more delicious flavour.
- If making the cake with three eggs, drop the baking soda to ¼ teaspoon.
- Try icing the top with ½ quantity Creamy Chocolate and Coconut Fudge Frosting (see page 253), and you could even split it in half and spread with raspberry jam.
- Try icing the cake with 1 quantity Quick and Simple Butter Icing (see page 257) flavoured with finely grated lemon zest or juice, or passionfruit. This will be enough to fill and ice the top and sides of the cake.

Pretty buttermilk cake

WHEAT FREE
SERVES 6–8

This wonderful wholemeal cake uses the technique created by baker Rose Levy Beranbaum (read about this in Fat and Crumb on page 54) that discourages the development of gluten. It is a perfect technique for a 100 per cent wholemeal plain crumb cake, and the result is an exceptionally moist and delicious crumb that stands up to any occasion. The cake is even more gorgeous when made with an unrefined white flour. It's a perfect base to use for a special occasion cake and makes a great batter for an upside-down pudding (see page 177).

Made with either wholemeal or white flour, this cake keeps exceptionally well at a moderate room temperature for up to 3 days and also freezes well. I've served it here with fresh peaches and delicious candied ginger and its syrup, but it would be equally good in winter with a high-quality peach or nectarine jam.

Glacé ginger and syrup
10 cm (4 inch) piece of ginger, peeled and very thinly sliced
37 g (1¼ oz/¼ cup) rapadura sugar

Pretty buttermilk cake
195 g (6¾ oz) wholemeal spelt flour or 175 g (6 oz) wholemeal
    wheat cake flour
½ teaspoon ground ginger (optional)
1 teaspoon baking powder
½ teaspoon baking soda (bicarbonate of soda)
a pinch of sea salt
105 g (3½ oz/½ cup) golden caster (superfine) sugar
4 egg yolks, at room temperature
2 teaspoons natural vanilla extract
170 ml (5½ fl oz/⅔ cup) cultured buttermilk
115 g (¼ oz) unsalted butter, softened

To decorate
fresh peaches
thin (pouring) cream

BAKING NOTES

• You can replace the golden caster (superfine) sugar with an equal amount of rapadura, but the cake will not be as light or rise quite as much.

• Cultured butter is a good choice here.

• This cake relaxes to 3.5 cm (1¼ inches) high. To make a higher cake with jam in the middle, make two 20 cm (8 inch) cakes instead using 2 quantities of batter.

For the glacé ginger and syrup, place the ginger, sugar and 150 ml (5 fl oz) of water in a small saucepan over low heat and simmer for 10 minutes or until the liquid has reduced to about 2 tablespoons. Remove the ginger and cut into small pieces for the cake batter. Reserve the syrup for drizzling over the cake after it is cooked.

For the pretty buttermilk cake, preheat the oven to 180°C (350°F/Gas 4). Line the base and sides of a 20 cm (8 inch) springform cake tin with baking paper.

Place the flour and ground ginger in the bowl of a stand mixer fitted with the paddle attachment. Sieve in the baking powder and baking soda, then add the salt and sugar.

Place the egg yolks, vanilla extract and buttermilk in a small bowl and whisk together.

Break the butter up into rough chunks and add to the flour mixture together with one-third of the buttermilk mix. Beat on low–medium speed and when it starts to come together, add the remaining buttermilk mixture and beat together on low speed. When it begins to come together, increase the speed to medium–high and beat until thick and creamy, about 30 seconds. Fold in the glacé ginger. Turn into the tin and gently smooth over the surface with an offset spatula.

Bake for 40–50 minutes or until a skewer inserted into the middle comes out clean. Remove from the oven and cool in the tin for 30 minutes before releasing the springform side of the cakes. Slide onto a wire rack (still in the paper) and leave to completely cool before decorating.

Peel and cut the peaches into 1 cm (½ inch) thick slices — I cut them straight off the stone into a bowl so the juices drip into the bowl. Add the ginger syrup, toss to combine and set aside.

Whip the cream to firm peaks and gently spread over the cooled cake. Top with the peaches and drizzle with the peach juices in the bowl.

White buttermilk cake

If you want to make this with white spelt flour, replace the wholemeal spelt with 195 g (6¾ oz/1½ cups) white spelt, reduce the baking powder to ¾ teaspoon, and omit the glacé ginger and ground ginger.

Raspberry and white chocolate layer buttermilk cake

WHEAT FREE
SERVES 10–12

Certainly a cake for special occasions! I've chosen to use the white flour version of the Pretty Buttermilk Cake as it has a much softer texture.

390 g (13¾ oz/3 cups) unbleached white spelt flour
1½ teaspoons baking powder
1 teaspoon baking soda (bicarbonate of soda)
210 g (7½ oz/1 cup) golden caster (superfine) sugar
¼ pinch of sea salt
8 egg yolks, at room temperature
1 tablespoon natural vanilla extract
330 ml (11¼ fl oz/1⅓ cups) cultured buttermilk
230 g (8 oz) unsalted butter, softened
160 g (5¾ oz) fresh or frozen raspberries (if frozen, do not thaw)
1 quantity raspberry better buttercream (see pages 258–260)
1 quantity white chocolate better buttercream (see pages 258–261)

Preheat the oven to 180°C (350°F/Gas 4). Line the base and sides of three 20 cm (8 inch) sandwich cake tins with baking paper.

Sieve the flour, baking powder and baking soda into the bowl of a stand mixer fitted with the paddle attachment. Add the sugar and salt.

Place the egg yolks, vanilla extract and buttermilk in a small bowl and whisk together.

Break the butter up into rough chunks and add to the flour mixture together with one-third of the buttermilk mix. Beat on low–medium speed and when it starts to come together, add the remaining buttermilk mixture and beat together on low speed. When it begins to come together, increase the speed to medium–high and beat until thick and creamy, about 30 seconds. Fold the raspberries in by hand. Divide the mix between the tins and gently smooth over the surfaces with an offset palette knife.

Bake for 40–45 minutes or until a skewer inserted into the middle comes out clean.

Remove from the oven and cool in the tins for 30 minutes before moving to a wire rack to completely cool.

To put together the cake, place one cake on a cardboard round, and place this on a rotating cake stand. Using an offset spatula, spread half of the raspberry buttercream on top of the cake. Place the next cake on top and spread with the remaining raspberry buttercream. Top with the final cake.

You need to apply the white chocolate buttercream two separate times — the first layer will seal in the crumbs and make a smooth surface for the second application. Spread an even coating of white chocolate buttercream around the edges of the cake and on the

BAKING NOTE

You will need a 20 cm (8 inch) cardboard cake round, a rotating cake stand, 15 cm (6 inch) straight and offset palette knives, and a stainless steel squared-off dough scraper.

top — I like to use a 15 cm (6 inch) straight spatula. You will most likely use most of the buttercream, but don't use it all now — the quantity of white chocolate buttercream is enough to coat this cake well, but you just can't afford to waste any. It doesn't have to be perfect — you are going to take care of any messy bits in a minute. Then using a squared-off dough scraper, place the squared side on the base of the cake stand and against the side of the cake and gently rotate the cake stand in an even manner with your other hand — making sure you only apply light pressure on the buttercream. This will give you a smooth spread of buttercream. Use your palette knife to even off the top, and again, it doesn't have to be perfect, just close. Place in the fridge or freezer (I use a very sturdy knife to get under the cardboard round to help pick up the cake and to help lower it onto the shelf) to firm up for a few minutes (or longer if in the fridge).

Remove the cake from the fridge and apply another layer of buttercream to the sides and top. Repeat the process with the dough scraper and palette knife until the cake is how you would like it. Remember that buttercream responds to temperature — in very hot weather, you may need to refrigerate the cake and bring it out about 40 minutes before serving for the cake and buttercream to relax (again, this depends on the ambient temperature of the room).

Leftovers keep very well stored under a cake dome for up to 2 days, depending on the temperature, or in an airtight container in the fridge, and they freeze well too.

Upside-down jewelled pudding

WHEAT FREE
SERVES 6–8

A delicious, gorgeous cake for a cold winter's afternoon tea or dessert. Perfect in mid to late winter when only apple and pears from the cool room are left. Dried fruit enables you to make use of the bounty of summer fruits.

- 250 g (9 oz) dried fruit (I use apricots, peaches, cherries and mango)
- 125 ml (4 fl oz/½ cup) apple juice (or you could use pear or orange juice or even a bit of vincotto diluted in water)
- 60 g (2¼ oz) unsalted butter
- 125 ml (4 fl oz/½ cup) maple syrup, or light or dark brown muscovado sugar
- 1 quantity pretty buttermilk cake batter (with or without the ground ginger and glacé ginger) (see page 172)
- thin (pouring) cream or custard, to serve

Preheat the oven to 180°C (350°F/Gas 4) or 165°C (320°F/Gas 2–3) if fan-forced.

Place the fruit in a saucepan, then add the juice and 125 ml (4 fl oz/½ cup) of water. Bring to the boil and simmer for 5–6 minutes or until the fruit is soft. Strain off the juice and keep for another use if desired.

Place the butter and maple syrup in a 20 cm (8 inches) across the base ovenproof frying pan or cast-iron skillet, at least 4 cm (1½ inches) deep, over low heat. Once the butter has melted, remove from the heat and swirl the butter so it is evenly distributed. Arrange the fruit in your desired pattern in the base of the pan and set aside.

Make the cake batter and dollop it over the fruit, then use a spoon to gently spread it evenly over the fruit as best you can.

Bake for 25–30 minutes — it's good to see the sugary juices boiling around the edges.

Remove from the oven, place a serving plate with a lip over the frying pan and *carefully* invert the pudding over the plate, taking great care as the sugar syrup will be very, very hot. Serve warm with cream or custard.

Sweet and sour dark chocolate buttermilk cake

WHEAT FREE
SERVES 8–10

I'm not sure whether you've noticed, but there's not a huge amount of chocolate in this book. I'm not a big fan, but when I am, I want it moist, dark and not too sweet, with a definite edge. Thanks to the buttermilk this is a light cake and I've used the very fine sugar crystal of a dark muscovado to give it a slight chew, but it's the icing that seals the deal. Dark, sweet and sour, with a very definite edge, it's a killer and irresistible combination whether it be in a cake, icing or a man.

195 g (6¾ oz/1½ cups) unbleached white spelt flour
55 g (2 oz/½ cup) unsweetened dutched cocoa powder
½ teaspoon baking powder
½ teaspoon baking soda (bicarbonate of soda)
2 teaspoons natural vanilla extract
185 ml (6 fl oz/¾ cup) cultured buttermilk
125 g (4½ oz) unsalted butter, softened
165 g (5¾ oz/1 cup) dark muscovado sugar
70 g (2½ oz/⅓ cup) golden caster (superfine) sugar
2 eggs, at room temperature
1 quantity dark chocolate and sour cream icing (see page 256)

Preheat the oven to 180°C (350°F/Gas 4). Line the base and side of a 20 cm (8 inch) springform cake tin with baking paper.

Sieve the flour, cocoa, baking powder and baking soda into a bowl and set aside.

Add the vanilla extract to the buttermilk and set aside.

Using a stand mixer fitted with the paddle attachment, beat the butter and sugars until light and fluffy, scraping down the sides from time to time. Add the eggs, one at a time, beating well after each addition. Add half of the flour mixture and half of the buttermilk and beat on the lowest speed until just mixed through. Add the remaining flour mixture and remaining buttermilk and beat on the lowest speed until just combined. Turn into the tin and gently smooth over the surface with an offset spatula.

Bake for 40–60 minutes or until a skewer inserted into the middle comes out clean.

Remove from the oven and cool in the tin for 30 minutes before releasing the springform side of the cake tin. Slide onto a wire rack (still in the paper) and leave to completely cool before icing.

Store in an airtight container in a cool, dark place for up to 5 days, or wrap well in plastic wrap and freeze for up to 4 weeks.

BAKING NOTES

• It can be tempting to think the mix needs a little extra milk, but don't do this as there is plenty of fat in this mix to give you a moist, lovely crumb. Too much liquid will collapse the cake.

• If piping the icing onto this cake using a star nozzle, it will need to be done as soon as the icing is made.

Coconut and palm sugar cake

WHEAT FREE / CAKE IS DAIRY FREE
MAKES 1 X 20 CM (8 INCH) CAKE TO SERVE 8–10 / MAKES 16 CUPCAKES

Coconut palm sugar shines here, providing deep, dark and complex flavour, which is relieved by the lime syrup and curd. It does, however, deliver a dense but moist cake, which the coconut palm syrup and icing help soften. It's best eaten on the day it's made, as the coconut oil will constrict the crumb somewhat, especially if stored in the fridge overnight. There are a couple of ways to serve this cake — with the coconut palm sugar syrup soaked into the cake layers as you make it or serve the syrup separately for people to pour it over the cake themselves once sliced. Either way, the role of the syrup is to help moisten the crumb, and my preference is to pour it on after. This is the perfect cake to bring life and sharp flavour into the winter months, as the Tahitian lime comes into season.

1 quantity coconut and cream cheese icing (see page 263),
    made with 2–3 tablespoons extra maple syrup
½ quantity luscious lime coconut curd (see page 264)

Cake
98 g (3½ oz/¾ cup) unbleached white spelt flour
73 g (2½ oz/½ cup) wholemeal spelt flour
32 g (1 oz/¼ cup) coconut flour
2 teaspoons baking powder
45 g (1½ oz/½ cup) desiccated coconut
finely grated zest of 1 lime
105 g (3½ oz/¾ cup) granulated coconut palm sugar
3 eggs, at room temperature
125 ml (4 fl oz/½ cup) coconut oil, melted and hot
250 ml (9 fl oz/1 cup) coconut milk
1 teaspoon natural vanilla extract

Coconut palm sugar syrup
50 g (1¾ oz) granulated coconut palm sugar

Lime drizzle syrup
60 ml (2 fl oz/¼ cup) freshly squeezed and strained lime juice
    (about 1–2 limes)
zest of 1 lime, removed in thin strands
1–2 tablespoons golden caster (superfine) sugar

BAKING NOTES
- Hot oil ensures that it doesn't firm and seize up when you add it to a cold mix, and is easier to incorporate evenly.
- Don't bake in two sandwich tins, as there will be too much cake exposed and it will dry out.
- For the best crumb, do not refrigerate the cake and aim to serve it within 1–2 hours of making.
- To make the entire cake dairy free, replace the Coconut and Cream Cheese Icing with the Creamy Cocoa Butter and Vanilla Frosting (see page 254), with finely grated lime zest added and 1–2 drops of Boyajian Lime Oil if you have it.

Preheat the oven to 180°C (350°F/Gas 4). Line a 20 cm (8 inch) round cake tin with baking paper.

For the cake, sieve the white spelt flour into a good-sized bowl that will make folding easy. Add the wholemeal flour, coconut flour, baking powder, coconut and lime zest. Whisk through to evenly distribute the ingredients.

Using a stand mixer fitted with the whisk attachment, whisk the palm sugar and eggs until thick and creamy and doubled in volume. The mixture is ready when you can lift the beaters and the mixture falls back into the bowl in a ribbon that rests on the surface for about 10 seconds. This should take about 5 minutes.

At this point, add the hot oil to the coconut milk and vanilla extract and whisk together.

Add the milk mixture to the flour mixture, then add two-thirds of the egg mixture and fold through as gently as possible until it is just combined, and then very gently fold in the remaining egg mixture. This final bit of egg mixture will give it some air. Turn into the tin.

Bake for 40–50 minutes or until a skewer inserted into the middle comes out clean. Remove from the oven and cool in the tin for 30 minutes, then move to a wire rack. Leave to completely cool before cutting in half and filling.

For the coconut palm sugar syrup, place the sugar in a small saucepan with 60 ml (2 fl oz/¼ cup) of water. Brush down any granules on the side of the pan with a pastry brush. Stir through and bring slowly to the boil as the sugar sinks to the bottom and takes a while to dissolve. Gently simmer over medium heat for 5 minutes. Remove and cool. You should have 80 ml (2½ fl oz/⅓ cup). If you find that the syrup solidifies when cool, just add a tiny bit of water to loosen it up. Pour the syrup into a jug for serving.

For the lime drizzle syrup, place the lime juice and zest and 1 tablespoon of the sugar in a small saucepan. Simmer over a fairly moderate heat — it should be a good, but not rolling boil. After 1 minute, taste for sweetness and add the remaining tablespoon as needed. Continue to simmer for 4–5 minutes or until you have a thick syrup.

To put the cake together, cut the cooled cake in half horizontally and place the bottom layer, cut side up, on a cardboard round, cake stand or serving platter. Spread half of the icing over the cake. Spread the curd over the top of the icing, leaving a 1.5 cm (⅝ inch) border because when the cake sits on top, the weight of it will push the curd to the edges. Place the remaining layer of cake, cut side down, onto the curd. Using a palette knife, gently spread the remaining icing in a circular motion over the top of the cake to create slight grooves that will trap the syrup. Drizzle the lime syrup over the cake. Cut into slices and serve with the coconut palm sugar syrup for pouring over.

This cake is best served fresh on the day of baking (but no leftovers have been turned away when offered!). Leftovers can be stored under a cake dome, or in an airtight container in the fridge if the weather is hot.

Cupcakes

Long after the cupcake craze has gone out of fashion, those that bake will still make, cherish and love them. They will remain an elegant, pretty and delicious way to deliver a beautiful cake in a mouthful and a perfect example that a small portion of something beautiful and delicious is all you need. They are also an excellent arena for gluten-, dairy- and/or egg-free cakes, where there is not so much surface area to support and bind together.

The cupcake family tree

CLASSIC VANILLA AND COCONUT CUPCAKES

* Nut free
* Rose–pistachio
* Dairy free and egg free (but not nut free)
* Egg free and nut free (with a dairy-free option)

CHOCOLATE AND COCONUT CUPCAKES

* Dairy free and egg free
* Nut free and egg free (with a dairy-free option)

GLUTEN-FREE CHOCOLATE CUPCAKES

* Raspberry and egg free
* Dairy free
* Dairy free and nut free

Clockwise from top left: Julie's rose–pistachio cupcakes with strawberry and rosewater better buttercream; dairy-free and egg-free vanilla and coconut cupcakes with creamy chocolate and coconut fudge frosting; gluten-free chocolate cupcakes with white chocolate better buttercream; classic vanilla and coconut cupcakes with quick and simple butter icing with passionfruit.

Classic vanilla and coconut cupcakes

WHEAT FREE / NUT FREE
MAKES 12

I love cupcakes but find many just too sweet, especially the icing. You can still get a gorgeous looking crumb, using less-refined ingredients. This recipe is easy to throw together, and infinitely flexible — it would be lovely with finely grated citrus zest (lime, lemon or orange) or the coconut can be replaced with ground nuts. With regards to the frosting, I really love these with the Better Buttercream as it's such a fabulous frosting — neither overly rich or sweet, but just perfect. These cupcakes freeze brilliantly.

195 g (6¾ oz/1½ cups) unbleached white spelt flour
¾ teaspoon baking powder
¼ teaspoon baking soda (bicarbonate of soda)
45 g (1½ oz/½ cup) desiccated coconut
105 g (3½ oz/½ cup) golden caster (superfine) sugar
a pinch of sea salt
2 eggs, at room temperature
100 g (3½ oz) unsalted butter, melted and cooled but still liquid
185 ml (6 fl oz/¾ cup) milk
2 teaspoons natural vanilla extract
1 quantity better buttercream (see page 258), for icing

Preheat the oven to 170°C (325°F/Gas 3). Line a 12-hole muffin tin with paper cases.

Sieve the flour, baking powder and baking soda into a bowl. Add the coconut, sugar and salt, and whisk through to distribute the ingredients evenly.

Place the eggs, butter, milk and vanilla extract in a bowl and whisk together well. Add to the dry ingredients and mix until just combined. Leave to sit for 1–2 minutes — the mixture will look wet but will firm up as it stands. Spoon ¼ cup of batter into each paper case.

Bake for 25 minutes or until golden and the centre of the middle cupcake is firm to the gentle touch and lightly golden in colour. I would prefer you didn't insert a skewer into one to test as removing them too early from the oven can cause them to collapse a little. Turn off the oven, open the door and leave the cupcakes in the oven for 5 minutes.

Remove from the oven and leave in the tin until almost cool, then move to a wire rack to completely cool before icing.

Store under a cake dome at room temperature for up to 2 days, or in an airtight container in a cool place for up to 4 days. If the weather is hot, store in an airtight container in the fridge, but take the cakes out 15–30 minutes before eating, so the crumb and buttercream can relax.

BAKING NOTE

These cupcakes require a slightly lower oven temperature, which helps to give a nicely even dome to the top of the cakes.

Julie's rose–pistachio cupcakes

My wonderful friend Julie adores rose-flavoured desserts — this is the cupcake I designed for her birthday. It lacks the cloying sweetness of many in this flavour family, and the choice of a strawberry buttercream is deliberate. A simple glaze would be too brown in colour (using golden icing/confectioners' sugar) but when whipped with butter, it will become paler and take on some colour — in this case, fresh, ripe strawberry purée. It's a beautiful cupcake, with rose, pistachio and strawberry making some very glorious music.

Replace the desiccated coconut with ½ cup of lightly roasted and ground pistachios and add 1 teaspoon of rosewater. Ice the cupcakes with 1 quantity Strawberry and Rosewater Better Buttercream (see page 260), then sprinkle with lightly roasted and coarsely chopped pistachios. You can also decorate each cupcake with an unsprayed rose petal.

Dairy-free and egg-free vanilla and coconut cupcakes

WHEAT FREE / DAIRY FREE / EGG FREE / CAN BE NUT FREE
MAKES 12

This is the cake batter I turn to when a dairy-free and egg-free cake is needed — it will give you a well-textured and moist crumb, it's quick and easy to make, and keeps and freezes well.

195 g (6¾ oz/1½ cups) unbleached white spelt flour
1 teaspoon baking powder
¾ teaspoon baking soda (bicarbonate of soda)
45 g (1½ oz/½ cup) desiccated coconut
2 teaspoons apple cider vinegar
2 teaspoons natural vanilla extract
185 ml (6 fl oz/¾ cup) maple syrup
125 ml (4 fl oz/½ cup) coconut milk
60 ml (2 fl oz/¼ cup) rice milk
80 ml (2½ fl oz/⅓ cup) macadamia nut or almond oil
1 quantity creamy cocoa butter and vanilla frosting (see page 254),
    or creamy chocolate and coconut fudge frosting
    (see page 253), for icing

Preheat the oven to 170°C (325°F/Gas 3). Line a 12-hole muffin tin with paper cases.
Sieve the flour, baking powder and baking soda into a bowl, add the desiccated coconut and whisk through.
Place the vinegar, vanilla extract, maple syrup, coconut and rice milks, and oil in another bowl and mix together. Add to the dry ingredients and mix until just combined. Leave to sit

for 1–2 minutes — the mixture will look wet but will firm up as it stands. Divide the batter among the paper cases.

Bake for 25–30 minutes or until a skewer inserted into one of the cupcakes comes out clean. Cool in the tin for 20 minutes or until almost cool, then move to a wire rack to completely cool before icing.

Nut free (with a dairy-free option)

Replace the macadamia nut or almond oil with 100 g of unsalted butter, melted, and omit the ¼ cup of rice milk (80 g melted butter gives 80 ml/2½ fl oz/⅓ cup, plus there is an extra 20 g/¾ oz of butter to ensure there is 80 ml fat, and this extra makes up for the ¼ cup rice milk).

You can also replace the macadamia nut or almond oil with 80 ml (2½ fl oz/⅓ cup) coconut oil, melted and cooled — the cake will be lovely while still fresh, but the crumb will toughen and constrict a little when it has sat for some time or been in the fridge.

Dairy-free and egg-free chocolate and coconut cupcakes

WHEAT FREE / DAIRY FREE / EGG FREE / CAN BE NUT FREE
MAKES 12

These cupcakes are a variation on my Dairy-free and Egg-free Vanilla and Coconut Cupcakes (opposite). They have ¼ cup fresh or frozen raspberries added to make up for the extra ¼ cup moisture that the cupcakes need.

130 g (4½ oz/1 cup) unbleached white spelt flour, plus
    1½ tablespoons
40 g (1½ oz/⅓ cup) unsweetened dutched cocoa powder
¾ teaspoon baking soda (bicarbonate of soda)
50 g (1¾ oz/½ cup) almond meal (ground almonds)
2 teaspoons apple cider vinegar
2 teaspoons natural vanilla extract
185 ml (6 fl oz/¾ cup) maple syrup
125 ml (4 fl oz/½ cup) coconut milk
80 ml (2½ fl oz/⅓ cup) macadamia nut or almond oil
30 g (1 oz/¼ cup) fresh or frozen raspberries (if frozen, thaw first
    in a sieve and discard the juices)
1 quantity creamy cocoa butter and vanilla frosting (see page 254),
    or creamy chocolate and coconut fudge frosting
    (see page 253), for icing

Preheat the oven to 180°C (350°F/Gas 4). Line a 12-hole muffin tin with paper cases.

Sieve the flour, cocoa and baking soda into a bowl. Add the almond meal and whisk through to distribute evenly.

Place the vinegar, vanilla extract, maple syrup, coconut milk and oil in a bowl and mix together. Add to the dry ingredients and mix until just combined. Gently fold through the raspberries. Spoon the mixture into the paper cases.

Bake for 25–30 minutes or until a skewer inserted into the middle comes out clean.

Remove from the oven and cool in the tin for 15 minutes, then move to a wire rack to completely cool before icing.

Nut free (with a dairy-free option)

Replace the almond meal with 45 g (1½ oz/½ cup) of desiccated coconut, and replace the macadamia nut or almond oil with 80 g (2¾ oz) of unsalted butter, melted.

You can also use 80 ml (2½ fl oz/⅓ cup) coconut oil, melted and cooled — the cake will be lovely while still fresh, but the crumb will toughen and constrict a little when it has sat for some time or been in the fridge.

Gluten-free chocolate cupcakes

GLUTEN FREE / WHEAT FREE / NUT FREE / CAN BE EGG FREE / CAN BE DAIRY FREE
MAKES 9–12

160 g (5¾ oz/1 cup) brown rice flour
30 g (1 oz/¼ cup) true arrowroot
45 g (1½ oz/½ cup) desiccated coconut
45 g (1½ oz) unsweetened dutched cocoa powder
¾ teaspoon baking soda (bicarbonate of soda)
2 teaspoons apple cider vinegar
2 teaspoons natural vanilla extract
185 ml (6 fl oz/¾ cup) maple syrup
125 ml (4 fl oz/½ cup) coconut milk
1 egg, at room temperature
80 ml (2½ fl oz/⅓ cup) melted butter or ghee
1 quantity raspberry or white chocolate better buttercream
    (see pages 260–261), for icing

Preheat the oven to 170°C (325°F/Gas 3). Line a 12-hole muffin tin with paper cases.

Place the rice flour, arrowroot and coconut in a mixing bowl. Sieve the cocoa and baking soda into the bowl and whisk through to distribute the ingredients.

Place the vinegar, vanilla extract, maple syrup, coconut milk, egg and butter in a bowl and whisk through well, to ensure the egg is beaten. Add to the dry ingredients and mix until just combined. Leave to sit for 1–2 minutes — it will look wet, but will firm up a little as it sits. Spoon the mixture into the paper cases.

Bake for 25–30 minutes. Remove from the oven and cool in the tin for 15 minutes, then move to a wire rack to completely cool before icing.

Raspberry and egg free

This will have a fragile crumb without the egg to bind. Replace the egg with ¼ cup fresh or frozen raspberries (if frozen, thaw first in a sieve and discard the juices). Gently fold the berries through the batter after it has sat for 1–2 minutes and firmed up.

Dairy free (but not nut free)

Replace the butter or ghee with the same amount of macadamia nut or almond oil. Ice with the Creamy Cocoa Butter and Vanilla Frosting (see page 254) or Creamy Chocolate and Coconut Fudge Frosting (see page 253).

Dairy free and nut free

Replace the butter or ghee with the same amount of coconut oil, melted and cooled — the cake will be lovely while still fresh, but the crumb will toughen and constrict a little when it has sat for some time or been in the fridge, and will be noticeably more crumbly. Ice with the Creamy Cocoa Butter and Vanilla Frosting (see page 254) or Creamy Chocolate and Coconut Fudge Frosting (see page 253).

Pastry

I'm not sure there is any better dessert than a slice of pie or tart, so full of fruit that the juices burst through the pastry, sizzling and caramelising on the hot tin — a delicious and glorious sight. I adore fruit, and a good pastry could be considered in the same vein as the phrase 'behind every successful man, there is a good woman'. Pastry holds and supports fruit while it cooks down to an intense burst of concentrated flavour. Or when the fruit is placed upon a cloud of pastry cream within a pre-baked shell, the pastry complements the fruit, allowing it to be all it can be.

Know thy pastry

Unfortunately many people miss out on the joys of homemade pastry — nothing seems to engender as much fear in the baker as pastry. Pastry is the misunderstood toddler who, when tired or hungry, falls apart and worse still has a tantrum — we've all had those pastry moments. Yet, when you understand your toddler, you don't let them get tired or hungry, or ask things of them when they are in this place. It's exactly the same for pastry. We don't try to roll it when it's too hot, or expect it to behave when it's been overworked.

So why even bother to make your own pastry when there are so many available commercially — and some very good ones at that? Because they are standardised, consistent and homogenised, and while some have good flavour they are without character. I don't want my puff pastry to rise one-metre high (okay, a slight exaggeration) and fall apart in fine shards as I cut it, and have an homogenised, shallow flavour. I want more. I want a bohemian puff that says to me: 'I am made from the earth, from grain that has swayed in the winds — some parts of me are light and breezy, but some parts of me may be hard to handle. My heart is full, my flavour and weight may be intense and heavy, I may not rise or puff as much, but I am real and true.' That's what I want in my puff, and in all my pastry, and to be honest, I'd say in my life.

This chapter is about understanding the characteristics of different pastries. Socrates' guiding rule, 'know thyself' applies just as much to pastry. Know thy pastry. Learn what it likes and what makes it crazy, and you will find pastry one of the easiest and quickest of things to make — ready to wrap, fold and support delicious, glorious ripe seasonal fruit. It seems the defining factor for healthy pastry these days is that it does not contain butter. This is a perspective I absolutely disagree with and butter is always my first choice for the most healthful, stable and delicious fat when baking (see more on page 31). However, for those times you can't use butter (for example, when cooking for those with allergies), you will also find alternatives in this chapter that are wholesome and healthy.

Before you begin this section, read up on the tart tins (see page 43) and other equipment you might need.

Sweet shortcrust pastry

This is the pastry I most commonly use, and it is an excellent all-round workhorse for fruit pies and rustic tarts. It does however have its limitations — containing little sugar or egg, it is never as delicious as when eaten within a few hours of baking. I'm not mad about it to bake blind as a shell for filling, and prefer to use a Rich Shortcrust Pastry (Pâte Sucrée) (see page 204) for that purpose, or if a dairy-free option is required, a Coconut Oil Sweet Shortcrust Pastry (see page 199).

The ingredients

Fat: often described as the shortening

The term 'shortening' describes one of the most important roles of fat in shortcrust pastry when using gluten flour — it minimises the development of gluten strands (shortening them), when moisture is added to the flour.

There are two aspects to fat that we must consider:

* **Amount of fat in the fat used** Primarily the role of fat in shortcrust pastry is to provide a tender and flaky texture. It does this by coating gluten flour (such as wheat or spelt) with fat, isolating the flour from the water when it is added, and thus reducing gluten development. To do this successfully the 'fattier' it is the better the result. Taking into account that butter has a percentage of water and milk solids, the higher percentage of butterfat in a butter, the better the pastry — this is the reason so many of the French butters make such excellent pastry. Lard and suet are also exceptionally good as they are 100 per cent fat and are renowned for a flake with exceptional shatter. Oils and ghee are 100 per cent fat. Butter also has the advantage of some liquid (buttermilk), which when left in some good-sized clumps within a shortcrust pastry will steam during baking, helping to lift the pastry and create a flakier result.
* **Saturated (solid) fats versus unsaturated (liquid) fats** Saturated fats will always provide the best flake. Once this kind of fat is incorporated into the pastry, it will set into a solid shape when cold. Once the pastry is put into the oven, that little piece of solid fat will melt (and in the case of butter, release steam). As the gluten in the flour sets around it, you are left with the tiniest air pocket — this is the flake. Liquid fat (oil) cannot form that little solid shape. But you can set a coconut oil into a solid form and use that.

The bottom line is the more fat you use, the flakier and more delicious the pastry will be. Puff pastry, for example is generally equal amounts of fat to flour.

Flour

As for most baking, I prefer using spelt for my pastry. If using wheat, lower-protein wheat flour (a cake or pastry flour) will make a softer and more delicious pastry than hard (or high-protein) wheat flour. And, to be fair, low-protein cake or pastry wheat flour will give you a shortcrust pastry with exceptional flake — this is because the type of gluten in wheat traps and holds the flake (air) far better than spelt. However, because the technique used to make shortcrust (encasing the flour with butter to minimise gluten), removes much of that possibility, you could consider using a plain (all-purpose) flour for shortcrust pastry, though I would recommend you up the quantity of fat by 20 g (¾ oz) to ensure that as much flour as possible is coated, and rely less on water to bind the mixture.

Using only wholemeal flours (wheat or spelt) makes a superb, nutty tasting pastry, but will have less rise. You can lighten this by using a mix of wholemeal and unbleached white flours.

Salt

A small amount of salt sharpens flavour. Take this into account if you are using salted butter. Bear in mind that the salt should be fine, so it combines with the flour easily.

Water

The role of water is to hydrate the flour, activate the gluten and bind. Water must always be iced, again to keep the fat from melting. It is critical not to add more water than you need — this is a common cause of tough pastry.

Acid: lemon juice or apple cider vinegar

A small amount of acid such as lemon juice or apple cider vinegar keeps the dough from oxidising and turning a dull colour. It also helps to relax the gluten strands, preventing the dough from becoming too tough or elastic, allowing you to roll it without the dough bouncing back. Personally, I don't include this when making a butter or lard pastry, but it won't hurt. I always include it when making coconut oil–based shortcrust.

Technique

Technique is a major stress point for good shortcrust, the golden rules are:

Conditions must be kept cool

Summer is a perfect season for pastry, with the abundance of fruit, but the biggest enemy (outside of the oven) of shortcrust pastry is heat. Your single aim when making shortcrust pastry is not to allow the butter to melt into the flour during making and rolling and 'becoming one' with the flour. This is why it's traditional to make and roll pastry on marble as it is cool to the touch. Use chilled butter, ice-cold water and ensure it has as little contact with your hands as possible. A pastry cutter is not expensive and does a great job of cutting the flour into the butter, keeping your hands and thus body warmth out of the bowl. You can also use a food processor to cut the butter into the flour, but be very careful not to overdo it — it's easy to 'cream' it into the flour.

In summer, you might like to pre-chill your ingredients: add the flour (and salt if using) to the bowl, toss small cubes of butter through the flour, and chill in the fridge before using or overnight, ready to make the next morning while it's still cool.

Don't overwork the pastry

Good pastry depends upon a gluten flour, and the more you work (that is mix, handle or play with the pastry) the more you develop the gluten, and the tougher the pastry will be. Never overwork rubbing the butter into the flour — the major cause of poor or tough pastry. You need to find a balance between small pea-sized bits (to help create some steam during baking) and small breadcrumbs. The commonly used description of rubbing butter into fine breadcrumbs can often end up in overworked dough. You also should not play with the dough when the water has been added.

Adding water

Be very careful about how much you add. You need enough to make a cohesive dough, that is neither crumbly nor sticky. Dry and crumbly dough is hard to roll out, and too wet/sticky will give you tough dough. If using spelt, know that it will relax and become softer than wheat flour when rested, so you need to be extra careful about judging how much water you use.

Resting the dough

Resting allows the moisture level in the dough to equalise and the gluten to relax, which makes it easier to roll.

Rolling shortcrust pastry

Along with technique, rolling is the other major stress point for good shortcrust. Consider the following points.

Keep it chilled

When you take the pastry from the fridge, it should feel well chilled to the top of the hand, and should still feel chilled when finished. Placing pastry in a freezer to hurry the initial rest and chill phase is useless, as the butter on the outside will be rock hard and the interior, soft, making it very difficult to roll. Patience during the rest period will be rewarded with effortless rolling.

How much flour to use

You need a perfect amount — neither too little nor too much. Too little and the pastry will stick to the rolling surface and pin as it grows bigger. Too much and it will upset the texture of the baked pastry. Most often, the pastry will stick to the rolling pin and surface when the butter is beginning to melt. If the pastry is very cold to start with and you have worked quickly, this should not be a problem. You should continually monitor the temperature of the dough as you roll. It should feel well chilled at all stages. If it doesn't, especially in summer, simply pick it up, place it on a tray lined with baking paper and place it in the freezer for a couple of minutes to reset the butter. Stop trying to reason with that over-tired toddler. The other reason a pastry sticks to a rolling pin is because it is too wet. You will need to sprinkle it with a little flour and remember to adjust this next time you make pastry.

Rolling technique

Use a good-quality, heavy, decent-sized rolling pin (see page 42). Rolling out pastry is exactly like handling a child — it must know you have sure, confident and in-charge hands. Have a good-sized palette knife (see page 42) ready to turn the pastry — keeping your warm hands off the pastry.

Make sure your rolling pin and surface are lightly coated with flour. Roll once or twice — introduce yourself to the pastry and assess it. If the pastry is very cold, it may not be ready to 'give' immediately, and pressing too hard will result in it cracking.

Run the palette knife underneath and move the pastry firmly and quickly, redust the rolling area with flour, redust the rolling pin if necessary and turn the dough over. Repeat this process, though as the dough gets bigger you will probably be able to give it two to three rolls each time. *If you do too many rolls at a time, the pastry will stick to both the surface and the rolling pin.* As you move the pastry, lift and turn the pastry over, it should feel chilled and hold its integrity — that is, it should not stretch out, but hold its shape. If it doesn't, or begins to stick to the rolling pin, it's too warm. Pick it up, place it on a tray lined with baking paper and place it in the freezer for a couple of minutes to reset the butter. Once it has become larger, you may need to fold it to help move it on. *Make your rolls count — try to use as few rolls as possible to achieve your result. Over-rolling contributes to overworked pastry.* If your pastry begins to contract after rolling, it's a sure sign the gluten is overworked.

Putting the pastry into the tin

Fold the pastry and using a palette knife and your hands, move it to the greased tin, placing the centre point of the pastry at the centre of the tin. Unfold and feed the pastry into the corners of the tin — do not stretch it into the tin. At this point use kitchen scissors to trim excess pastry but make sure to leave enough for your purposes — you can trim again later.

Classic sweet shortcrust pastry

WHEAT FREE / EGG FREE
MAKES ENOUGH TO LINE A 24–26 CM (9½–10½ INCH) ROUND BY 2.5–3.5 CM (1–1¼ INCH) DEEP TART TIN /
ROLLS OUT TO A 30–35 CM (12–14 INCH) ROUND/
1½ QUANTITIES IS ENOUGH FOR A 24 CM (9½ INCH) PIE (TOP AND BOTTOM) /
2 QUANTITIES IS ENOUGH FOR A 26 CM (10½ INCH) PIE (TOP AND BOTTOM)

180 g (6¼ oz) cold unsalted butter, cut into small chunks
130 g (4½ oz/1 cup) unbleached white spelt flour
145 g (5¼ oz/1 cup) wholemeal spelt flour
2 tablespoons golden caster (superfine) sugar
a pinch of fine sea salt
90–170 ml (3–5½ fl oz) ice-cold water
1½ teaspoons lemon juice or apple cider vinegar (optional)

Stage 1: Add the dry ingredients to the bowl

By hand Use your fingertips and thumb to rub the butter with the flour combined with the sugar and salt. The aim is to press the butter into flat chips, coated with flour. I tend to lift the butter and flour that I am working on, and let it fall back into the bowl. This helps to aerate and keep the flour cool. You must work quickly and lightly, so the heat from your hands doesn't start to melt the butter. When ready, chunks and chips of butter should range from small breadcrumbs, to small lentils, to a small navy bean.

Using a pastry cutter Cut the butter into the flour combined with the sugar and salt until it is incorporated into the flour, using a butter knife to cut the mix from the blades, from time to time. When ready, chunks and chips of butter should range from small breadcrumbs, to small lentils, to a small navy bean.

Using a food processor Pulse the butter and flour combined with the sugar and salt one or two times or until ready and turn out into a bowl. You are better to pulse — this throws the pastry up, and then drops it, aerating and cooling it. When ready, chunks and chips of butter will be finer than those if done by hand or using a pastry cutter, which is fine. Don't be tempted to add the water to the food processor as it is too easy to overwork the pastry, but rather turn it out into a bowl first.

Stage 2: Add the water (and acid if using), hydrate the dough

Using a butter knife, begin to mix the cold water (and acid mixture, if using) into the flour and butter. This is the step most people need to keep practising — you will rarely use the same amount of water twice — it depends on the freshness of the flour, the humidity, the temperature and if any of your butter has melted. Also, the higher the percentage of wholemeal flour, the more water is needed. The idea is to add a small amount of water, and begin to cut and mix it in with a knife. As you continue to add the water, little bit by little bit, you are cutting the wet bits into the dry bits, cutting, mixing and stirring. *Only use as much water as you need, with an average of 100 ml (3½ fl oz) being perfect.* By cutting the

USE IN
- Sweet shortcrust and rich shortcrust tarts and pies
- Cherry Pie for Body and Soul (see page 213)

wet dough into the dry bits, you avoid using too much water (another reason for tough pastry). Once all the mix looks moist, bring it together into a ball, *do not knead or play with it.* Flatten the ball, wrap and chill long enough to take the softness off the butter — at least 1 hour or overnight. The dough can be frozen at this point also.

When using higher ratios of butter, less water is required to bind the dough. Add just enough — making a dough that will come together when pressure is applied with your hands to bring it into a cohesive ball.

Use as directed in the recipe.

Barley and spelt sweet shortcrust pastry

LOW GLUTEN / WHEAT FREE
MAKES ENOUGH TO LINE A 24–26 CM (9½–10½ INCH) ROUND BY 2.5–3.5 CM (1–1¼ INCH) DEEP TART TIN /
ROLLS OUT TO A 30–35 CM (12–14 INCH) ROUND/
1½ QUANTITIES IS ENOUGH FOR A 24 CM (9½ INCH) PIE (TOP AND BOTTOM) /
2 QUANTITIES IS ENOUGH FOR A 26 CM (10½ INCH) PIE (TOP AND BOTTOM)

Low-gluten barley adds an honest and rustic appeal to shortcrust, with a warm flavour and soft crumb. With less gluten, egg helps to bind the dough and butter is reduced. Do give this a try — it just might become your favourite.

150 g (5½ oz) cold unsalted butter, cut into small chunks
130 g (4½ oz/1 cup) unbleached white spelt flour
110 g (3¾ oz/1 cup) barley flour
1½ tablespoons golden caster (superfine) sugar
1 egg
1 tablespoon ice-cold water, plus 1 tablespoon extra, if needed

Stage 1: Add the dry ingredients to the bowl
By hand Use your fingertips and thumb to rub the butter with the flour combined with the sugar. The aim is to press the butter into flat chips, coated with flour. I tend to lift the butter and flour that I am working on, and let it fall back into the bowl. This helps to aerate and keep the flour cool. You must work quickly and lightly, so the heat from your hands doesn't start to melt the butter. When ready, chunks and chips of butter should range from small breadcrumbs, to small lentils, to a small navy bean.

Using a pastry-cutter Cut the butter into the flour combined with the sugar until it is incorporated into the flour, using a butter knife to cut the mix from the blades, from time to time. When ready, chunks and chips of butter should range from small breadcrumbs, to small lentils, to a small navy bean.

Using a food processor Pulse the butter and flour combined with the sugar one or two times, or until ready and turn out into a bowl. It is better to pulse — this throws the pastry up and then drops it, aerating and cooling it. When ready, chunks and chips of butter will be finer than those if done by hand or using a pastry cutter, which is fine. Don't be tempted to add the egg and water to the food processor as it is too easy to overwork the pastry, but rather turn it out into a bowl.

Stage 2: Add the egg and water, hydrate the dough
Beat the egg and 1 tablespoon of water together and add to the flour. Using a butter knife, begin to mix the cold water into the flour and butter. Try to avoid using more water, only add extra if absolutely needed — 1 tablespoon should be enough. Once all the mix looks moist, bring it together into a ball, do not knead or play with it. Flatten the ball, wrap and chill long enough to take the softness off the butter — at least 1 hour or overnight. The dough can be frozen at this point also.

Use as directed in the recipe.

Coconut oil sweet shortcrust pastry

WHEAT FREE / DAIRY FREE / EGG FREE
MAKES ENOUGH TO LINE A 24–26 CM (9½–10½ INCH) ROUND BY 2.5–3.5 CM (1–1¼ INCH) DEEP TART TIN /
2 QUANTITIES IS ENOUGH FOR A 24 CM (9½ INCH) PIE (TOP AND BOTTOM) /
ROLLS OUT TO A 26–29 CM (10½–11½ INCH) ROUND

Because it is solid when chilled, coconut oil will make a much better dairy-free pastry than oil — it will behave in a very similar fashion to butter, with regard to how it takes up space in the pastry, melts and thus contributes to flakiness and mouthfeel. It will, however, taste different. It is a taste that will never match the beauty or flavour that good butter imparts, but if butter is not for you, this is the next, most wholesome option. The addition of a small amount of baking powder helps to lighten the pastry, as does the addition of a little acid. Remember this is a better pastry when warm, as the crumb will constrict when cold.

While never as good as a Classic Sweet Shortcrust Pastry (see page 197), this pastry will make an excellent pre-baked tart shell when a dairy-free and egg-free option is required.

60–90 ml (2–3 fl oz) ice-cold water
1 teaspoon apple cider vinegar
98 g (3½ oz/¾ cup) unbleached white spelt flour
a pinch of fine sea salt
1 tablespoon golden caster (superfine) sugar
¼ teaspoon baking powder
80 g (2¾ oz/½ cup) coconut oil, solid and preferably frozen or
    at least well chilled and solid
½ teaspoon vanilla extract

BAKING NOTES

• I do think you get the best result using a food processor with this pastry, as it breaks down the coconut oil quickly, before it has a chance to melt, giving you a better result. The recipe calls for 50% wholemeal, but you can make this either with 100% wholemeal or 100% white.

• If using wheat flour, make sure you read Baking with Wheat Versus Spelt on page 14.

Mix together 60 ml (2 fl oz/¼ cup) of the water and the vinegar and chill. Chill the remaining water.

Mixing by hand or pastry cutter Mix the flour, salt, sugar and baking powder in a bowl.

Grate the frozen or well-chilled solid coconut oil into the mix. Add the vanilla extract and 60 ml (2 fl oz/¼ cup) of the cold water and vinegar mixture, using a butter knife to mix it. This is the step most people need to practise — you will never use the same amount of water twice — it depends on the freshness of the flour, the humidity, the temperature and if any of your butter has melted. Also, the higher the percentage of wholemeal flour, the more water is needed. The idea is to add a small amount of water and begin to cut and mix it in with the knife. As you continue to add the water, little bit by little bit, you are cutting the wet bits into the dry bits, cutting, mixing and stirring. Only use as much water as you need — I usually use 1 tablespoon extra. By cutting the wet dough into the dry bits, you avoid using too much water (another reason for tough pastry). Once the mixture looks evenly moist, bring it together into a ball, do not knead or play with it. Flatten the ball, wrap (I use a plastic bag) and chill for at least 1 hour or overnight.

Mixing by food processor — the best method Place the flour, salt, sugar and baking powder in a food processor. Using a butter knife or small knife, break up the very cold, hard coconut oil into chunks as best you can and add these to the processor. Pulse a few times or until the mixture resembles fine breadcrumbs — smaller is better for this pastry.

Add the vanilla extract and 60 ml (2 fl oz/¼ cup) of the water and vinegar mixture. Pulse one or two times to bring the pastry together — take care not to overprocess and overwork the pastry. Add extra water as needed, using as little as possible — I usually use 1 tablespoon extra. Once the mixture looks evenly moist, bring it together into a ball, do not knead or play with it. Flatten the ball, wrap (I use a plastic bag) and chill for at least 1 hour or overnight. Use as directed in the recipe.

Rich shortcrust pastry (pâte sucrée)

This is the easiest pastry to make — it's very difficult to stuff up, but it is more difficult to roll. Adding egg yolk and sugar to the flour changes the structure of the pastry and makes it a sturdier and more biscuit-like pastry. It is the egg yolk and the sugar that makes it tender, rather than the butter. Because of the amount of sugar, it will be more evenly golden in colour, and is a perfect pastry for holding a filling — such as a pie filled with cooked or raw fruit, or a partly baked tart shell filled with a custard (as in the Labne Tart, see page 218, or Cherry and Macadamia Nut Frangipane Tart, see page 216), or fully baked and filled with My Classic Pastry Cream (see page 244) and topped with luscious fresh fruit. It is always my first choice for tartlets. While the texture of a sweet shortcrust will deteriorate after sitting for some time, this pastry retains its integrity.

The ingredients

Fat

Butter is the best fat to use here, as it creams well and gives the best flavour.

Flour and sugar

You can use wholemeal spelt flour and rapadura sugar here — the colour will be darker, but you will still get a light, delicious pastry.

Salt

Salt can be used as desired, but take into account if you are using salted butter. Bear in mind that the salt should be fine, so it combines with the flour easily.

Water

Most rich shortcrust recipes don't include water. I find a small amount helps to actually develop a little gluten, and gives me a slightly stronger pastry — easier for rolling, and a sturdier pastry to support a fruit filling, which comes in mighty handy when you're making 40 dozen fruit mince pies.

Technique

Other than making sure that the butter is lovely and soft, there's little to worry about when making this pastry — you can literally whip it up in seconds by hand with a wooden spoon or with electric beaters. The tricky part is rolling it.

Adding water

Use no more than the recipe suggests. If your butter is hard, it can be tempting to add more than what is called for; it is essential that your butter is soft, but not melted.

Mixing the dough together

Once you've added the flour and water to the mix, it's fine to use electric beaters to bring it together, and sometimes this may take a few seconds — don't worry that this will overwork the pastry, it can stand up to this, but only beat until you just see the pastry coming together, then bring it together into a ball with your hands.

Resting the dough

Resting allows the moisture level in the dough to equalise and the gluten to relax, which makes it easier to roll.

Rolling rich shortcrust pastry

Find the temperature sweet spot

When you take the pastry from the fridge, it should feel well chilled to the top of the hand and at this temperature, it will be very difficult to roll and will crack. Rich shortcrust rolls best when it is chilled, but not very cold; but if it is too warm, it is impossible — it has a definite temperature sweet spot.

How much flour to use

You need a perfect amount — neither too little nor too much. Too little and the pastry will not roll easily in between baking paper as it grows bigger. Too much and it will upset the texture of the baked pastry. Most often, the pastry will stick to the baking paper when the butter is beginning to melt, especially in summer. If this does happen though, simply slide a baking tray under the pastry (still in between the baking paper) and place it in the freezer for a couple of minutes to reset the butter. Stop trying to reason with that over-tired toddler.

Rolling technique

Use a good-quality, heavy, decent-sized rolling pin (see page 42). This pastry is best rolled between two sheets of baking paper. Sprinkle one piece of baking paper with a little flour, a bit on the top of the pastry and cover with another piece of baking paper. Make sure the paper is big enough for the pastry to grow. Roll once or twice — introduce yourself to the pastry and assess it. If the pastry is very cold, it may not be ready to 'give' immediately, and pressing too hard will result in it cracking. Many a time, especially in winter, I have placed my warm hands on this pastry to help it heat up a little and become compliant. After two to three rolls, and as the pastry becomes bigger, it will stick to the paper. Lift the paper off, sprinkle the pastry with a little flour, gently turn the whole thing over (paper and all) and then peel what was the underneath paper off and sprinkle the pastry with flour — you are ready to roll again. If you don't do this, the pastry will just stick to both pieces of paper and won't get any bigger (that is, it won't roll). This pastry will work best at 3 mm ($\frac{1}{8}$ inch) thick.

Putting the pastry into the tin

Peel the top paper off the pastry, and invert this onto your buttered tin. Gently peel the paper off and feed the pastry into the tin — do not stretch it into the tin. Ensure the pastry is chilled before doing this, as warm pastry will simply fall apart and be too sticky. At this point use kitchen scissors to trim excess pastry — this will help stop extra weight from any excess breaking the shell. Make sure though to leave enough for your purposes — you can trim again later. If any bits do break, they are easy to patch up. Keep a small amount of scrap pastry just in case you need to patch up any cracks during baking blind.

Cutting tartlets

Make sure the pastry is very cold at all stages of cutting and moving the cut pastry — it's easy to slide a tray under the baking paper and place it in the freezer for a couple of minutes and this makes the process so much easier. Use a palette knife to move the cut tartlet shell (that is, keep your warm hands off it as much as possible) — this will stop it stretching as you move and place it. Place it into a buttered tart shell that has two strips of baking paper that cross over the tartlet tin (read more about this on page 206). Use the baking paper to fold the pastry scraps over themselves (and thus keeping your hands off them), wrap up the scraps and place them in the fridge for a few minutes to firm up before re-rolling. Keep a small amount of scrap pastry, should you need to patch up any bits during baking blind.

Rich shortcrust pastry (pâte sucrée)

USE IN PARTLY BLIND-
BAKED TARTS AND
TARTLETS

• Cherry and Macadamia
Nut Frangipane Tart
(see page 216)

• Labne Tart (see
page 218)

USE IN PRE-BAKED TART
SHELL OR TARTLETS

• Filled with My Classic
Pastry Cream (see page
244) (and whipped
cream) or for a lighter
option, Vanilla Bean
Almond Cream (see page
246), topped with fresh
fruit and glaze

• Seasonal Fruit Tart or
Tartlets with Pastry Cream
and Glaze
(see page 215)

• Tahitian Lime Curd and
Meringue Tart (see
page 219)

• Variation of Chocolate
tart filled with dark
berries and Cocoa Nib
Panna Cotta
(see page 158)

USE IN FRUIT PIES
WITH A COOKED OR
UNCOOKED FRUIT
FILLING

• Dried Apricot pie
(see page 214)

• Fruit Mince Tartlets for
Christmas (see page 220)

• Cherry Pie For Body and
Soul (see page 213)

WHEAT FREE
MAKES ENOUGH TO LINE A 24 CM (9½ INCH) ROUND BY 3.5 CM (1¼ INCH) DEEP TART TIN /
1½ QUANTITIES IS ENOUGH FOR A 20 CM (8 INCH) PIE (TOP AND BOTTOM) /
2 QUANTITIES IS ENOUGH FOR A 24 CM (9½ INCH) PIE (TOP AND BOTTOM) /
1 QUANTITY IS ENOUGH TO MAKE 12 TARTLET SHELLS (6.5 CM/2½ INCHES IN DIAMETER AT THE TOP,
4.5 CM/1¾ INCHES AT THE BASE AND 2 CM/¾ INCH DEEP) AND 1½ QUANTITIES IS ENOUGH TO MAKE LIDS
/ ROLLS OUT TO A 30–33 CM (12–13 INCH) ROUND

80 g (2¾ oz) unsalted butter, softened
55 g (2 oz/¼ cup) golden caster (superfine)
    or rapadura sugar
1 egg yolk
½ teaspoon natural vanilla extract
163 g (5¾ oz/1¼ cups) unbleached white spelt flour or
    wholemeal spelt flour
a pinch of fine sea salt
1–1½ tablespoons ice-cold water

Using a stand mixer fitted with the paddle attachment, or a wooden spoon, beat the butter and sugar until creamy. Add the egg yolk and vanilla extract and beat until well combined. Add the flour and salt and beat gently until it just begins to come together, then add 1 tablespoon of water and continue to beat gently until it begins to come together. It should be firm, but not hard, soft but not moist. Only add the extra water if the dough is not hydrated (if your spelt has a large amount of germ and bran, you may need this). Press the dough into a ball and flatten. Cover well and refrigerate for 30 minutes. Use as directed in recipes.

Chocolate rich shortcrust pastry

Replace 32 g (1 oz/¼ cup) of the flour with 30 g (1 oz/¼ cup) of dutched process cocoa.

Baking your tarts and pies

To bake Classic Sweet Shortcrust Pastry, Barley and Spelt Sweet Shortcrust Pastry, Coconut Oil Sweet Shortcrust Pastry, Rich Shortcrust Pastry (Pâte Sucrée) and Low-gluten Oat and Barley Rich Shortcrust Pastry (see page 222), keep in mind the following tips.

Use the right dish

Tin and enamel distribute the heat rapidly to raw pastry, enabling the gluten to set before the butter has fully melted, giving you a better flake and crumb. China will diffuse the heat and can result in pastry being soggy on the bottom (read more about tart tins on page 43). When making pies, it can be difficult to get a crisp bottom. Everyone has their own 'trick' to achieve this — some more successful than others. I place a baking tray (and prefer my black enamel–coated tin one which holds more heat) in the very hot oven to heat up and place the pie on this. Sitting on the hot tray helps cook the base of the pie.

Very cold pastry goes into a hot oven

You will always get the best results from very cold pastry. Once your pastry is in the tin, or your rustic tart or pies are ready (with the fruit in place), place it in a very cold fridge for 15–30 minutes, or the freezer for 10–15 minutes before going into a hot 200°C (400°F/Gas 6) oven. This sets the fat and provides a better flake and lighter pastry.

Hot first, then reduce to a moderate heat

An initial burst of high heat sets the gluten and contains the butter within the pastry, resulting in a light and flaky texture. Depending on the size of your tart or pie, it needs to stay at a high temperature for about 10–20 minutes, before reducing the oven to a moderate heat, about 180°C (350°F/Gas 4). As a general rule with a butter shortcrust pastry, any butter seeping out should be sizzling by the pastry, and not at all running away from the pastry. Butter seeping out indicates the temperature is not hot enough.

Keep an eye on that temperature

From about 10 minutes after you place your tart or pie in the oven, you want to be looking into the oven every now and then to check. If there is butter running out, then increase the heat. If the pie top or the top of the tart sides are burning, but it has only been in the oven for a short while — thus the filling will not have had time to cook properly — you will need to reduce the heat.

Tarts or tartlets should be baked blind before filling

Baking blind is when you cover and weight the pastry, and either partly or fully bake it, by itself, without any filling. The weighting mimics the weight of the filling, keeping the pastry in place as it cooks. Pastry is partly cooked to help seal it, avoiding seepage of a liquid filling through the uncooked pastry (for example, a custard tart) and it also helps to ensure a crisp and well-cooked bottom pastry.

To bake blind, carefully place a sheet of baking paper over the interior of the lined tart tin, or if filling small tartlets, each individual tartlet. Fill with beans or pastry weights. Make sure the weights come all the way up to the top and that the paper is pressed well into the bottom shape of the tart. Chill well, before placing in the oven.

Bake in a preheated oven at 190°C (375°F/Gas 5) for 10–15 minutes or until you see a very light blush of golden colour around the edge of the pastry. Reduce the oven to a moderate temperature of 180°C (350°F/Gas 4), remove the weights and cook for 10 minutes more (or less if a very small tart or tartlet) until the pastry is partly cooked and no longer looks overly raw. If the pastry begins to bubble up at this point, reduce your oven temperature. If this doesn't work, let it finish its time, and remove from the oven. Let it cool slightly before adding the filling and custard — it should flatten of its own accord. Or, if you are not adding an overly liquid filling, prick the base of the tart with the tines of a fork.

Should you be filling the tart with a custard (such as the Labne Tart, see page 218) check for any breaks or cracks that custard could leak through. If there are any, patch them up with extra raw pastry.

For a fully cooked shell, continue to cook at a moderate temperature until lightly golden, taking care not to overdo the rich shortcrust, or you will get too crispy a shell for cutting.

Glazing the top of a pie

I rarely glaze as I think pastry looks beautiful just as its own self. If you would like to do so, brush it with either egg white, or egg mixed with a little water. With fruit pies, I often top them with a sprinkle of sugar and cinnamon.

Baking tartlets in the oven either blind or filled

These benefit from having a cross of baking paper underneath them — made from 2 strips of baking paper that cross over in the middle of the tartlet tin — the width can vary from 1.5–5 cm (⅝–2 inches) depending on the size of the tartlet tin. I use a tartlet tin 6.5 cm (2½ inches) in diameter at the top, 4.5 cm (1¾ inch) at the base and 2 cm (¾ inch) deep, and there are 12 in a tray. My strips measure 1 x 12 cm (½ x 4½ inches) and they help you to lift the tartlet out of the tin as they will often stick, especially when filled with a sugar or fruit filling. Once they come out of the oven, leave them to sit for a few minutes, but don't let them cool too much, or the sticky juices will glue them to the tin. Use the baking paper tabs to help lift them out.

Tarts are cooked when …

The pastry is glistening and lightly browned with flakes evident. At this point they should be left in the oven just that little bit longer — that is, when you have looked at it and thought, 'Oh, yep that's ready'. When you look at it, you see the pastry that is directly exposed to the heat, but the pastry on the side and on the bottom are sealed by the tin and filling and will need a little longer. Usually another 5–7 minutes makes for a better finished product, unless there is some serious browning and drying out going on (this will be because your oven is too hot).

Pies are cooked when …

The pastry that you can see (on top) is glistening, lightly browned and with flakes evident, and you think, 'Ooh, yep that's ready', however leave it just that little longer for the sides and bottom to really cook.

Leave to sit

Once cooked, tarts and pies should always be allowed to sit for about 10–15 minutes (more if very large), allowing the filling and pastry to set a little.

Sweet shortcrust and rich shortcrust tarts and pies

From quick and simple-to-put-together rustic tarts to something special for a celebration, these tarts and pies are all worthy of a second slice. Enjoy warm from the oven and add a scoop of good-quality vanilla bean ice cream or cultured cream (see pages 250–251) on the side as you please.

A rustic tart of seasonal fruits: rhubarb and strawberry

WHEAT FREE, DAIRY FREE AND/OR EGG FREE DEPENDING ON WHICH PASTRY USED
SERVES 10–12

This is what I make the most — one piece of pastry rolled out with the edges folded over a mountain of gorgeous fruit. I prefer this to a fruit pie with top and bottom pastry, as the bottom pastry crisps wonderfully and you get more fruit and less pastry in each slice. It's especially quick to put together if you already have pastry in the freezer. Almost any fruit, as long as it is ripe, is delicious in this tart.

1 quantity classic sweet shortcrust pastry (see page 197), barley
    and spelt sweet shortcrust pastry (see page 198), or coconut oil
    sweet shortcrust pastry (see page 199), rested and well chilled
1 tablespoon raw or golden caster (superfine) sugar, extra, for
    sprinkling (optional)

Filling
600 g (1 lb 5 oz) rhubarb, trimmed of leaves and bases, washed
    and cut into 2–3 cm (¾–1¼ inch) pieces
500–600 g (1 lb 2 oz–1 lb 5 oz) ripe strawberries, hulled, washed
    and larger ones halved or quartered (use less berries if using
    coconut oil sweet shortcrust pastry)
55 g (2 oz/¼ cup) raw sugar or 60 ml (2 fl oz/¼ cup) maple syrup
2 tablespoons cornflour (cornstarch) or kudzu (kuzu), or spelt or
    wheat flour

Preheat the oven to 200°C (400°F/Gas 6). Line a baking tray with baking paper.
    Roll out the pastry to a 30–35 cm (12–14 inch) diameter circle (or smaller if using the coconut oil sweet shortcrust). Move the pastry to the baking tray (I generally fold it) and

BAKING NOTES
• I've suggested you use 1–1.3 kg (2 lb 4 oz–3 lb) of fruit. Be bountiful, and remember the fruit will cook down. I tend to use closer to 1 kg when using winter fruits with less liquid in them (apples and pears) and more with the wetter summer stone fruits and berries. You must always assess the amount of sugar and thickener you add to the fruit. Taste your fruit and see how sweet it is, adding between 1½–3 tablespoons of sugar. Know also that fruits such as rhubarb will also require more. Wet fruit, such as stone and berries, especially, will require more flour/starch than dry winter fruits, about 1½–2 tablespoons, but I tend to err on the side of less, preferring juice that is just bound, but runs.

• Note that while the Classic Sweet Shortcrust Pastry and Barley and Spelt Sweet Shortcrust Pastry will roll out to about 30–35 cm (12–14 inches) in diameter, the Coconut Oil Sweet Shortcrust Pastry will roll out to only 26–29 cm (10½–11½ inches) and will need only 1 kg (2 lb 4 oz) of fruit.

centre it — depending on the size of the tray, it may overhang the sides a little. Don't worry about this as you will be folding this over the fruit. If the weather is warm, or the pastry has softened, place it in the fridge at this point to chill while you prepare the fruit.

Place the rhubarb and strawberries in a bowl, together with the sugar or maple syrup and cornflour and toss through gently. Don't do this step too early, as the juices will weep from the fruit and you want them to do this in the oven, where they will be immediately bound by the cornflour.

Remove the pastry from the fridge — it should be chilled but not so firm that you can't fold the sides inward. If you do not already have a tray under the pastry, slide one under now. Either arrange the prepared fruit in an attractive pattern, or simply pile it into the middle and gently spread to leave a border of about 8 cm (3¼ inches). Fold the pastry border over the fruit, peeling it from the paper underneath as you go. Try not to fold the pastry over itself as this gives you too many layers and it will not cook properly. Use kitchen scissors if needed to cut any pastry that is too wide. Sprinkle with the extra sugar if desired. If required, trim the sides of the baking paper to fit the tray. Place the tart in the freezer for 5–10 minutes to chill up.

Place the tart in the oven. You can tell if your temperature is right by how the butter is behaving; if it is running out of the pastry, you need to turn it up — it should be sizzling on the pastry or at the base of it. Bake for 15–20 minutes before reducing to 180°C (350°F/Gas 4) for about 35 minutes or until the pastry is lightly golden, and juices are bubbling, which indicates that the starch has cooked out. I also like to see that the juices have begun to ooze from the tart. If this has not happened, but the pastry is beginning to burn, reduce the oven temperature slightly. Don't be worried if the juices look too watery, they will thicken as they cool a little.

Individual tartlets

Divide the Classic Sweet Shortcrust or Barley and Spelt Sweet Shortcrust into six, or the Coconut Oil Sweet Shortcrust into four, and roll to a diameter of 18 cm (7 inches). You will need 100–150 g (3½–5½ oz) fruit per tart. Once folded, they will be about 12 cm (4½ inches) in diameter. Sprinkle with a little sugar, if desired. Bake at 200°C (400°F/ Gas 6) for 15 minutes, then reduce the oven temperature to 170°C (325°F/Gas 3) and continue baking for 20–25 minutes.

A rustic tart of quince and dried fruit compote with goat's cheese

LOW GLUTEN / WHEAT FREE
MAKES A 22 CM (8½ INCH) TART / SERVES 8–10

A not too sweet, ever so slightly savoury tart, perfect for a dessert after a bowl of soup on a cold day.

1 quantity barley and spelt sweet shortcrust pastry (see page 198)
200 g (7 oz) young goat's curd (I use Ringwould Blanc)
1 tablespoon raw or golden caster (superfine) sugar, extra,
    for sprinkling (optional)

Poached quinces
2 ripe quinces
1–2 tablespoons raw honey
½ vanilla bean, halved lengthways

Dried fruit compote
10 dried apricot halves
7 dried peach halves, halved if very large
6 dried figs, woody stem cut off and halved or quartered
    depending on size
1 cinnamon quill
½ vanilla bean, halved lengthways
60 ml (2 fl oz/¼ cup) vincotto
1 orange
2–3 teaspoons rapadura sugar or raw honey

For the poached quinces, peel the skin and cut the fruit into eighths, taking great care when removing the core as they are tough and it's easy to cut yourself doing this. Place into a pan — I absolutely prefer cast-iron here — and add the honey, vanilla and enough water to cover the quinces for the entire cooking time. Cover with a tight-fitting lid and cook over a heat low enough for a gentle simmer, without losing steam through the lid. Cook for 5 hours or until rosy — the longer you cook them, the darker in colour they will become. Check there is enough water from time to time, taste and adjust the sweetening if desired. When ready, if you have too much liquid, remove the lid, increase the heat and reduce to a thick syrup, about 60–125 ml (2–4 fl oz/¼–½ cup). The high amount of pectin in quince will also help to thicken any juices.

For the dried fruit compote, place the dried fruit, cinnamon, vanilla and vincotto into a saucepan. Remove the peel from half of the orange and add to the pan. Juice the orange. Place the juice in a 250 ml (9 fl oz/1 cup) measure and top up with water to make up to 250 ml. Add the juice mixture and an extra 60 ml (2 fl oz/¼ cup) of water to the fruit, cover and simmer over gentle heat for 20 minutes from the time it comes to the boil. Remove the lid, taste and add the sugar to taste. Increase the heat and simmer for 10 minutes or until the liquid is thick and syrupy, but not at all dry — you should have about 125–185 ml (4–6 fl oz/½–¾ cup). Leave to cool.

Preheat the oven to 200°C (400°F/Gas 6). Line a baking tray with baking paper.

Roll out the pastry to a 26–29 cm (10½–11½ inch) diameter circle — the pastry shouldn't be too thin, about 3 mm (⅛ inch) is ideal. Move the pastry to the baking tray (I generally fold it) and centre it — depending on the size of the tray, it may overhang the sides a little. Don't worry about this as you will be folding this over the fruit. If the weather is warm, or the pastry has softened, place it in the fridge at this point to chill.

Remove the pastry from the fridge — it should be chilled but not so firm that you can't fold the sides inward. If you do not already have a tray under the pastry, slide one under now. Leaving about 5–7 cm (2–2¾ inches) of pastry for folding, make a 22 cm (8½ inch) diameter area to place the fruit. Use a spoon to scoop out the fruit compote and place it on the pastry. Some juice will come with the fruit and that is fine — you just don't need it all.

Spoon the quince onto the fruit compote, arrange it attractively, then pour the thick quince juice over, but no more than 60 ml (2 fl oz/¼ cup).

Dollop over the goat's curd and fold the pastry border over the fruit, peeling it from the paper underneath as you go. Try not to fold the pastry over itself as this gives you too many layers and will not cook properly. Use kitchen scissors if needed to cut any pastry that is too wide. Sprinkle with a little extra sugar, if desired. If required, trim the sides of the baking paper to fit the tray. Place the tart in the freezer for 5–10 minutes to chill.

Bake for 15–20 minutes before reducing to 180°C (350°F/Gas 4) for about 35 minutes or until the pastry is golden and juices are running. There is a fine line here between the juices running and the goat's curd melting too, so try to grab it just before the curd does this. Leave to cool for 15 minutes before serving.

Cherry pie for body and soul

WHEAT FREE OR LOW GLUTEN, DAIRY FREE AND/OR EGG FREE DEPENDING ON PASTRY
MAKES A 24 CM (9½ INCH) DIAMETER BY 2.5–3.5 CM (1–1¼ INCH) DEEP PIE / SERVES 10

You can make a good fruit pie with a Classic Sweet Shortcrust Pastry or Coconut Oil Sweet Shortcrust Pastry. However, my preference is a Rich Shortcrust Pastry, which will hold its shape better and last longer. Fruit pie is about ripe fruit — the pastry is simply there to encase and support it, so use lots of fruit, knowing it will cook down, and any fruit can be used. Cherry pie on a hot summer night, with ice cream, is a pretty good moment in time.

unsalted butter, for greasing
1½ quantities classic sweet shortcrust pastry (see page 197), or
    2 quantities rich shortcrust pastry (pâte sucrée) (see page 204), or
    or 2 quantities coconut oil sweet shortcrust (see page 199)
1.5 kg (3 lb 5 oz) cherries or seasonal fruit (weighed whole)
35–90 g (1¼–3¼ oz/¼–½ cup) raw sugar, to taste, plus
    ½–1 tablespoon extra, for sprinkling
2 tablespoons cornflour (cornstarch) or kudzu (kuzu) or you could
    use spelt flour
1 teaspoon vanilla paste or natural vanilla extract

Preheat the oven to 200°C (400°F/Gas 6). Grease the base and side of a 24 cm (9½ inch) diameter by 2.5–3.5 cm (1–1¼ inch) deep loose-based tart tin with a little butter. Place a baking tray in the oven.

Roll out half the pastry (see introduction to both Sweet Shortcrust, page 197, and Rich Shortcrust, page 204) to 3 mm (⅛ inch) thick and line the tin, trimming the pastry to about 3 cm (1¼ inches) above the edge of the tin. Place in the fridge for at least 20 minutes to chill. Cover the remaining pastry and place in the fridge.

Meanwhile, wash and pip the cherries and place into a mixing bowl. Taste the fruit and assess the sweetness, then add the sugar to taste, the cornflour and vanilla and gently toss through. Don't do this step too early, as the juices will weep from the fruit and you want them to do this in the oven, where they will be immediately bound by the cornflour.

Remove the lined tart tin from the fridge and evenly spread the fruit mixture in it.

Roll out the remaining pastry to a 25 cm (10 inch) circle, carefully cover the pie and gently press the edges together to seal. If desired, fold the edges over, and crimp together with your fingers. Cut a small slit in the top to allow steam to escape. Place in the fridge for 30 minutes or the freezer for 15 minutes. Success will come only from very cold pastry going into a very hot oven. Sprinkle with the extra sugar.

Place on the tray in the oven and bake for 30–45 minutes. Check after about 30 minutes and if the pastry is browning too quickly, reduce the oven temperature to 180°C (350°F/Gas 4). Cook for another 30–45 minutes or until the top is golden. It is important that the base is cooked, so leave in the oven for a little longer, about 5 minutes, beyond this point to ensure the pastry on the side and bottom is cooked. Leave to sit for about 10 minutes before serving.

BAKING NOTE

Cherries have always been a bit of a luxury in Western Australia, but this year they were fat, plentiful and cheap. I bought freely, came home and pitted madly, those cherry juices dripping down my hand as I went. It was all worth it. It's fine to use frozen fruit, but bigger pieces won't relax and fit into the pie shell well, so just thaw them enough to make them more pliable.

Dried apricot pie

WHEAT FREE / CAN BE DAIRY FREE
MAKES A 20 CM (8 INCH) DIAMETER BY 2.5 CM (1 INCH) DEEP PIE / SERVES 6–8

This is my version of the wonderful dried apricot pie my best friend Nene used to bring to school — a highlight of my lunchtimes. Use the best-quality dried apricots. Dried Turkish apricots (though they may be organic) just won't give you the flavour. I only use unsulphured, organic dried Australian apricots — they are not cheap, so this is a bit of a treat pie. Add sweetness and lemon juice to taste as each time will be different. I hope you enjoy it as much as my family does.

unsalted butter, for greasing
300 g (10½ oz) dried apricots
½–1 tablespoon rapadura sugar
1–3 teaspoons lemon juice
1½ quantities rich shortcrust pastry (pâte sucrée) (see page 204)
1 egg, lightly beaten
1 teaspoon golden caster (superfine) sugar,
    for sprinkling

DAIRY FREE

Replace the pastry with 1½ quantities coconut oil sweet shortcrust pastry (see page 199) and grease the tin with oil.

Preheat the oven to 200°C (400°F/Gas 6). Grease the base and side of a 20 cm (8 inch) diameter by 2.5 cm (1 inch) deep loose-based tart tin with a little butter. Place a baking tray in the oven.

Place the apricots and 500 ml (17 fl oz/2 cups) of water in a saucepan, bring to a gentle simmer and cook for 20–30 minutes or until soft. Add the rapadura sugar and lemon juice, taste and adjust as desired. It will look as if there is a lot of water, but as you begin to mash the fruit, it will thicken from the apricots. Set aside to completely cool.

Roll out two-thirds of the pastry (see introduction page 202) to line the tin, trimming the pastry to about 3 cm (1¼ inches) above the edge of the tin. Place in the fridge for a few minutes to chill, while you roll out the remaining pastry for the top.

Remove the lined tart tin from the fridge. Place the apricot mixture in it and even it out. Carefully cover the pie and gently press the edges together, trimming to about 2 cm (¾ inch) above the edge of the pie. If desired, fold the edges over and make an attractive pattern. Cut a small slit in the top to allow steam to escape. Brush with the beaten egg and sprinkle with the sugar. Place in the freezer for 5 minutes. Success will come only from very cold pastry going into a very hot oven.

Place on the tray in the oven and bake for 20–30 minutes. Check after about 15 minutes and if the pastry is browning too quickly, reduce the oven temperature to 180°C (350°F/Gas 4). Cook for another 30 minutes or until the top is golden. It is important that the base is cooked, so once it's golden, leave in the oven for a little longer, about 5 minutes. Leave to sit for about 10 minutes before serving.

Seasonal fruit tart or tartlets with pastry cream and glaze

WHEAT FREE IF SPELT FLOUR USED / CAN BE DAIRY FREE AND EGG FREE
MAKES A 24 CM (9½ INCH) DIAMETER BY 2.5–3.5 CM (1–1¼ INCH) DEEP TART /
MAKES 12 TARTLETS (6.5 CM/2½ INCHES IN DIAMETER AT THE TOP, 4.5 CM/1¾ INCHES AT THE BASE
AND 2 CM/¾ INCH DEEP) (PICTURED PAGE 231)

This is my favourite way to use rich shortcrust pastry — as a fully cooked tart or tartlet shell, filled with a delicious cream and topped with fresh fruit at the peak of its glory and flavour. But for a dairy-free option, using the Coconut Oil Sweet Shortcrust Pastry (see page 199) filled with Vanilla Bean Almond Cream (see page 246) gives an equally delicious result. The dairy tart and tartlets are best served within 2 hours of making and the dairy-free within 1 hour of making.

1 quantity rich shortcrust pastry (pâte sucrée) (see page 204)
1 quantity berry glaze or passionfruit glaze (see page 275)
   unsalted butter, for greasing
125–185 ml (4–6 fl oz/½–¾ cup) thin (pouring) cream, if making
   one tart, or 60 ml (2 fl oz/¼ cup) if making tartlets
1½ quantities my classic pastry cream (see page 244) if making
   one tart, or ½ quantity if making tartlets
½ teaspoon vanilla paste
about 600–800 g fresh, best, ripe seasonal fruit, prepared
   (see Baking Notes)

Preheat the oven to 190°C (375°F/Gas 5). Grease the base and side of a 24 cm (9½ inch) diameter by 2.5 cm (1 inch) deep loose-based tart tin or 12 tartlet tins with a little butter and line the tartlet tins with baking paper crosses (see page 206).

Roll out the pastry (see introduction, page 202) to 3 mm (⅛ inch) thick and line the tin/s, trimming the pastry to about 3 cm (1¼ inches) above the edge of the tin. Place in the fridge for at least 20 minutes to chill.

Carefully place a sheet of baking paper over the interior of the lined tart tin/s (see page 206). Fill with beans or pastry weights. Make sure the weights come all the way up to the top and that the paper is pressed well into the bottom shape of the tart. Chill well, before placing in the oven.

Bake for 10–15 minutes or until you see a very light blush of golden colour around the edge of the pastry. Reduce the oven temperature to 180°C (350°F/Gas 4), remove the weights and cook for another 10 minutes (or less for tartlets) or until the pastry is partly cooked and no longer looks overly raw. If the pastry begins to bubble up at this point, reduce the oven temperature or prick the base of the tart/s with the tines of a fork. Continue to cook until just lightly golden, taking care not to overcook the pastry or it will be too crispy a

BAKING NOTES

• When cooked, the tart or shell can be brushed with melted chocolate.
• I like to add an extra ½ teaspoon of vanilla paste to the pastry cream when mixing it with the whipped cream for extra flavour.
• The pastry cream can be infused with cocoa nib (see Cocoa Nib Whipped Cream, page 248) or rose geranium.
• The amount of fruit will depend on how much you like on top of your tart (too much can weight the pastry cream down). I like to use: berries; peeled and thinly sliced peaches; nectarines, thinly sliced (depending on size); apricots, cut into quarters or smaller depending on size; figs, peeled (or not) and cut into quarters or more depending on size; 1–2 mangoes, peeled and thinly sliced.

• If I am using berries in the tart, I like to make a glaze using the same berry, adding just enough sugar to take the edge off the berry. Really, the glaze is a berry essence. Or sprinkle with a little icing (confectioners')sugar. When using tropical fruits, I prefer a passionfruit glaze.

• Sliced fruits dry out and discolour as they sit, so ensure these are well coated with the glaze.

• There are two glaze options for this recipe. The berry glaze is in essence a pseudo jam, reduced to the desired consistency. The passionfruit glaze is agar set and needs to be used when it is still a little warm and still liquid, with just a tiny bit of set to it — it will set up on the fruit. If it has set too firm, place it back on the heat to relax it to a warm (not hot) consistency.

shell for cutting. Remove from the oven and leave to completely cool in the tin for the tart; but tartlets should be moved to a wire rack to completely cool.

While the pastry is baking, prepare the glaze.

For the pastry cream, whisk the thin cream to a thick but not firm consistency — just enough to hold its shape. Remove the set pastry cream from the fridge, add the vanilla paste and whisk to a smooth consistency. Gently fold in the whipped cream.

If making a tart, when the pastry is absolutely cool, carefully remove the tart from the tin by pushing it up from the base, so it stays on its base. Hold it from underneath and just above a serving platter, then run a palette knife the base of the tart and the tin base, moving the tart shell onto the platter. If coating the tart shell with chocolate, do so now and leave to cool for 5 minutes. Place the pastry cream in the tart and gently spread to even out.

If making tartlets, leave these on the wire rack. Divide the pastry cream among the tartlets.

Arrange the fruit as desired on your tart or tartlets and top with the glaze. Serve immediately.

Dairy free

Replace the pastry with 1 quantity coconut oil sweet shortcrust pastry (see page 199), and replace the pastry cream with 1 quantity vanilla bean almond cream (see page 246) or creamy cocoa butter and vanilla frosting (see page 254). If making tartlets, you will only need ½ quantity of the cream or the frosting but it would be better to make the full quantity, otherwise it will be difficult to blend and achieve the silky smooth texture you are after.

Cherry and macadamia nut frangipane tart

WHEAT FREE
MAKES A 24 CM (9½ INCH) DIAMETER BY 2.5 CM (1 INCH) DEEP TART / SERVES 10–12

I can't think of anywhere better than a frangipane for coconut palm sugar to shine — and frangipane made with macadamia nuts instead of the more traditional almonds is more delicious than you could imagine. You can use any moist fruit here — stone fruit and berries are best, and if frozen place in a bowl to thaw slightly before using. This can also be made as individual tartlets (6.5 cm/2½ inches in diameter at the top, 4.5 cm/1¾ inches at the base and 2 cm/¾ inch deep).

unsalted butter, for greasing
1 quantity wholemeal rich shortcrust pastry (pâte sucrée)
　　(see page 204)

Frangipane
100 g (3½ oz) unsalted butter, softened
100 g (3½ oz) granulated coconut palm sugar
2 eggs
1 tablespoon true arrowroot
1 teaspoon vanilla paste
100 g (3½ oz) lightly roasted macadamia nuts (see page 280),
　　finely ground but not into a paste
300 g (10½ oz) pitted cherries (if frozen, thaw in a sieve and
　　discard the juices)

Preheat the oven to 190°C (375°F/Gas 5). Grease a 24 cm (9½ inch) diameter by 2.5 cm (1 inch) deep tart tin.

Roll out the pastry to a 30–33 cm (12–13 inch) diameter round (see introduction, page 202), then line your tin with the pastry, patching as necessary, then trim the sides. Carefully place a sheet of baking paper over the interior of the lined tart tin. Fill with beans or pastry weights. Make sure the weights come all the way up to the top and that the paper is pressed well into the bottom shape of the tart. Chill well, before placing in the oven.

Bake for 10–15 minutes or until you see a very light blush of golden colour around the edge of the pastry. Reduce the oven temperature to 180°C (350°F/Gas 4), remove the weights and paper, return to the oven and cook for another 10–20 minutes or until the pastry is just about but not fully cooked. If the pastry begins to bubble up at this point, reduce the oven temperature. Remove from the oven and leave to cool in the tin for 15–20 minutes.

For the frangipane, using a stand mixer fitted with the paddle attachment, cream the butter and sugar until light and fluffy. Add the eggs, one at a time, beating well after each addition. Add the arrowroot, vanilla paste and ground macadamias and mix through. If the frangipane is very soft, place it in a bowl and press a piece of baking paper onto the surface, then refrigerate it to firm up a little. You don't want it too hard, as it will be too difficult to spread, but you certainly don't want it sloppy or have the butter melt, which can happen in very hot weather (cherry weather).

Reduce the oven temperature to 165°C (320°F/Gas 2–3).

When the tart shell has cooled down, place the cherries on the base, top with the frangipane and gently smooth over the surface. Bake for 30 minutes or until the frangipane has set — it will be gently firm to the touch. Check it after 15 minutes of cooking. At no time should the frangipane be bubbling — this indicates the temperature is too high, so it will need to be reduced. Remove from the oven and leave to cool in the tin for at least 15 minutes before serving.

BAKING NOTE

The frangipane can be made well ahead of time, and will keep covered in the fridge for a couple of days. Before using, let it soften a little. This will depend on the ambient temperature of the room — you don't want a melted sloppy mess. A half quantity of frangipane is enough to fill 12 tartlets.

Labne tart

WHEAT FREE
MAKES A 24 CM (9½ INCH) DIAMETER BY 2.5 CM (1 INCH) DEEP TART / SERVES 10–12

This is my idea of a perfect tart, inspired by a recipe by my favourite baker Alice Medrich. I prefer to make my own labne from full-cream, non-homogenised yoghurt (it's incredibly easy and quick), and to use the glorious perfume and sexiness of maple syrup. Serve this with nothing more than a deep and dark, absolutely ripe berry — mulberry is the true soul mate here.

unsalted butter, for greasing
1 quantity rich shortcrust pastry (pâte sucrée) (see page 204)
3 eggs, at room temperature
60 ml (2 fl oz/¼ cup) maple syrup
1 teaspoon vanilla paste
500 g (1 lb 2 oz/1½ cups) labne (see page 249)

BAKING NOTE

This tart is best served within 5 hours of making. Leftovers can be kept in the fridge, but the baked labne loses some of its height and beauty.

Preheat the oven to 190°C (375°F/Gas 5). Grease a 24 cm (9½ inch) diameter by 2.5 cm (1 inch) deep tart tin.

Roll out the pastry to a 30–33 cm (12–13 inch) diameter round (see introduction, page 202), then line your tin with the pastry, patching as necessary, then trim the sides. Carefully place a sheet of baking paper over the interior of the lined tart tin. Fill with beans or pastry weights. Make sure the weights come all the way up to the top and that the paper is pressed well into the bottom shape of the tart. Chill well, before placing in the oven.

Bake for 10–15 minutes or until you see a very light blush of golden colour around the edge of the pastry. Reduce the oven temperature to 180°C (350°F/Gas 4), remove the weights and paper, return to the oven and cook for another 10–15 minutes or until the pastry is just about but not fully cooked. If the pastry begins to bubble up at this point, reduce the oven temperature.

While the pastry is cooking, prepare the filling. Whisk the eggs, maple syrup and vanilla paste until well combined. Add the labne and whisk until smooth.

When the tart shell is ready, remove it from the oven and set aside. Place a baking tray in the oven to heat — the tray will help you to move the filled tart more easily. Leave the tray for 10 minutes, then remove from the oven and immediately reduce the oven temperature to 160°C (315°F/Gas 2–3).

Place the tart shell on the hot tray. Pour the filling into the tart shell, gently place in the oven and bake for 25–30 minutes or until ever so slightly wobbly in the centre. At no point should the mixture rise too high or boil — this indicates that your temperature is too high. Remove from the oven and leave to completely cool in the tin before slicing.

Tahitian lime curd and meringue tart

WHEAT FREE
MAKES A 35 CM X 12 CM X 2.5 CM (14 X 4½ X 1 INCH) RECTANGULAR TART / SERVES 8–10

Tahitian limes come into season in the cold months, and when ripe are nuanced with coconut — they make an exceptional curd, and bring some summer brightness into the dark winter. This one is an extremely rich, sublime, silky smooth lime curd, where the butter is actually added after the eggs and sugar are cooked, and based on the curds made by my two favourite bakeries — Miette and Tartine, both in San Francisco. Topped with Italian Meringue for better sitting, this is a special occasion tart that I like to make in a rectangle, for easy cutting.

unsalted butter, for greasing
1 quantity rich shortcrust pastry (pâte sucrée) (see page 204)
1 quantity Italian Meringue (see page 262)

Tahitian lime curd
180 g (6¼ oz) golden caster (superfine) sugar
4 eggs
2 tablespoons finely grated lime zest
185 ml (6 fl oz/¾ cup) freshly squeezed but unstrained Tahitian
    lime juice
300 g (10½ oz) unsalted butter, softened

For the lime curd, place the sugar and eggs in the top pot of a double boiler and whisk until well combined. Add the lime zest and juice and whisk well, before placing over medium heat (the water shouldn't boil). Stir frequently with a straight-edged wooden spoon until the mixture has thickened and coats the back of the spoon — once you see the mixture begin to steam, you know that it's not far off.

Strain the mix through a fine sieve over a bowl and discard the zest and pulp that remains. Whisk the strained curd to cool down and leave to sit for 5 minutes — it must be ever so slightly warm, but not too hot.

Transfer the mix to a food processor and add the butter 1 tablespoon at a time while blending on high speed. Once the butter has emulsified it will be smooth and creamy. Turn into an airtight container, press a piece of baking paper onto the surface and leave to set in the fridge for at least 5 hours or overnight. Makes 2½ cups.

Preheat the oven to 190°C (375°F/Gas 5). Grease a 35 cm x 12 cm x 2.5 cm (14 x 4½ x 1 inch) rectangular tart tin. Roll out the pastry into a rectangle to fit your tin (see introduction on page 202), then line your tin with the pastry, patching as necessary, then trim the sides. Carefully place a sheet of baking paper over the interior of the lined tart tin. Fill with beans or pastry weights. Make sure the weights come all the way to the top and that the paper is pressed well into the bottom shape of the tart. Chill well, before placing in the oven.

Bake for 10–15 minutes or until you see a very light blush of golden colour around the edge of the pastry. Reduce the oven temperature to 180°C (350°F/Gas 4), then remove the

BAKING NOTES

- Very ripe Tahitian limes will give you the best result, but if you use regular limes and are unhappy with the flavour of your curd when it's finished, a drop or two of Boyajian Lime oil just might save the day.

- The curd can be made ahead, and will keep covered in an airtight container in the fridge for up to 5 days.

weights and paper, return to the oven and cook for another 15–20 minutes or until the pastry is just cooked and a very light golden colour — keep an eye on the pastry so it doesn't overcook, otherwise it can be a bit crispy to cut. If the pastry begins to bubble up at this point, reduce the oven temperature. Remove from the oven and leave to completely cool in the tin.

To fill, remove the tart shell from the tin, spoon the cooled curd into the shell and spread evenly. In warmer weather, you will need to place it in the fridge for the curd to set up a little, about 10–30 minutes, before topping with meringue.

Make the meringue and spread all over the top of the tart. Using a kitchen blowtorch, gently brown the meringue peaks. If you don't have a blowtorch, place the tart under a hot grill (broiler) for 30 seconds or until just browned.

Fruit mince tartlets for Christmas

MAKES 12 TARTLETS (6.5 CM/2½ INCHES IN DIAMETER AT THE TOP, 4.5 CM/1¾ INCHES AT THE BASE AND 2 CM/¾ INCH DEEP)

This is the loveliest fruit mince I know, making a light and fragrant tart that is not too heavy with dried fruit. This mince makes these kind of tartlets so much lovelier in Australia's hot Christmas weather — it always seems to be around the very high thirties or low forties here! They will keep for two days in a cool, dark place, but are best the day they are made — this never seems to be a problem. Remember to save some for Santa.

unsalted butter, for greasing
1½ quantities rich shortcrust pastry (pâte sucrée) (see page 204)

Fruit mince
150 ml (5 fl oz) apple juice
125 ml (4 fl oz/½ cup) apple juice concentrate
500 g (1 lb 2 oz) apples, peeled, cored and finely diced
½ teaspoon mixed spice
⅛ teaspoon freshly grated nutmeg
¼ teaspoon ground cinnamon
110 g (3¾ oz) seedless raisins, roughly chopped
60 g (2¼ oz) currants
85 g (3 oz/½ cup) sultanas
30 g (1 oz) blanched almonds, finely chopped
finely grated zest of ½ lemon
75 ml (2¼ fl oz) brandy

BAKING NOTE

You can use any type of apple for this, but one that breaks down, such as a granny smith (green) are best.

For the fruit mince, place all of the ingredients except the brandy in a saucepan. Cover and bring to a gentle simmer, then cook for 30–40 minutes or until the apples have sweated out their juices and the mixture looks very moist and loose. Remove the lid and continue to simmer for another 30 minutes or until the mixture is thick and the apples have cooked down. I try and mash the apple pieces as I am stirring it. Stir frequently, especially towards the end of cooking. Remove from the heat and cool a little. Stir in the brandy. Store in sterilised jars in the fridge for up to 1 year. Makes about 3 cups.

I would recommend when making the pastry, to form two-thirds in a disc and the remaining third into a disc too. Chill both. This will make cutting and rolling so much easier.

Preheat the oven to 190°C (375°F/Gas 5). Grease 12 tartlet tins with a little butter and line with baking paper crosses (see page 206).

Roll out the larger disc of pastry to a 30–33 cm (12–13 inch) diameter round, about 3 mm (⅛ inch) thick (see page 202). Using a 7.5 cm (3 inch) plain cutter, cut out rounds for the bases — you should get 10–11 out of this. Place the rounds in the tartlet tin, then place in the freezer (to keep cool). Roll out the smaller disc of pastry, cut 1–2 more rounds out and place in the tin. Using a 6 cm (2½ inch) fluted cutter, stamp out 12 rounds from the pastry to use as tops. Fill each tartlet shell with fruit mince as full as you can, without them overflowing or mounding up high, about 1 generous tablespoon. Gently place a pastry top on each tartlet but don't seal them. Place in the freezer to firm up for 5 minutes, then pop them immediately into the oven.

Bake for 15 minutes, then reduce the oven temperature to 180°C (350°F/Gas 4) and cook until lovely and golden, about another 20 minutes.

When they come out of the oven, let them sit for a couple of minutes to get themselves together, then gently lift them (using the baking paper strips) from the tray. If the fruit mince has oozed out and stuck, you may need to use the tip of a small, sharp knife to cut the seal. Leave to cool on a wire rack. Store in an airtight container in a cool, dark place.

Low-gluten oat and barley rich shortcrust pastry

LOW GLUTEN / WHEAT FREE
MAKES ENOUGH TO LINE A 20 CM (8 INCH) DIAMETER BY 2.5 CM (1 INCH) DEEP PIE (TOP AND BOTTOM)

This pastry is a variation of that used for the Oat and Barley Fig Pillows (see page 84), for at its basic level, many a rich shortcrust is just that — a biscuit dough. Made with oatmeal rather than flour, this has slightly more stability — it is still a fragile dough and will likely fall apart as you move a slice from pie to plate, but it will be delicious. You can use any pre-cooked, thickened fruit in this shell, including the filling for the Dried Apricot Pie (see page 214).

110 g (3¾ oz/1 cup) barley flour, plus extra, for rolling
67 g (2¼ oz/½ cup) oatmeal
½ teaspoon baking powder
80 g (2¾ oz) unsalted butter, softened
75 g (2½ oz/½ cup) rapadura sugar
1 egg
1 teaspoon natural vanilla extract

Place the flour, oatmeal and baking powder in a small bowl and whisk through to evenly distribute the ingredients and lighten.

Using a stand mixer fitted with the paddle attachment, beat the butter and sugar until light and fluffy. Add the egg and beat until creamy. Add the vanilla extract and flour mixture and beat on very low speed until the flour is just incorporated into the egg mix and you have a dough. Divide the very soft dough into two-thirds and one-third. Form each into a ball, using a little extra barley flour to help, and flatten lightly. Place each in a plastic bag and chill for 1–2 hours. It is important that the dough is well chilled.

Use as directed in the recipe.

Cinnamon apple pie with oat and barley rich shortcrust

LOW GLUTEN
MAKES A 20 CM (8 INCH) DIAMETER BY 2.5 CM (1 INCH) DEEP PIE / SERVES 6–8

1.2 kg (2 lb 10 oz) apples (about 7–8 large)
60–125 ml (2–4 fl oz/¼–½ cup) maple syrup, to taste
185 ml (6 fl oz/¾ cup) apple juice
½–1 teaspoon ground cinnamon
1 teaspoon natural vanilla extract
1 tablespoon kudzu (kuzu) or cornflour (cornstarch)
unsalted butter, for greasing
1 quantity low-gluten oat and barley rich shortcrust pastry
   (opposite)

BAKING NOTE
A firm apple that does not break down is best here. I like using the golden delicious.

Peel, core and cut the apples into eight wedges or less if very large. Place in a saucepan with the maple syrup, 125 ml (4 fl oz/½ cup) of the apple juice, the cinnamon and vanilla extract. Cover and cook over medium heat for 8 minutes, stirring occasionally or until the apples are just tender. Combine the kudzu and remaining apple juice in a small bowl and mix to a smooth slurry. Add to the hot apple mixture, stirring as you do and bring to the boil, stirring constantly. Set aside to cool.

Preheat the oven to 190°C (375°F/Gas 5). Grease a 20 cm (8 inch) diameter by 2.5 cm (1 inch) deep pie tin. Place a baking tray in the oven.

Remove the larger ball of pastry from the fridge (keep the remaining pastry chilled while you work). This is a very fragile dough so be prepared to possibly have to give it a couple of minutes in the freezer during the process. Roll the pastry between two sheets of baking paper until big enough to fit the tin, lightly flouring with barley flour as you go. As the pastry becomes bigger, it will stick to the paper. Lift the paper off, sprinkle with a little flour, and replace the paper. Gently turn the whole thing over (paper and all) and then repeat with the paper underneath; if you don't do this, the pastry will just stick to the paper and won't get any bigger. If at any time the pastry tears and does not peel from the paper easily put it in the freezer for a couple of minutes to chill up. Peel the top paper off, invert the pastry over the tart tin and feed it into the tin. Neaten the edges and trim to 2 cm (¾ inch) above the rim. Place in the fridge to chill, while you roll out the remaining pastry to make the top.

Remove the lined tart tin from the fridge, place the apple mixture in the tin and even it out. Carefully cover the pie with the pastry top and gently press the edges together, trimming to about 2 cm (¾ inch) above the edge of the pie. If desired, fold the edges over and make an attractive pattern. Cut a small slit in the top to allow steam to escape. Place in the freezer for 5 minutes. Success will come only from very cold pastry going into a very hot oven.

Place on the tray in the oven and bake for 15 minutes, then reduce the temperature to 180°C (350°F/Gas 4) and cook for 30 minutes or until the top is golden. Leave in the oven for another 10 minutes to ensure the side and bottom are cooked. Cool in the tin for 10 minutes.

Dairy-free, egg-free and/or gluten-free pastry

You can still get great pastry, though somewhat different in texture without dairy, egg or gluten flours. Made with oils, they are better used as close to making as possible and, while they can sit in an airtight container overnight, they will be more crumbly to use.

I would never recommend using margarine, or any of the numerous vegan oil-based shortenings, no matter how 'natural' and 'healthy' they sound. They are highly processed products and the fats are very damaged. In the following recipes, ghee, the highly stable oils olive and coconut, and the still fine but not as stable oils, macadamia nut and almond, can all be used interchangeably, though coconut will give you a different texture when cool. While this texture is not as marked in the following pastries as it is in the Coconut Oil Sweet Shortcrust Pastry (see page 199), it will most certainly still have an impact.

These pastries are, on the whole, best pressed into the tin. Once cooked, large tart shells are best filled and eaten on the day — many of the softer mousse fillings will soften the pastry as they sit. Pre-baked and unfilled tartlet shells keep exceptionally well in an airtight container in a cool, dark place for up to 3 days.

Almond, spelt and maple syrup shortcrust pastry

DAIRY FREE / EGG FREE / WHEAT FREE
MAKES ENOUGH TO LINE A 24–26 CM (9½–10½ INCH) DIAMETER BY 3.5 CM (1¼ INCH) DEEP TART TIN /
½ QUANTITY MAKES ENOUGH TO LINE A 20 CM (8 INCH) DIAMETER BY 2.5 CM (1 INCH) DEEP TART TIN /
MAKES ENOUGH TO LINE 20 TARTLETS (6 CM/2½ INCHES IN DIAMETER AT THE TOP, 4 CM/1½ INCHES
AT THE BASE AND 2 CM/¾ INCH DEEP)

This is a highly fragrant dough based on the Almond, Coconut and Maple Syrup Biscuits (see page 90). It's easy to make, slightly temperamental to roll, but once cooked and unfilled, it keeps exceptionally well. When cool, this will lift out of the tin and off the base easily.

98 g (3½ oz/¾ cup) unbleached white spelt flour
110 g (3¾ oz/¾ cup) wholemeal spelt flour
¼ teaspoon baking powder
a pinch of fine sea salt
100 g (3½ oz) lightly roasted almonds (skins on) or hazelnuts
    (skins removed), finely ground
90 ml (3 fl oz) maple syrup
90 ml (3 fl oz) coconut oil, must be liquid
1½ teaspoons natural vanilla extract

Place the flours, baking powder, salt and nuts in a bowl and whisk together to evenly distribute the ingredients and break up any lumps — the nuts especially tend to stick together due to their oil content.

Place the maple syrup, coconut oil and vanilla extract in a small bowl and whisk together. Add to the dry ingredients and mix until it comes together. Flatten into a disc, place in a plastic bag and chill for 30 minutes.

Take the pastry from the fridge and leave to warm a little for 10 minutes, depending on the ambient temperature — warmer is better for this dough as the coconut oil becomes difficult when very cold. In winter I sometimes put my hands on the dough to warm it a little; if the dough is at the right temperature, it is an easy dough to roll; if not it will fracture and crumble.

Roll the pastry between two sheets of baking paper. As the pastry becomes bigger, it will stick to the paper. Lift the paper off and replace the paper — this breaks its seal. Gently turn the whole thing over (paper and all) and then repeat with the paper underneath; if you don't do this, the pastry will just stick to the paper and won't get any bigger. Roll to about 3 mm (⅛ inch) thick.

Peel off the top layer of paper and invert it over the tin. Gently peel off the paper and feed the pastry into the tin — it may well break off, but no matter, simply patch it up and use the warmth in your fingers to stick it back together. Chill well for 30 minutes, then trim the sides to the edge of the tin. Bake for 15–18 minutes or until light golden and dry. Remove from the oven and leave to cool in the tin for 15 minutes, then move to a wire rack to completely cool — if you leave it too long it can stick to the tin.

Unfilled, the tart shell will keep for 2–3 days in an airtight container in a cool, dark place; the fridge is not the best place for this as it is made with coconut oil.

Chocolate almond shortcrust pastry

Add 50 g (1¾ oz) finely chopped dairy-free chocolate to the dry ingredients. The baked tart shell would be lovely filled with Vanilla Bean Almond Cream (see page 246) and fresh fruit.

BAKING NOTES

- Making this shortcrust in summer is very different from making it in winter. In the warmer weather the coconut oil melts quickly. The pastry should give a very slight resistance when rolling and needs to have some chill to hold the coconut oil. The pastry should not look oily. It will only behave when it's at a temperature sweet spot, so during summer there might be a bit of rolling and popping in the fridge for a minute or so — just don't be tempted to use flour for rolling.

- I love this pastry as a cooked tart shell filled with either the Dark Chocolate and Coconut Ganache (see page 265) or filled with the Vanilla Bean Almond Cream (see page 246) and topped with luscious fresh fruit.

- You can also stamp out with cutters for tartlets.

Dark chocolate and coconut ganache tart

CAN BE DAIRY FREE IF DAIRY-FREE CHOCOLATE IS USED / EGG FREE / WHEAT FREE
MAKES A 20 CM (8 INCH) DIAMETER BY 2.5 CM (1 INCH) DEEP TART / SERVES 12–14

This is a rich, but oh so delicious tart. It keeps very well in an airtight container kept in a cool, dark place, though the pastry softens after a day or so. Serve with fresh, gloriously ripe berries.

½ quantity almond, spelt and maple syrup shortcrust pastry
   (see page 224)
200 g (7 oz) dark chocolate (55–60%), finely chopped
270 ml (9½ fl oz) coconut milk
2 teaspoons natural vanilla extract
2 tablespoons maple syrup

BAKING NOTE

This recipe is designed for a 55–60 per cent dark chocolate — any more or less, and you won't get the right ganache texture. I use Rapunzel Organic dark chocolate (55%), which is dairy free.

Preheat the oven to 180°C (350°F/Gas 4). Grease a 20 cm (8 inch) diameter by 2.5 cm (1 inch) deep tart tin.

Roll out the pastry to about 3 mm (⅛ inch) thick (see introductions on pages 195 and 202), then line your tin with the pastry, patching as necessary. Chill well for 30 minutes, then trim the sides to the edge of the tin. Bake for 15–18 minutes or until light golden and dry. Remove from the oven and leave to cool in the tin for 15 minutes, then move to a wire rack to completely cool — if you leave it too long it can stick to the tin.

Place the chocolate in a small mixing bowl. Bring the coconut milk to the boil, pour over the chocolate and stir until the chocolate is completely melted. Stir in the vanilla extract and maple syrup. Gently pour into the cooled tart shell and leave to firm up at room temperature, about 3–4 hours. In summer, you can firm it up in the fridge, but take care not to let it over-set — you want a slightly soft texture to this tart.

Oat and macadamia nut pastry

DAIRY FREE / EGG FREE / WHEAT FREE / LOW GLUTEN (OR CAN BE GLUTEN FREE IF USING UNCONTAMINATED OATS)
MAKES ENOUGH TO LINE A 24 CM (9½ INCH) DIAMETER X 2.5–3.5 CM (1–1¼ INCH) DEEP TART TIN

This recipe has served me well over many years and I love how the nuts roast up in the oven, adding so much flavour. It's quick and easy to make and can be lifted out of the tart tin still on the bottom tin base, but it is too fragile to remove from that base. While I've paired it with a passionfruit orange and lemon mousse in the following recipe, it is also perfect with a simple filling of Vanilla Bean Almond Cream (see page 246) and topped with fresh fruit. This shell is also delicious filled with the dairy-free Passionfruit Bavrois from Wholefood.

202 g (7 oz/1½ cups) oatmeal
65 g (2¼ oz/½ cup) shredded or desiccated coconut
40–75 g (1½–2½ oz/¼–½ cup) macadamia nuts
2½–3 tablespoons macadamia nut or almond oil, or 3 tablespoons
    coconut oil, liquid, plus extra, for greasing
1½–2½ tablespoons maple syrup
1 teaspoon natural vanilla extract

Preheat the oven to 180°C (350°F/Gas 4) or 165°C (320°F/Gas 2–3) if fan-forced. Lightly oil a 24 cm (9½ inch) diameter by 2.5–3.5 cm (1–1¼ inch) deep tart tin.

Using a food processor, lightly process the oatmeal, coconut and nuts until the nuts are just broken. Try not to over-process them as they are best in good-sized pieces. Add 2½ tablespoons of the oil and 1½ tablespoons of the syrup and pulse until combined, adding the remaining oil and syrup as needed. Pick up a little and check for consistency — it should stick together well when pressed together. Press the pastry into the tart tin starting with the side, taking care to press into the edge and not making the side too thick, then evenly cover the base — this pastry is not suitable for rolling. Bake for 15–20 minutes or until just lightly golden.

Remove from the oven and leave to cool but not completely in the tin, then remove from the tart tin, but make sure to leave on the tart base. Made with oats, this tart shell should be used on the day of baking. If it has cooled too much and stuck to the base, place in a warm oven for a couple of seconds to loosen.

BAKING NOTE

Any nut can be used, but hazelnuts should have the skin removed.

Passionfruit, orange and lemon mousse tart

DAIRY FREE / EGG FREE / WHEAT FREE / LOW GLUTEN (OR CAN BE GLUTEN FREE IF USING UNCONTAMINATED OATS IN TART SHELL)
MAKES A 24 CM (9½ INCH) DIAMETER BY 2.5–3.5 CM (1–1¼ INCH) DEEP TART / SERVES 10–12

This is a bright and refreshing dairy-free and gluten-free filling for a tart shell (or tartlets). Once the shell is filled, it's best eaten that same day, as it will soften the shell considerably as it sits after 24 hours.

125 ml (4 fl oz/½ cup) passionfruit pulp (about 6 passionfruit)
185 ml (6 fl oz/¾ cup) orange juice, strained (about 2 oranges)
125 ml (4 fl oz/½ cup) lemon juice, strained (about 1 lemon)
125 ml (4 fl oz/½ cup) agave nectar
250 ml (9 fl oz/1 cup) coconut milk
1 teaspoon vanilla paste
1½ teaspoons agar powder
1 tablespoon kudzu (kuzu) or cornflour (cornstarch)
1 oat and macadamia nut pastry tart shell, baked and cooled
   (see page 227)

BAKING NOTE

The best air in this mousse (and thus lightness) comes from a mixture that is just beginning to set — warm, but not cold. This is tricky because agar starts to set at room temperature, and you do not want to add a set mixture to the mixer, but one that is beginning to set. The colder the mix without it setting, the better the air.

Strain the passionfruit pulp through a sieve placed over a bowl. Press and mix through with a large spoon to extract as much juice as possible. You will need 80 ml (2½ fl oz/⅓ cup).

Place the passionfruit juice in a saucepan with the orange and lemon juices, agave nectar, coconut milk and vanilla paste, then whisk in the agar powder. Bring to the boil over low heat, stirring frequently to stop the agar from sinking to the bottom and sticking. Continue to cook at a gentle simmer for 8 minutes from the time it comes to the boil, stirring frequently. Remove from the heat.

Place the kudzu in a small bowl, add 1 tablespoon of water and mix until smooth. Whisk this into the hot juice mixture, return the pan to the heat and bring to the boil, stirring constantly. As soon as the mixture comes to the boil, remove from the heat.

Pour into the bowl of an electric mixer fitted with the whisk attachment and leave to sit on the bench or in the fridge until it looks as if it is starting to set (you may need to put it in a smaller metal bowl first). You want it to still be a little slushy, but have body. Whisk for 5 minutes, which allows it to cool down quickly and thus thicken, producing great air bubbles. Immediately pour into the tart shell and leave to set at room temperature.

Gluten-free and dairy-free shortcrust pastry

GLUTEN FREE / DAIRY FREE / EGG FREE
MAKES ENOUGH TO LINE A 24 CM (9½ INCH) DIAMETER BY 2.5-3.5 CM (1-1¼ INCH) TART TIN /
MAKES ENOUGH TO LINE 16 TARTLETS (6 CM/2½ INCHES IN DIAMETER AT THE TOP, 4 CM/1½ INCHES
AT THE BASE AND 2 CM/¾ INCH DEEP)

Gluten-free and dairy-free pastry will invariably be slightly denser, but with the high amount of nuts and coconut, this is a delicious pastry. It is also a slightly strong-tasting pastry (thanks to the quinoa) and thus, best sliced from a 24 cm (9½ inch) tart with lots of filling, rather than making it into tartlets with a small amount of filling. If you do want to make tartlets, then use the chocolate version of this pastry.

90 g (3¼ oz/¾ cup) quinoa flour
40 g (1½ oz/¼ cup) brown rice flour
25 g (1 oz/¼ cup) desiccated coconut
60 g (2¼ oz/½ cup) lightly roasted macadamia nuts,
     finely ground (but not to a paste)
80 ml (2½ fl oz/⅓ cup) macadamia nut or almond oil
80 ml (2½ fl oz/⅓ cup) maple syrup
1 teaspoon natural vanilla extract

Preheat the oven to 180°C (350°F/Gas 4).

Place the flours, coconut and nuts in a mixing bowl and whisk together to evenly distribute the ingredients.

Whisk together the oil, maple syrup and vanilla extract. Add to the dry ingredients and stir together until combined. This is a soft and moist mix, but it will firm up a little as it sits.

For a tart

Lightly oil a 24 cm (9½ inch) diameter by 2.5 cm (1 inch) deep tart tin. Press the pastry into the tart tin, starting with the side, taking care to press into the base edge of the tin and not making a thick edge, to evenly cover the base and side. Bake for 15–20 minutes or until light golden. Remove from the oven and leave to cool in the tin for 15 minutes (if you leave it too long, it can stick), then remove from the tin (but leave on the tin base) and move to a wire rack. This is best left on the tart base, and used on the same day of baking.

For tartlets

Lightly oil 16 tartlet tins (but you don't need to line them with baking paper crosses as these will come out easily). Divide the pastry into 16 portions. Press the pastry into the tins, creating an even thickness, trying not to make the bottom edges too thick. Neaten the top edges. Bake for 15–20 minutes or until lightly golden. Leave to cool in the tins for 5 minutes before removing from the tin — you may need to use the tip of a sharp knife to break the seal, but they should come away easily. Place on a wire rack to completely cool. These keep well in an airtight container for 2–3 days, retaining their crispness, but once filled will begin to soften and are best used the same day.

BAKING NOTES

- Any nut can be used, but hazelnuts should have the skin removed.

- In summer, cover the pastry and leave to sit in the fridge for 30 minutes before pressing into the tin. If very hot, it may need to go into the freezer for 5 minutes before baking.

- Serve with Vanilla Bean Almond Cream (see page 246) and with fresh, ripe, seasonal fruit.

- Use to make Passionfruit, Orange and Lemon Mousse Tartlets (8–12 cm/3¼–4½ inches; opposite)

- Use the chocolate variation (see page 230) to make the Strawberry Mousse Tart (see page 230)(must be 24 cm/ 9½ inch diameter tart not tartlets).

- This is meant to be a soft and moist mixture, even as you press it into the tin. If you find it becoming sticky and oily as you're pressing it in, place it (tin and all) in the fridge for 5–10 minutes. Make sure your hands are clean also.

Chocolate gluten-free and dairy-free shortcrust pastry

60 g (2¼ oz/½ cup) quinoa flour

40 g (1½ oz/¼ cup) brown rice flour

30 g (1 oz/¼ cup) unsweetened dutched cocoa powder

25 g (1 oz/¼ cup) desiccated coconut

75 g (2½ oz/½ cup) lightly roasted hazelnuts (skins removed),
  finely ground (but not to a paste)

80 ml (2½ fl oz/⅓ cup) macadamia nut oil

90 ml (3 fl oz) maple syrup

1 teaspoon natural vanilla extract

Place the flours, cocoa, coconut and hazelnuts in a mixing bowl and whisk together to evenly distribute the ingredients.

Whisk together the oil, maple syrup and vanilla extract, add to the dry ingredients and stir together until combined. This is a soft and moist mix, but will firm up as it sits. Bake for 20–25 minutes.

Strawberry mousse tart

GLUTEN FREE / DAIRY FREE / EGG FREE
MAKES A 24 CM (9½ INCH) DIAMETER BY 2.5–3.5 CM (1–1¼ INCH) DEEP TART / SERVES 10–12

Bright with strawberry flavour, this tart is light and delicious. Once the shell is filled, it's best eaten that same day, as after 12 hours, the filling will soften the pastry as it sits.

1 x 24 cm (9½ inch) chocolate gluten-free and dairy-free shortcrust
  pastry tart shell, baked and cooled (see above)
250 g (9 oz) ripe strawberries, halved

Strawberry mousse
80 g (2¾ oz/½ cup) blanched almonds
30 g (1 oz/¼ cup) cornflour (cornstarch) or kudzu (kuzu)
1 teaspoon vanilla paste
1½ tablespoons maple syrup
250 g (9 oz) ripe strawberries, hulled and roughly chopped
1½–2 tablespoons raw or golden caster (superfine) sugar,
  or to taste
¾ teaspoon agar powder
60 ml (2 fl oz/¼ cup) coconut milk

Strawberry mousse tart; and seasonal fruit tartlets with pastry cream and glaze (see page 215).

Glaze
250 g (9 oz) ripe strawberries, hulled and roughly chopped
1–3 tablespoons golden caster (superfine) sugar
½ teaspoon agar powder

For the strawberry mousse, place the blanched almonds and 435 ml (15¼ fl oz/1¾ cups) of water in a blender and process well. Peg 4 layers of muslin onto a jug or bowl and pour the almond mix through and strain. Squeeze the almond milk from the muslin — you will need 375 ml (13 fl oz/1½ cups) almond milk.

Place the cornflour, vanilla and maple syrup in a saucepan and mix to a smooth paste. Add a small amount of almond milk to form a thin paste, then add the remaining milk. Place the saucepan over low heat, and slowly bring to a boil, stirring constantly. The mixture needs to bubble, ensuring the cornflour is cooked out, but only just. Remove from the heat, transfer to a small bowl and press a piece of baking paper onto the surface. Refrigerate until cold.

Meanwhile, place the chopped strawberries, sugar, agar powder and 60 ml (2 fl oz/¼ cup) of water into a small saucepan, stirring to mix the agar. Cover and cook over very, very low heat for about 10 minutes or until the juices sweat out from the berries. Taste and adjust the sweetness as desired. Once this has happened, increase the heat so the mix comes to a gentle boil, and continue to simmer for 6 minutes from this time, stirring frequently as the agar likes to sink to the bottom and stick. Set aside to cool slightly for only 5 minutes.

Place the cold almond cream, coconut milk and strawberry mix into a blender and process until light and smooth. You need to work quickly through the next phase, as the agar will begin to set. Place a strainer over a bowl (small enough to catch the strawberry seeds), then pour the mixture through the strainer, using a spatula to press as much mixture through as possible. Discard the seeds. Immediately pour the mousse into the cooked and cooled tart shell and gently even it out. Place in the fridge to set for 30 minutes or until set, before topping with strawberries and glaze.

To make the glaze, place the strawberries and 60 ml (2 fl oz/¼ cup) of water in a small saucepan. Cover and cook over low heat for 10–15 minutes. Strain the mixture through a fine sieve, gently pressing onto the solids to extract as much juice as possible, but not too much or it will be cloudy. Discard the pulp. You should have 250 ml (9 fl oz/1 cup) of juice. If you don't have quite enough, add a bit of water or try to extract a little more juice.

Place the juice in a small saucepan with 1 tablespoon of the sugar and whisk in the agar. Bring to a gentle boil, whisking frequently as the agar begins to dissolve. Taste and adjust the sweetness as desired. Simmer for 6 minutes from this time, stirring frequently as the agar likes to sink to the bottom and stick. Set aside to cool but do not refrigerate.

To put the tart together, arrange the strawberries in an attractive pattern on the top of the mousse, then gently spoon the glaze (do not pour) over the berries, ensuring they are coated by the glaze. Leave to sit at room temperature until the glaze begins to firm up, then place in the fridge for 30 minutes before serving.

Choux pastry

I am lucky enough not to have a problem with gluten, and use my Classic Sweet Shortcrust Pastry (see page 197) and Rich Shortcrust Pastry (Pâte Sucrée) (see page 204) with delight. When I want a light as a cloud and very delicious gluten-free option, this is what I turn to. I don't try to replicate those pastries (which generally only end up heavy and not all that delicious), but rather choose a lateral approach to achieving my goal — always nourishment, deliciousness in taste and mouthfeel.

Choux puffs with orange-scented pastry cream and chocolate ganache

GLUTEN FREE
MAKES 30 SMALL PUFFS

1 quantity dark chocolate and coconut ganache (see page 265)

Choux pastry
25 g (1 oz) potato starch
55 g (2 oz) white rice flour
⅛ teaspoon baking powder
a pinch of fine sea salt
3 teaspoons rapadura sugar
58 g (2¼ oz) unsalted butter
½ teaspoon natural vanilla extract
1–2 eggs

Orange-scented pastry cream
125 ml (4 fl oz/½ cup) thin (pouring) cream
1 quantity my classic pastry cream (see page 244)
finely grated zest of 1–2 medium oranges
1 teaspoon vanilla paste

For the choux pastry, preheat the oven to 210°C (415°F/Gas 6–7). Line a baking tray with baking paper.

Place the potato starch and rice flour, baking powder, salt and sugar in a bowl and whisk through to evenly distribute the ingredients.

Place the butter, vanilla extract and 125 ml (4 fl oz/½ cup) of water in a saucepan and bring to the boil over medium heat. Immediately add the flour mixture, reduce the heat to low and, using a wooden spoon, mix vigorously until the mixture forms a ball and comes

BAKING NOTE

The amount of egg you need to add varies — you may not need to add all the eggs, or you may need a little extra. If the mixture is too stiff (not enough egg) then the choux pastry will be too heavy, but if the mixture is too wet (too much egg), the puffs will not hold their shape when spooned or piped onto the tray — you want the mixture to fall off your spoon but still hold its shape.

away from the sides. Remove the mixture and place in the bowl of an electric mixer fitted with the paddle attachment or medium mixing bowl if using hand-held electric beaters. Leave to cool for 5–10 minutes or until the dough is warm, but not in any way hot — stirring it from time to time can help to cool it down more quickly.

Add an egg to the warm dough, beating very well to incorporate. Assess if you need to add the other egg (see Baking Note). Once the last egg has been added, beat until the mixture has softened, is nice and shiny and has a dropping consistency — this will be at least 2 minutes.

Either spoon 1 tablespoonful amounts onto the tray, leaving about 3 cm (1¼ inches) in between each, or place the mixture in a piping (icing) bag fitted with a plain 1–1.5 cm (½–⅝ inch) nozzle and pipe onto the tray.

Bake for 15 minutes, then reduce the oven temperature to 170°C (325°F/Gas 3) and bake for another 10–15 minutes. If they look like they are browning too much, reduce the oven temperature. This stage is important, as they are drying out. Remove from the oven, reduce the oven temperature to 150°C (300°F/Gas 2) and quickly prick each puff with a skewer, rough is fine and you will often find a natural crack or break to do this. Immediately return to the oven for another 5 minutes. Turn the oven off, open the oven door and leave until cool. When cool, move the puffs to a wire rack.

For the orange-scented pastry cream, whip the thin cream to soft peaks and fold into the pastry cream together with the orange zest and vanilla paste. Spoon the mixture into a piping bag fitted with a small nozzle (about 3 mm/⅛ in diameter), and fill each puff, inserting the nozzle into the hole you've made.

Make sure the ganache is soft and runny. Spoon some on top of each puff. Leave to set for a few minutes before serving.

Puff pastry

I'd hate to think that you are deterred from making puff pastry because it's too hard, or takes too long. This recipe is based on one by American chef Michel Richard and just about every one of my students has success the first time they make it. It's not complicated or time consuming to make — it just needs to spend a lot of time resting and chilling. The reward is the best puff you've ever tasted — one that 'bites' almost perfectly and doesn't shatter into tiny shards, or is so dense that you need to really bite into it.

Spelt puff pastry

WHEAT FREE / EGG FREE
MAKES 4 SHEETS (EACH ABOUT 24 CM/9½ INCHES SQUARE)

260 g (9¼ oz/2 cups) unbleached white spelt flour, or 130 g
    (4½ oz/1 cup) unbleached white spelt flour and 145 g
    (5¼ oz/1 cup) wholemeal spelt flour
pinch of fine sea salt
185 ml (6 fl oz/¾ cup) ice-cold water, plus 1–2 tablespoons
1 x 250 g (9 oz) block unsalted butter, well chilled
65 g (2¼ oz/½ cup) unbleached white spelt flour, extra

BAKING NOTES

- The most important thing about making this puff pastry is to take care that the butter does not melt into the flour dough — it needs to be firm at all times. Essentially, you are layering dough, butter and air, many times over. If, when rolling, the butter starts to soften and smear through, immediately put your pastry on a baking paper–lined tray, then cover it with another sheet of baking paper and refrigerate until chilled and firm again. If the butter happens to smear or break through during rolling, your course of action will depend on what stage of rolling you are at: If it is long enough, I would fold the pastry as described, wrap and chill it and, in essence, just give it an extra fold.

- If it isn't long enough and you've only just started, I would keep on and get it long enough to do that extra fold. This way, by folding, the butter is encased.

- It is very important you don't place the pastry in the freezer to speed up the chilling process. This often makes the butter set too hard in some spots while leaving other spots soft, and makes rolling impossible.

- It's a great pastry to use in summer, but an easier one to make in winter. In summer I make it early in the morning, freeze my rolling pin (I have a copper one) and chill it well between rolls.

- You can make this with 100% white spelt, or 50% white and 50% wholemeal. The quality of your wholemeal here is important. Choose one that is very finely ground. This is usually stone-ground and the bran is very small. If the bran is too large, it can 'cut' and slice through the layers you are trying to build as you roll.

Place the flour and salt in a bowl. Using a butter knife, gradually cut the water into the flour. You may need to use 1–2 tablespoons more water as different batches of spelt flour will absorb different amounts of water. Add enough to form a dough that holds together, but is not at all wet. Form the dough into a ball (do not knead or play with it), wrap in a tea towel, then flatten a little and chill in the fridge.

Place the butter between two sheets of baking paper and beat with a rolling pin until it forms a rough square about 20 cm (8 inches) and is 1 cm (½ inch) thick. You may need to lift the paper from both sides from time to time to release the butter and allow it to get bigger — it doesn't matter if the butter ends up more of a rectangle. Return the butter (paper and all) to the fridge to chill.

Place the extra flour in a bowl, near where you will be rolling, to use for dusting. Place the dough on a lightly floured work surface. Sprinkle a small amount of flour over the pastry and rolling pin. Roll the dough into a square, about 26 cm (10½ inches) — again, it doesn't matter if it ends up more a rectangle, about 28 cm x 25 cm (11¼ x 10 inches). To prevent sticking, keep the pastry and rolling surface lightly dusted with flour, even turning the pastry from time to time.

Starting from the centre of your square, roll out each corner to make an 'ear', creating a kind of 'cross' shape. Remove the top piece of baking paper from the butter and invert it onto the centre of the pastry. Remove the remaining paper and fold over the 'ears' of the pastry, so they completely cover the butter. They will overlap and that is fine. You should end up with a completely sealed parcel of butter. If the pastry and butter at this stage still feels cold and chilled, you can start to roll. If not, cover and place in the fridge to chill.

You are now commencing to make turns. (You'll be rolling the dough lengthways, so make sure you have plenty of space.) Making sure your rolling surface and pin are dusted with flour, begin to roll out the dough. When the butter is very chilled, this might take a couple of times — simply press along the pastry to gently flatten it evenly. As the pastry begins to give, continue to roll out until you have a long rectangle about 67 cm x 26 cm (26½ x 10½ inches) — you are only ever rolling lengthways.

As you roll, you will need to continually move the pastry and redust it with flour underneath and on top. As you are moving the pastry, take care not to hold it for too long, as your body warmth will soften the butter. Work swiftly to avoid the butter softening. Try to avoid ending up with pointy, uneven bits at the two edges at the ends of the pastry — use the rolling pin to push it (not press or roll it) back into a more even line. Otherwise you can incorporate the pointy ends into the fold (in the next step).

You are now ready to commence the first turn. Fold the pastry into thirds, from the bottom, then down from the top. Rotate the pastry so the closed fold is to your left. Repeat the rolling to make a rectangle about 67 cm long, following the guidelines above. Fold the pastry as described, rotate so the closed fold is to your left and mark it with two little dents. This lets you know you have completed two turns.

Place the pastry on a tray lined with baking paper, top with baking paper and cover, sealing well to avoid it drying out. Place in the fridge to rest and chill for 2 hours. Repeat the above rolling and folding twice — you have now completed four turns. Mark the pastry with four little dents. Place the pastry on a tray lined with baking paper, top with baking paper and cover, sealing well to avoid it drying out. Chill in the fridge for another 2 hours.

Repeat the above rolling and folding twice more. It can often be quite hard when it comes out of the fridge and crack along the folded edges as you roll. If this happens, just leave it for a few minutes until the butter has relaxed a bit. You now have completed six turns and the pastry is ready. Place on a tray lined with baking paper, top with baking paper and cover, sealing well to avoid it drying out. Place in the fridge to rest and chill. You can now freeze the pastry, but I prefer to cut it into quarters and roll the pastry into four sheets about 24 cm (9½ inches) square ready for use. To roll out, keep the rolling surface, pin and top of pastry lightly dusted with flour. Try to keep the shape fairly even as you roll, but don't worry too much as you can trim it to shape later. The pastry should be about 2–3 mm (¹⁄₁₆–⅛ inch) thick. As each quarter is rolled, place it on a tray (I use a cake cardboard) covered with a sheet of baking paper, then top with baking paper. Finish with a sheet of baking paper, cover and seal well with plastic wrap and freeze.

Puff pastry fruit danishes

WHEAT FREE
MAKES 10

I often make these for Christmas morning, as you can prepare most of the elements well ahead of time. They take about 15 minutes to put together and are always very well received, and honestly so much nicer than those you buy.

2 tablespoons golden caster (superfine) or raw sugar
2 sheets ready-rolled frozen or very cold spelt puff pastry
    (see page 235)
spelt flour, for dusting
½ cup my classic pastry cream (see page 244)
your choice of fruit

Preheat the oven to 200°C (400°F/Gas 6). Line a baking tray with baking paper and sprinkle it with 1 tablespoon of the sugar.

Lay the frozen or very cold puff pastry sheets on a lightly floured surface and, using a 10 cm (4 inch) cutter, cut rounds from the sheets. (Keep any pastry scraps, layering them together, and wrap and freeze for another time.) Taking one round at a time, place a lightly dusted rolling pin in the centre of the pastry and roll out the middle a tiny bit to make an oval — you only need to do one or two light rolls, so don't make it paper thin. Don't roll all the way to the ends either as you want the ends to be a little thicker so that they'll puff up higher around the fruit. Place the pastry on the tray and brush off any flour from the tops.

Place a generous teaspoon of pastry cream in the centre of each pastry and top with the fruit, taking care to keep the fruit along the centre line of the pastry, where you have rolled. Sprinkle with the remaining sugar. Bake for 20–30 minutes or until puffed and golden.

BAKING NOTES

- In spring and summer, ripe stone fruit is the obvious choice. Apricots, peaches and nectarines will need to be lightly poached, as do pears in autumn. Lightly poach these first in a little water, with a vanilla bean and sugar — they should only be poached until they offer just a little resistance when pierced with the tip of a sharp knife.

- Fresh ripe berries need no cooking, and small stone fruit, such as cherries, can be simply pitted.

- Depending on the size of the fruit, per danish you will need 2–3 slices of pear, or 2 apricot/nectarine/plum halves, or 1 peach half, or about 10 berries.

Apple and blackberry turnovers

WHEAT FREE / EGG FREE
MAKES 4

It's so sad that you just do not see these beauties around anymore — and if you do, the puff is chewy and as thick as cardboard. Biting into these turnovers, made with your own puff, you'll be rewarded with the lightest, crisp and flaky pastry, encasing pure fruit — they are delicious and especially so when served with high-quality vanilla bean ice cream. Blackberry is a wonderful pairing with the apple but any berry could be used.

4 small apples (about 350 g/12 oz)
1 tablespoon rapadura sugar
finely grated zest of 1 lemon
1 sheet ready-rolled frozen spelt puff pastry (see page 235)
50 g (1¾ oz) fresh or frozen blackberries (if frozen, do not thaw)
1–2 teaspoons golden caster (superfine) sugar, plus 2 tablespoons
  extra, for sprinkling
2 teaspoons cornflour (cornstarch) or true arrowroot
1 egg, lightly beaten (optional)
thin (pouring) cream, to serve

Peel, core and cut the apples into quarters, then cut into smaller slices about 1 cm (½ inch) thick. Place in a saucepan with 2 tablespoons of water and the rapadura sugar, cover with a lid and cook over very gentle heat until the apples have sweated out their juice. Continue to cook for 10–15 minutes or until just soft. If there is any liquid at this time, remove the lid and increase the heat to high to evaporate it off. Set aside to cool.

Preheat the oven to 210°C (415°F/Gas 6–7). Line a baking tray with baking paper.

Remove the puff pastry from the freezer and leave to soften — just enough so it is easy to fold and seal, but don't let it get too warm or soft or it will be impossible to move. Cut the pastry into four equal squares.

Place the cooled apples in a mixing bowl with the lemon zest. Taste them and assess the sweetness, taking into account the ripeness of the berries. Add the caster sugar to taste, the cornflour and berries and toss together gently.

Making one turnover at a time, place one-quarter of the fruit mix on an imaginary diagonal fold line of the pastry, fold the pastry over — it's okay to stretch it a little to make it fit (this is easier when the berries are not frozen) — and press the edges with the tines of a fork to seal. You should have a triangle. Swiftly and gently pick up and place on the tray. If your pastry is too thawed, this can be difficult. Repeat with the remaining fruit and pastry. If the weather is very hot, place the tray in the freezer to firm up for 5 minutes.

Brush the turnovers with the beaten egg (if using) and sprinkle with the extra caster sugar. Bake for 30–35 minutes or until the pastry is very golden and the juices are running from the fruit — this indicates that the berries are cooked. Remove from the oven and leave them to cool a little before biting into as the fruit can be too hot and burn. Serve with the cream.

BAKING NOTE

An apple that breaks down here is best — a granny smith (green) is perfect. Blackberries can be fresh or frozen, and any fruit can be used. If using all berries, increase the cornflour to 1 tablespoon to thicken the larger amount of juice coming from the berries.

Peach and raspberry rustic puff tart

WHEAT FREE / EGG FREE
SERVES 2

These are the quickest things to make, and the most delicious. The juice will ooze out of the fruit as they cook and caramelise. The recipe is for two, but you could easily cut the pastry in half and make individual ones. Don't try to double it and make it for four on one sheet of pastry as the middle will just end up soggy — instead, just make two lots of this recipe.

2–3 teaspoons golden caster (superfine) sugar
1 sheet ready-rolled frozen or very cold spelt puff pastry
   (see page 235), trimmed to 24 cm x 9 cm (9½ x 3½ inches)
1–2 medium peaches (about 200 g/7 oz), peeled
100 g (3½ oz) fresh raspberries (if frozen, do not thaw)
pinch of ground cinnamon

BAKING NOTE

Most ripe fruits will work here. I have used pineapple and strawberry, mango and berry, apricot and blueberry, even apricot and peach by themselves. If using denser fruits, such as apples, make sure they're sliced exceptionally thin.

Preheat the oven to 200°C (400°F/Gas 6). Line a baking tray with baking paper and sprinkle 1 teaspoon of the sugar on the tray to cover an area the same size as the pastry. Place the pastry on top of the sugar and return to the freezer while you slice the peaches.

Cut the peaches into 1.5 cm (⁵/₈ inch) thick slices. Lay the slices down the length of the pastry along the centre. You will end up with a border around the edges of the tart. Scatter the berries over the peaches, taking care to stay within the border. Sprinkle the remaining sugar over the whole of the tart — some will end up on the baking paper, which is fine. Sprinkle the tart with the cinnamon.

Bake for 10 minutes, then reduce the heat to 190°C (375°F/Gas 5) and bake for another 20–25 minutes or until the pastry is puffed and golden, and the fruit is even slightly singed. As the tart cooks, some juices will weep, mingle with the sugar and caramelise, making it extra delicious.

Custards, creams, icings

and spreads

*It is very often the custard, cream filling, icing or frosting that brings
a cake or pie together, providing delicious moistness and mouthfeel —
they absolutely are the 'icing on the cake'. Personally, I find many a time
they are too rich, and I don't believe this is really necessary. You will find
in this chapter a range of fillings with less (and better) sugars and less
fat, and that vary in richness. They will leave you feeling happy and
satiated, instead of heavy.*

Custards and creams

Using whole and true ingredients — full cream, non-homogenised organic milk, real cream, beautiful vanilla beans — will result in surprising depth of flavour in your creams and custards. It is this that will add the many extraordinary and complex nuances of deliciousness to your scone, cake or pie.

My classic pastry cream

MAKES 1 CUP

Invariably many recipes call for cream cheese or mascarpone, which I simply find too rich and overwhelming; a pastry cream is so delicious and far lighter. This is my faithful pastry cream and it is easy to make. It does set to a fairly firm consistency, which I either beat to break down a little or lighten with whipped cream. Again, flavour can be infused into the milk (see Baking Notes for Vanilla Bean Almond Cream on page 246).

    35 g (1¼ oz/scant ¼ cup) golden caster (superfine) sugar
    2 egg yolks, at room temperature
    2 scant tablespoons cornflour (cornstarch)
    250 ml (9 fl oz/1 cup) milk
    ½–1 vanilla bean, halved lengthways and seeds scraped
        or 1½ teaspoons vanilla paste
    a tiny pinch of sea salt

Place the sugar, egg yolks and cornflour in a heavy-based saucepan and mix to a smooth slurry with a small amount of the milk. Add the remaining milk and whisk together well. Add the vanilla beans (you can keep the bean to make vanilla sugar, see page 30). (If you're using vanilla paste, you will add it later.) Cook over a gentle heat, stirring constantly with a wooden spoon until it comes to the boil, at which point it should have thickened and the spoon will leave track marks as you stir. Remove from the heat, remove the vanilla bean halves and immediately pour into a bowl, stirring a little to cool it down (if using vanilla paste, stir it through now). Press a piece of baking paper onto the surface, stand until cool, then refrigerate for 3 hours or until cold. Whisk well to a smooth consistency before using.

- I like to lighten my pastry cream with whipped cream, which gives a perfect consistency for filling tarts or even for using in trifle. For 1 quantity of pastry cream, simply whisk 125 ml (4 fl oz/½ cup) thin (pouring) cream with vanilla paste until soft peaks form — just enough to lightly hold its shape. Once the pastry cream has set, whisk the cold pastry cream (still in the bowl) to break it up, and then gently whisk through the whipped cream.

- 60 ml (2 fl oz/¼ cup) thin cream, whipped to soft peaks, combined with ½ quantity my classic pastry cream will fill 12 small tartlets.

- 185 ml (6 fl oz/¾ cup) thin cream, whipped to soft peaks, combined with ½ quantity my classic pastry cream will fill a 24 cm (9½ inch) pre-baked tart shell.

Vanilla bean almond cream

GLUTEN FREE / DAIRY FREE / EGG FREE
MAKES 500 ML (17 FL OZ/2 CUPS)

This is a multi-use dairy-free and egg-free cream, and with only a slight variation can also give you a custard cream, with the texture between whipped cream and custard. By adding cocoa butter, you can also make a delicious dairy-free frosting (see pages 253–255).

Agar and kudzu (kuzu) or cornflour (cornstarch) are used together to provide a thick but light cream. Kudzu thickens the mixture, but it is the agar that allows it to hold air when whipped.

Flavour is infinitely variable — you can infuse cocoa nibs or rose geranium leaves into the milks before adding the agar.

This cream has a thicker texture, holding its shape like a whipped dairy cream, and can be used whenever you would use My Classic Pastry Cream (see page 244), such as to fill a tart, to layer a cake or to fill choux pastry (see page 233).

The custard cream variation (opposite), meanwhile, has more flow, like a traditional custard with more air and body. It is perfect for pouring over a piece of plain cake, served with fruit or used in a trifle.

> 375 ml (13 fl oz/1½ cups) freshly prepared almond milk
>   (see page 278)
> 250 ml (9 fl oz/1 cup) coconut milk
> 70 ml (2¼ fl oz) maple syrup
> 1½ teaspoons agar powder
> 1 vanilla bean, halved lengthways and seeds scraped
>   or 1 teaspoon vanilla paste
> 1½ tablespoons kudzu (kuzu) or cornflour (cornstarch)

Place 310 ml (10¾ fl oz/1¼ cups) of the almond milk, the coconut milk and maple syrup in a medium saucepan. Sprinkle the agar over the top and whisk well to distribute the agar. Add the vanilla seeds and bean halves. (If using vanilla paste, you will add this later.) Whisk together and bring to a gentle boil. Continue to simmer very gently, stirring frequently to prevent the mixture sticking on the base, for 6 minutes.

Meanwhile, mix the remaining almond milk and the kudzu to form a paste. When the agar has dissolved, remove the pan from the heat, and take out and discard the bean halves. Add the kudzu mix to the pan, whisking rapidly as you do so — it will begin to thicken as soon as you add it. Place back over low heat, whisking constantly as it comes to the boil. Remove from the heat (and if using vanilla bean paste, whisk it through now). Pour into a clean bowl and allow to cool slightly. Press a piece of baking paper onto the surface and refrigerate for at least 2 hours or until set.

When set, put what will be a fairly solid mix in the blender. To this, add 1½ tablespoons of water (or any remaining almond milk). Blend for 5 minutes or until silky smooth, scraping down the sides from time to time.

Place the mixture in an airtight container, press a piece of baking paper onto the surface, and seal in an airtight container and refrigerate for at least 3 hours, or preferably overnight, before using. The cream will keep refrigerated for up to 2 days.

BAKING NOTES

- While it involves a little more effort, vanilla bean will give you the best flavour.
- To infuse flavour, add the almond and coconut milks to a small saucepan with either 38 g (1½ oz/ ¼ cup) of cocoa nibs (if whole, chopped into small pieces) or three fresh unsprayed rose geranium leaves, roughly chopped. Heat to the point of just steaming, remove from the heat and leave to sit for 15–20 minutes. Strain through a fine sieve, pressing on the solids to remove every bit of flavour. Make sure you measure your milk quantity again before you start — you may find you have lost a small amount — it is essential that you have the exact amount specified for a successful result, so add a little extra milk, if necessary, to make up the difference.

Vanilla bean almond custard cream

Increase the almond milk to 435 ml (15¼ fl oz/1¾ cups) and the coconut milk to 310 ml (10¾ fl oz/1¼ cups). Follow the method opposite, using 375 ml (13 fl oz/ 1½ cups) of the almond milk, and 250 ml (9 fl oz/1 cup) of the coconut milk and the maple syrup. Combine the remaining 60 ml (2 fl oz/¼ cup) of almond milk with the kudzu.

When set, put what will be a fairly solid mix in the blender. To this, add 60 ml of water (or any remaining almond milk) and the remaining 60 ml coconut milk. Blend for 5 minutes or until silky smooth, scraping down the sides from time to time.

Makes 750 ml (26 fl oz/3 cups).

Cocoa nib whipped cream

GLUTEN FREE / EGG FREE
MAKES ABOUT 500 ML (17 FL OZ/2 CUPS)

This deliciousness is based on a recipe by cookbook author Alice Medrich. Nothing absorbs the subtle flavour of chocolate quite as well as fat and when infused with cocoa nibs, you are left wondering — is this chocolate I am tasting? White chocolate perhaps? It's neither, but somewhere in between and it's seriously good. This would be a delicious whipped cream to spread on a plain, chocolate or nut Génoise Sponge Cake (see page 151) and topped with fresh, dark berries (logan, young, et cetera). It would also be a wonderful replacement for the icing on the Sweet and Sour Dark Chocolate Buttermilk Cake (see page 178), again served with fresh, dark berries.

250 ml (9 fl oz/1 cup) thin (pouring) cream
2 tablespoons cocoa nibs, if whole roughly chopped into smaller
    pieces
½–1 teaspoon golden icing (confectioners') sugar (optional)
½–1 teaspoon vanilla paste (optional)

Place the cream and cocoa nibs in a small saucepan and bring to just under the boil — the cream will be just steaming. Turn off the heat, cover and leave to infuse for 30 minutes.

Strain the cream mixture through a fine mesh sieve into a small bowl, pressing lightly on the nibs to extract all the liquid and flavour, then discard the nibs. Cover the cream and place in the fridge until well chilled.

Whip the chilled cream, sweetening with a small amount of icing sugar and/or vanilla paste if desired. Store in a clean glass jar with a lid for 2–3 days in the fridge.

Labne

GLUTEN FREE / EGG FREE
MAKES ABOUT 500 G (1 LB 2 OZ) LABNE AND 500 ML (17 FL OZ/2 CUPS) WHEY DEPENDING ON YOGHURT

Real yoghurt is a fairly thin consistency (read more about this in Cultured Yoghurt and Cultured Buttermilk on page 35). It's incredibly easy and quick to thicken real yoghurt yourself by straining the yoghurt in muslin to drip off the whey. What you have left is labne (also called yoghurt cheese). This is a classic labne but you can sweeten it and flavour it as you please (see Honey and Cinnamon Labne, below). The whey that drips from the yoghurt into the bowl will keep for weeks in a sealed container (glass is best) in the fridge and is perfect for adding to the water used to soak grains and legumes or use in salad dressings and culturing vegetables.

1 kg (2 lb 4 oz) real, full-cream, non-homogenised yoghurt

Place a sieve lined with four layers of muslin (cheesecloth) over a bowl. Pour or spoon in the yoghurt and allow it to drain in the fridge for 2–3 hours. When the weather is milder, leave it to drip at room temperature, or when warmer, place in the fridge. The longer it sits, the firmer it will become. Store in a clean glass jar with a lid in the fridge for up to 5 days.

BAKING NOTE

The yoghurt must be real and not contain added milk solids.

Honey and cinnamon labne

GLUTEN FREE
MAKES ABOUT 375 G (13 OZ/1½ CUPS)

Extremely simple to make, this is a sweetened version of the classic labne (see above). Use yoghurt that is not already sweetened, and does not have added milk solids — it will be thinner, and this is as a real yoghurt should be.

600 ml (21 fl oz) real, full-cream, non-homogenised yoghurt
1 tablespoon raw honey (or maple syrup), or to taste
½ teaspoon natural vanilla extract or vanilla paste
a pinch of ground cinnamon (optional)

Place a sieve lined with four layers of muslin (cheesecloth) over a bowl. Pour or spoon in the yoghurt and allow it to drain in the fridge for 2–3 hours. The longer it sits, the firmer it will become.

Sweeten the labne to taste with honey and vanilla, stirring through to combine. Flavour with cinnamon if desired. Store in a clean glass jar with a lid in the fridge for up to 5 days.

Give that cream some culture

Cultured cream is naturally thicker and has a most delicious flavour and wonderful edge. As a bonus, it is a rich source of those good bacteria that are so important for good health — an excellent excuse to have it! There are a couple of ways to do this using kefir or cultured buttermilk, but whichever you choose, you should only combine it with the best-quality runny thin (pouring) cream, not a thick (double/heavy) or thickened (whipping) cream, and certainly not ultra-pasteurised.

The following recipes for kefir cream and crème fraîche differ in the method of making. Kefir cream is certainly easier to make as there is no need to heat the milk, and it will have the broader and more aggressive (in a good way) range of bacteria, while making crème fraîche is more of a yoghurt process, but easier in the sense that you don't have to strain the result.

Both processes involve live bacteria, hence warmth is a critical factor, with body temperature being the ideal temperature for them to grow. In winter you will need to find somewhere warmer — I wrap a quilt around the jar (leaving the muslin-covered top open, as it is an aerobic process) and place it on a stool next to the fridge engine. In summer (it gets up to 45°C/113°F where I live), you will need to cool it down — I leave it out overnight if it's cool and often this is enough; if not, it will just take a little longer. Then it goes into the fridge during the day.

Lacto-fermentation is easy to do at home. Fundamentally, it is the process of encouraging the growth of lactic-acid producing *bacilli*. As they proliferate, they produce lactic acid — one of the oldest ways of preserving food. During the growth or culturing process, many good things happen — B vitamins and enzymes are created, and proteins and sugar are pre-digested, making them easier for you to digest.

Crème fraîche (buttermilk cream)

GLUTEN FREE / EGG FREE
MAKES 185 G (6 OZ/¾ CUP) SLIGHTLY THICK CREAM

250 ml (9 fl oz/1 cup) thin (pouring) cream
2 teaspoons cultured buttermilk or left-over crème fraîche

Combine the cream and buttermilk in a small saucepan and gently heat to 30°C (86°F), then immediately remove from the heat and pour into a clean and dry glass jar. Partially cover (I use a few layers of muslin) and leave to sit in a warm place overnight or for 24 hours, checking it and stirring it every now and then until thickened. Remember, the warmer it is, the quicker this will happen. When thickened, cover with a lid, and place in the fridge for 24 hours for the flavour to fully develop. Store for up to 1 week in the fridge.

Kefir cream

GLUTEN FREE / EGG FREE
MAKES ABOUT 185 G (6 OZ/¾ CUP) THICK CREAM

When well cultured, this makes a thick cream with a delicious flavour. Cookbook author and natural foods chef Holly Davis introduced this to me — and oh my goodness it is so delicious. Though called kefir 'grains' they are not grains as we know what a grain to be, but rather a colony of good bacteria and yeasts (yes, good ones). You can buy them on the internet, or get them from someone who has extra to spare. You use the grains to culture milk (and its fat) — as the bacteria grow, they consume much of the milk sugar (lactose) and protein. The longer it's left, the more they consume, making the result more digestible. In the case of cream, there is still enough of the milk sugar and protein left to feed the bacteria. When ready, you strain the grains (putting them aside to make another batch) and use the kefir cream as you please. Culturing is aerobic, that is, it needs oxygen, so the process does not require a lid, but the jar does need to be covered with muslin.

You can buy kefir powder, but honestly I wouldn't use it — it's nasty and often doesn't work. I'm sure if you ask around you will find somebody who has it in grain form and has more than they know what to do with.

½–1 tablespoon kefir grains
250 ml (9 fl oz/1 cup) thin (pouring) cream

Place the kefir grains in a clean, dry jar, pour over the cream and cover with muslin (cheesecloth). Leave to culture in a warm place. The rule here is the warmer it is, the quicker it will culture. The longer it cultures, the more sour the taste becomes. Thus, in summer it may only take 5 or so hours, while in winter it may take 24 hours or more. As the culture develops, the cream will begin to lighten — looking and feeling like whipped cream — and it does not separate into curds and whey (as it does when making kefir milk, see page 276). This is when it's ready to use and ready for straining.

Place a colander over a jug and tip the entire contents of the jar into it. Then use a stainless steel spoon to gently lift up the grains, allowing the liquid to seep through, until there are only grains left in the colander. What is in the jug is yours to use. And the grains in the colander? You're ready to make another batch of cream — just add the grains back to a clean jar; if you're not quite ready to use them straight away, cover them with some milk and place in the fridge.

Place the kefir cream in a clean jar with a lid and store in the fridge. At this stage the bacteria continue to proliferate and ripen. It will last for 3–4 days refrigerated, but will get more sour in taste.

BAKING NOTE

It's best to strain this using a colander as it is easier for the thick cream to get through. Take care not to overwork the cream as you are straining it as it may begin to separate into butter and cultured buttermilk (another reason for using a colander). If that happens, you can't stop it, so you may as well keep going and use your wonderful cultured buttermilk to bake muffins, scones or a cake!

Icings

You will notice that I prefer to use a golden icing (confectioners') sugar, a semi-refined sugar, in many of the icing recipes. This is far less sweet (but plenty sweet enough) and darker coloured icing sugar that, when simply mixed with a little juice or water, will tint your icing a soft beige. It can be a little much when you are topping an already golden-tinged cake. It also makes colouring difficult as you now have brown in the colour mix. When I don't make my own food colourings. I use natural fruit and vegetable-based commercial food colourings, but you can also make your own. They tend to tint the icing softly, rather than giving you the opaque colours you may be used to, but there are many other ways to bring colour into a cake. I use a couple of tricks. If it's a simple icing such as the one described above, I will lift the icing with a bit of colour, and top it with bright nuts (pistachios are fabulous here), fresh blossoms and leaves. But, whenever I can form the icing base with butter, I do, as the air that is incorporated into the beaten butter (together with the icing sugar) lightens the result considerably for a creamy coloured frosting, and if adding colour, it will be more fully realised.

Piping

Piping requires a few tricks and a bit of experience:

* Choose a decent-sized piping (icing) bag — if the bag is too small, it will be difficult to handle (read more about this in Piping Bags and Nozzles on page 44).
* Fill the bag halfway to two-thirds full. This will give you enough icing to push the lower icing through the nozzle and it makes it easier on your hand.
* All icing has a temperature sweet spot — too cold and it will be very difficult to push through the nozzle (the smaller the nozzle, the harder it will be and harder again if you're using a star or other patterned nozzle). When it reaches that sweet spot, it will flow with just a bit of pressure, smoothly and easily. But it will then pass that sweet spot and become too warm to hold its shape well. If it has butter in it, the butter can melt and separate from the mix. Many things warm the icing, such as ambient room temperature, but by far the greatest impact comes from warm hands.
* Bring the icing from the fridge. If it is a fairly soft icing already (such as the Creamy Cocoa Butter and Vanilla Frosting, see page 254) it is ready to use as soon as you take it out of the fridge. But when taken from the fridge, Creamy Chocolate and Coconut Fudge, Quick and Simple Butter Icing, Better Buttercream, Maple Syrup Meringue Buttercream, Dark Chocolate and Coconut Ganache, Coconut and Cream Cheese Frosting and Honey and Cream Cheese Icing will all require a little time to sit and soften up a little — the time will depend on the ambient room temperature and their individual make up. In the case of Better Buttercream made in cool weather, it is possibly ready to use immediately after making.

Creamy chocolate and coconut fudge frosting

DAIRY FREE IF DAIRY-FREE CHOCOLATE USED / EGG FREE / NUT FREE /
CAN BE VEGAN DEPENDING ON THE CHOCOLATE USED
MAKES ABOUT 2½ CUPS — ENOUGH TO ICE AND FILL A 20–22 CM (8–8½ INCH) CAKE,
OR TO PIPE ICING ONTO 18 CUPCAKES / ½ QUANTITY WILL BE ENOUGH TO ICE 12 CUPCAKES BY HAND,
BUT YOU'LL NEED ABOUT 2 CUPS IF USING A PIPING (ICING) BAG

This is a rich and delicious frosting, which can be made ahead of time, as it keeps well for up to 1 week in an airtight container in the fridge and even freezes. It's perfect for spreading and piping (I think the piped icing looks shinier and prettier!). It's also perfect to fill the Quinoa, Cocoa Nib and Hazelnut Chocolate Sandwiches (see page 97) or the Almond, Coconut and Maple Syrup Biscuits (see page 90).

300 ml (10½ fl oz) coconut milk
3 teaspoons agar powder
1½ tablespoons cornflour (cornstarch)
60 g (2¼ oz/½ cup) unsweetened dutched cocoa powder
375 ml (13 fl oz/1½ cups) maple syrup
1 teaspoon natural vanilla extract
100 g (3½ oz) dairy-free dark chocolate, roughly chopped

Place 250 ml (9 fl oz/1 cup) of the coconut milk in a saucepan and whisk in the agar powder. Place over medium heat and bring to the boil, whisking frequently to prevent the agar sticking to the base. When the mixture comes to the boil, reduce the heat to low and simmer for 6–7 minutes, whisking frequently. After a couple of minutes, stirring rather than whisking is all that's needed.

Meanwhile, place the cornflour in a small bowl with the remaining coconut milk and mix to a smooth paste. Remove the agar mixture from the heat, whisk in the cocoa and maple syrup, then add the cornflour mixture and whisk to combine well. Return the pan to the heat and bring to the boil, whisking constantly. The mixture will thicken and lose its cloudy look as it starts to boil — although it can be tricky to see whether the mixture is boiling as it is almost too heavy for the bubbles to rise up through.

Remove from the heat, add the vanilla extract and chocolate and stir until melted and smooth. Pour into a bowl, leave to cool for 15 minutes, then press a piece of baking paper onto the surface and refrigerate for 1 hour or until set.

Break what will be a firm mixture into pieces and process in a blender or food processor until smooth and silky — you will need to scrape the sides down frequently and it takes some time. Store in an airtight container for up to 5 days in the fridge or up to 4 weeks in the freezer.

BAKING NOTES

- I use Dagoba Chocodrops, which contain 73 per cent, are free of soy lecithin, are dairy free and are made with rapadura sugar. You can soften the taste and intensity of the frosting — you may prefer something lighter, about 60 per cent, but these can be hard to find dairy free. Tropical Source and Rapunzel both have dairy-free options.

- There is a temperature sweet spot for this frosting, especially when you want to pipe it (read about Piping, opposite).

Creamy cocoa butter and vanilla frosting

GLUTEN FREE / DAIRY FREE / EGG FREE
MAKES 2 CUPS — ENOUGH TO ICE A 20–22 CM (8–8½ INCH) CAKE,
OR TO PIPE ICING ONTO 10–12 CUPCAKES, OR TO ICE 12 CUPCAKES BY HAND

I've been trying to develop a vanilla, dairy-free creamy frosting for some time now, but I have never been 100 per cent happy with the result. Every recipe I came across either used tofu (horrible) or a vegetable oil–based shortening (and there is no way I will ever use those with their damaged fats) or coconut oil (which will melt as soon as you take it out of the fridge, is overwhelming in flavour and you'll need dried milk powders of some sort to pad it out — mostly soy, which I won't use in that form). Smelling cocoa butter one day last year I wondered if that could work — here is the result. This has an amazing consistency and will hold to be piped exceptionally well, while at the same time it serves wonderfully as a cream filling. As a frosting, it is best eaten closer to the time of piping as when exposed to air, it will dry out slightly. Having said this, piped onto a cake and covered with a cake dome overnight, it still looks amazing, holds its integrity and tastes wonderful the next day. Task accomplished — and it only took twelve years.

120 g (4¼ oz/¾ cup) blanched almonds
250 ml (9 fl oz/1 cup) coconut milk
70 ml (2¼ fl oz) maple syrup
1½ teaspoons agar powder
1 vanilla bean, halved lengthways and seeds scraped or
   1 teaspoon vanilla paste
1½ tablespoons kudzu (kuzu) or cornflour (cornstarch)
30 g (1 oz) best-quality cocoa butter, pulsed in the food processor
   to very fine

Place the almonds and 435 ml (15¼ fl oz/1¾ cups) of water in a blender and blend very well until smooth. Peg four layers of muslin (cheesecloth) onto a jug or bowl and pour the almond milk through. Pick up the muslin and twist to squeeze out the remaining milk. This should make 375 ml (13 fl oz/1½ cups) of almond milk. If you don't have this amount, add a little more water to the muslin and ground almonds and squeeze out more. If you have extra, don't throw it away as you can use it in the final step.

Place 310 ml (10¾ fl oz/1¼ cups) of the almond milk, the coconut milk and maple syrup in a medium saucepan. Sprinkle the agar over the top and whisk well to distribute the agar. Add the vanilla seeds and bean halves to the pan. (If using vanilla bean paste, you will add it later.)

Whisk together and bring very gently to the boil. Continue to cook at a very gentle simmer for another 6 minutes. Take care to stir frequently with a whisk or spoon to prevent the mixture from sticking to the base.

Meanwhile, mix the remaining 60 ml (2 fl oz/¼ cup) of almond milk and the kudzu to a paste.

When the agar has dissolved, remove from the heat, and take out and discard the vanilla bean halves. Add the kudzu mix to the pan, whisking rapidly as you do so — it will begin to thicken as soon as you add it. Place it back on the stove over low heat, whisking constantly as it comes to the boil. Remove from the heat, add the cocoa butter (and the vanilla bean paste, if using) and whisk until the cocoa butter has melted and is well combined. Pour into a clean bowl and allow to cool slightly, then press a piece of baking paper onto the surface and refrigerate for at least 3 hours or until set.

When set, place what will be a fairly solid mix into the blender and blend for 5 minutes or until silky smooth, scraping down the sides from time to time. Place the frosting in an airtight container, press a piece of baking paper onto the surface, seal and refrigerate for at least 5 hours, or preferably overnight, before using. In winter, it is best left at room temperature for 10–15 minutes before piping. Store in an airtight container for up to 2 days in the fridge.

BAKING NOTES

- This frosting would be wonderful piped (with an 11 mm/½ inch star nozzle) as a mousse and served with fresh berries, especially blackberries. The texture is smooth and luscious.
- The texture after overnight refrigeration is beautiful — smooth and luscious and better because of the long chill. It is best piped straight from the fridge as it pipes more firmly, which, when you are using a star nozzle, is better as the lines are more clearly delineated. It is a softer consistency than the Creamy Chocolate and Coconut Fudge Frosting (see page 253), but still sturdy.

Dark chocolate and sour cream icing

GLUTEN FREE
MAKES 1½ CUPS — ENOUGH TO ICE A 20–22 CM (8–8½ INCH) CAKE,
OR TO PIPE ICING ONTO 10–12 CUPCAKES, OR TO ICE 12 CUPCAKES BY HAND

This icing is best spread as soon as possible after making. If you have stored it in the fridge, however, you will find it will have set to a ganache consistency and will become more spreadable when left to sit at room temperature for a bit; while it will still taste divine, the texture is not as lovely, though using a hot palette knife to smooth over the icing will help.

150 g (5½ oz) dark chocolate (70%), chopped
60 g (2¼ oz) unsalted butter, softened
185 g (6½ oz/1¼ cups) golden icing (confectioners') sugar
1 tablespoon unsweetened dutched cocoa powder
a pinch of sea salt
125 g (4½ oz/½ cup) sour cream, plus 1 tablespoon

Melt the chocolate in a heatproof bowl over a saucepan of just-simmering water, making sure the bottom of the bowl doesn't touch the water. Remove from the heat and leave to cool a little; if it is too hot, the butter will melt when added.

Using a stand mixer fitted with the paddle attachment, beat the butter until light and creamy — this won't take long. Sieve in the icing sugar and cocoa, then add the salt and beat on medium speed, stopping the machine and scraping down the sides every so often, until light and fluffy. Add the sour cream and beat until well combined.

Add the melted chocolate, taking care to beat as soon as possible as the chocolate can begin to set when it mixes with cold butter, beating on medium–high speed for 1 minute or so, until very creamy, soft and light. Use immediately.

Quick and simple butter icing

GLUTEN FREE / EGG FREE
MAKES 2¼ CUPS — ENOUGH TO ICE AND FILL A 20–24 CM (8–9½ INCH) CAKE,
OR TO PIPE ICING ONTO 18 CUPCAKES / ½ QUANTITY WILL BE ENOUGH TO ICE 12 CUPCAKES BY HAND

This is a classic butter icing — quick to make, and always delivers great results. If you prefer an icing with less sugar, I would suggest making the Better Buttercream (see page 258).

125 g (4½ oz) unsalted butter, softened
450 g (1 lb/3 cups) golden icing (confectioners') sugar, sieved
1–3 tablespoons milk (make sure the milk is not too cold)
1 teaspoon natural vanilla extract
1 teaspoon lemon or lime juice
natural food colouring, as desired

Beat the butter, icing sugar and 1 tablespoon of the milk using hand-held electric beaters (the paddle attachment is best) on low speed until the mixture begins to come together. Increase the speed to medium and beat for 3–4 minutes or until the mixture is smooth, thick and creamy. Add extra milk as needed, taking care not to add too much. Add the vanilla extract and lemon juice and colouring, if desired, and beat until smooth. If you find the mixture has curdled, add extra icing sugar and beat.

BAKING NOTES

- The butter must be very, very soft, with the texture of face cream — this will enable you to achieve a light result.
- Because this icing is a butter base, it is very flexible. You can incorporate flavours as desired into this — raspberry purée; lemon, lime or orange zest; rosewater and passionfruit are all delicious, but you will need to reduce the amount of milk. Add it with the vanilla extract to the creamed butter and sugar.
- If at any time you find the mixture curdling, add more icing (confectioners') sugar until the problem is resolved and make sure the mix is not too cold.
- There is a temperature sweet spot for this frosting, especially when you want to pipe it (read about Piping on page 252).

Variation

You can replace the dairy milk with coconut milk if desired.

Better buttercream

GLUTEN FREE / EGG FREE
MAKES 1½ CUPS — ENOUGH TO ICE A 20–22 CM (8–8½ INCH) CAKE,
OR TO PIPE ICING ONTO 10–12 CUPCAKES, OR TO ICE 12 CUPCAKES BY HAND

This is the icing I turn to for special occasions as it always gives a reliable, delicious result. It has a beautiful cream colour, and is incredibly flexible — taking on natural flavours and colours with ease. When made with raspberries, it is the prettiest pink and so tasty. When made with passionfruit, it has a soft glow and a fresh, light passionfruit flavour. When made with white chocolate, it is simply divine.

Buttercream icing can be very rich, but it is one of the best. This icing is based on New York's famous Magnolia Bakery's vanilla buttercream, but I use a thickened milk mixture to reduce the amount of butter. I've played with it a little to suit my needs — a less-rich milk, more coconut, lime or raspberry to cut the sweetness and a less-refined sugar. All in all, it's delicious and nowhere near as rich.

1 tablespoon cornflour (cornstarch)
60 ml (2 fl oz/¼ cup) rice milk
60 ml (2 fl oz/¼ cup) coconut milk
125 g (4½ oz) unsalted butter, softened
75 g (2½ oz/½ cup) golden icing (confectioners') sugar, sieved
2 teaspoons natural vanilla extract or
   1 teaspoon vanilla bean paste
2 teaspoons lime juice

Place the cornstarch in a small saucepan, add the rice milk and stir until smooth, then add the coconut milk. Place over medium heat, stirring constantly until boiling and thickened — because it is so thick, you won't see bubbles to indicate a boil, but rather a gentle lift at the base of the pan. Spoon into a small bowl and press some baking paper directly onto the surface to prevent a skin from forming. Cool to room temperature.

Using a stand mixer fitted with the paddle attachment, beat the butter until it is light and fluffy, then add the icing sugar and beat for a few more minutes or until well combined. Add the cooled milk mixture (in small chunks), vanilla extract and lime juice and beat for another 2–3 minutes or until the icing is beautifully smooth and fluffy, scraping down the sides from time to time.

Place in the fridge to set just a little before using, but don't leave it too long, or the butter will set hard. If the buttercream has become too firm to use, let it sit at room temperature to soften before using. In winter, the cool air from the beaters may begin to set the butter, so you might need to use a little more coconut milk (about 1 tablespoon) to bring it to a good consistency for spreading and piping.

BAKING NOTES
• Your frosting will be smoother and creamier if the milk mixture is just cooled to room temperature and not set hard in the fridge as this makes it easier to cream with the butter.
• When the weather is cooler, it's very important that the butter is soft.
• Both of these points make it easier to incorporate the water-based fruit purées.

*Clockwise from top right: raspberry better buttercream;
quick and simple butter icing with passionfruit; strawberry
and rosewater better buttercream; creamy chocolate and
coconut fudge frosting; white chocolate better buttercream;
creamy cocoa butter and vanilla frosting.*

BAKING NOTE

When the weather is cooler, you may need to wrap a hot towel around the bowl. This will help soften the butter and emulsify the water-based fruit juices and purées.

Passionfruit better buttercream

Scoop the pulp from 2–4 passionfruit into a sieve placed over a small bowl. Press down with the back of a large spoon to extract as much juice as possible — you will need 2 tablespoons of passionfruit juice. Omit the lime juice from the recipe and use only 1 teaspoon of vanilla extract.

Beat the butter until it is light and fluffy, then add the icing sugar and beat for a few more minutes or until well combined. Add the just-cool milk mixture (in small amounts) and beat for another 2–3 minutes or until the icing is beautifully smooth and fluffy, scraping down the sides from time to time.

Add 1 tablespoon of the passionfruit juice and the vanilla extract to the butter mixture and beat for 2–3 minutes or until smooth and fluffy, adding the remaining passionfruit juice, if necessary, to bring to the desired consistency.

Raspberry better buttercream

Place 90 g (3¼ oz/¾ cup) of raspberries in a fine sieve and place over a bowl. (You can use frozen raspberries, but thaw them first, in a sieve over a small bowl; use the watery juice that drips out for something else.) Using the back of a spoon, press the berries into the sieve to get a lovely purée. You will need 3 tablespoons of purée. Discard the seeds and pulp. Omit the lime juice from the recipe.

Beat the butter until it is light and fluffy, then add the icing sugar and beat for a few more minutes or until well combined. Add the just-cool milk mixture (in small amounts) and beat for another 2–3 minutes or until the icing is beautifully smooth and fluffy, scraping down the sides from time to time.

Add 2 tablespoons of the purée and the vanilla extract to the butter mixture and beat for 2–3 minutes or until smooth and fluffy, adding the remaining purée, if necessary, to bring it to the desired consistency.

Strawberry and rosewater better buttercream

Purée 150 g (5½ oz) of hulled and washed strawberries in a blender until smooth, then strain through a fine mesh sieve, pushing down on the solids to extract as much purée as possible. Discard the seeds and set the purée aside. You will need 3 tablespoons of juice. Omit the lime juice from the recipe and use 1 teaspoon of vanilla bean paste instead of the vanilla extract.

Beat the butter until it is light and fluffy, then add the icing sugar and beat for a few more minutes or until well combined. Add the just-cool milk mixture (in small amounts) and beat for another 2–3 minutes or until the icing is beautifully smooth and fluffy, scraping down the sides from time to time.

Add 2 tablespoons of the purée, 1 teaspoon of vanilla bean paste and 1 teaspoon of rosewater to the butter mixture and beat for 2–3 minutes or until smooth and fluffy, adding the remaining purée, if necessary, to bring it to the desired consistency.

White chocolate better buttercream

Place 100 g (3½ oz) of chopped good-quality white chocolate (I use Green & Blacks) in a heatproof bowl set over a saucepan of just-simmering water, making sure the bottom of the bowl doesn't touch the water, and melt until smooth; if the water is too hot, the chocolate will scorch and not melt. Reduce the quantity of lime juice to 1 teaspoon and when the buttercream is smooth and fluffy, add the warm melted chocolate at the end. Continue to beat until the chocolate is well incorporated.

Dairy milk better buttercream

Replace the rice and coconut milk with 125 ml (4 fl oz/½ cup) full-cream, non-homogenised milk .

Maple syrup meringue buttercream

GLUTEN FREE
MAKES 2 CUPS

This is a true buttercream — made with a meringue base, and with a silky smooth texture. It keeps extraordinarily well both in the fridge and the freezer. Wildly delicious, it works well with the Apple and Pecan Cake (see page 150), or a Pecan Génoise Sponge Cake (see page 151–153) and is used in the Bûche de Noël (see page 156).

170 ml (5½ fl oz/⅔ cup) maple syrup
2 egg whites, at room temperature
130 g (4½ oz) unsalted butter, softened
1 teaspoon natural vanilla extract or vanilla paste
1 tablespoon whisky (optional)

Place the maple syrup in a small saucepan and bring to the boil over medium heat until it reaches 114–116°C (237–241°F) on a candy thermometer — this takes a good 8–10 minutes. As the temperature approaches 110°C (230°C), begin to whisk the egg whites using a stand mixer until they just form stiff peaks, but take care that while you are waiting for the syrup to come to temperature they are not overwhipped.

When the maple syrup reaches the correct temperature, immediately remove it from the heat and while beating on medium speed, drizzle the syrup in a very slow stream (if it is too fast, the syrup will flick out to the side of the bowl) onto the whipped egg white. Continue to beat and when all the syrup is incorporated, scrape down the side of the bowl. Continue to beat on medium speed until the mix has cooled down. This is important, as you don't want the butter to melt when you add it.

Add the butter, 1 tablespoon at a time, beating well after each addition, adding the vanilla

BAKING NOTES

- I have made this using raw honey and it was divine, but I generally err in doing that as according to Ayurveda, cooking honey is said to make it toxic. If you'd like to give it a try, you will need 185 ml (6 fl oz/ ¾ cup) runny honey.

- I've also added 1 tablespoon of whisky to the maple syrup version at times.

- You will need a candy thermometer for this recipe.

and whisky (if using) in small portions halfway through. Continue beating until all the butter has been added and the buttercream looks smooth and silky. If it does begin to look curdled, don't worry too much, as it cools down, it will smooth out — just keep on beating.

You may well need to let the buttercream set in the fridge before using. It can be very soft after making, especially when the weather is hot. If the buttercream is too hard for use when it comes out of the fridge, leave it to sit at room temperature until it is the right consistency. Store in an airtight container in the fridge for up to 5 days or up to 4 weeks in the freezer.

Italian meringue

GLUTEN FREE / DAIRY FREE
MAKES ENOUGH TO TOP A 24 CM (9½ INCH) ROUND TART; OR A 35 CM X 12 CM (14 X 4½ INCH) RECTANGULAR TART; OR 12 TARTLETS (4 CM/1½ INCH BASE DIAMETER, 6 CM/2½ INCH TOP DIAMETER, 2 CM/¾ INCH DEPTH)

This is my favourite meringue, and for not too much extra trouble you get one that is exceptionally stable — I like stability. A lot. This meringue will sit atop a tart and not weep, and will still look just as good the next day — as I said, it's stable, and silky smooth on the tongue. Read the recipe through before you start, and with a candy thermometer, you'll be fine — just take care not to get any of that hot sugar syrup on you as it burns badly. Once you have topped the tart with the meringue, use a kitchen blowtorch to gently colour it.

With the addition of a little vanilla paste or extract, this can double as an icing — often known as boiled icing or marshmallow icing.

150 g (5½ oz) golden caster (superfine) sugar
3 egg whites, at room temperature

Place the sugar and 60 ml (2 fl oz/¼ cup) of water in a small saucepan over medium heat and bring to the boil — brushing the sides of the pan down with a wet brush if there is sugar on the side, sitting above the water level. Do not stir, otherwise the sugar may crystallise. When the sugar has dissolved, increase the heat to a rapid boil, place a candy thermometer in it and cook until it reaches 121°C (250°F).

Place the egg whites in the bowl of a stand mixer. As the thermometer approaches 115°C (239°F), begin to beat the whites on medium speed until you have soft peaks — take care not to overbeat them.

When the syrup reaches 121°C, immediately remove it from the heat and, while beating on medium speed, drizzle the syrup in a very slow stream (if it is too fast the syrup will splatter to the sides of the bowl, and not too close to the beaters or it will flick it out to the sides of the bowl) onto the whipped egg white. Continue to beat for 5 minutes or until the meringue has cooled down and is soft and silky. Use immediately.

BAKING NOTES
• This amount of sugar is for egg whites weighing 27–30 g (1 oz), which is a common weight for a large egg. If you are worried yours are exceptionally large, weigh them, and add extra sugar as required. This recipe works on a ratio of 50 g (1¾ oz) golden caster (superfine) sugar per 27–30 g egg white. This meringue is best used as soon as it is made. If disaster strikes and you've left it for 3–4 hours, give it a good mix with a spoon — it will deflate and not look as perky, but it will still be a silky smooth and shiny mix, and still taste and look glorious.
• You will need a candy thermometer.

Coconut and cream cheese icing

GLUTEN FREE
MAKES 2 CUPS ICING — ENOUGH TO ICE AND FILL A 20–22 CM (8–8½ INCH) CAKE,
OR TO PIPE ICING ONTO 12 CUPCAKES

This is one of my favourite icings. The coconut gives it a rich and delicious flavour. I've paired it with the Coconut and Palm Sugar Cake (see page 181), but it would work equally well with the Banana and Coconut Bread (see page 136) and indeed any of the cupcakes.

250 g (9 oz) cream cheese, at room temperature
120 g (4¼ oz) well-chilled coconut milk
1 teaspoon lime zest
1 teaspoon natural vanilla extract or vanilla paste
60 ml (2 fl oz/¼ cup) maple syrup

Using a stand mixer fitted with the paddle attachment, beat the cream cheese until smooth, then add the remaining ingredients and beat until deliciously creamy, scraping down the sides from time to time. Cover and place in the fridge to firm a little before using, but take care not to leave it too long or it will be too hard. If it is too firm, soften at room temperature. Store in an airtight container in the fridge for up to 5 days.

BAKING NOTE

To chill the coconut milk, place a 400 g (14 oz) tin of coconut milk in the fridge or freezer until the creamy part of the milk has firmed up — there will be a clear separation of solid (cream) and liquid. Spoon this solid portion from the tin until you have 120 g (4¼ oz). The remainder can be kept and used for smoothies and other cooking. Bear in mind that the coconut milk must be full strength (not light) and not stabilised.

Honey and cream cheese icing

GLUTEN FREE
MAKES 2 CUPS — ENOUGH TO ICE AND FILL A 20–22 CM (8–8½ INCH) CAKE
OR TO PIPE ICING ONTO 12 CUPCAKES

I've also made this icing in a ratio of 125 g (4½ oz) each of cream cheese, unsalted butter and very fresh goat's curd. The texture is a bit grittier, but I love the earthiness of it.

250 g (9 oz) cream cheese, at room temperature
125 g (4½ oz) unsalted butter, softened
80 ml (2½ fl oz/⅓ cup) runny raw honey, or to taste
1 teaspoon natural vanilla extract
1 teaspoon finely grated lemon zest

Using a stand mixer fitted with the paddle attachment, beat the cream cheese and butter until pale in colour and creamy, scraping down the sides from time to time. Add the honey, vanilla and lemon zest and beat until very pale in colour, creamy and somewhat fluffy. Taste and add extra honey as desired. Store in an airtight container for up to 1 week in the fridge.

SERVE WITH

I've paired this icing with the Apple and Pecan Cake (see page 150), and it would also make a wonderful icing for the Walnut and Yoghurt Cake For Easter (see page 140).

Spreads

Spreads are the range of scarves and jewellery in your wardrobe to add delicious nuances of flavour, texture and in some cases, moisture to your biscuit, cake or tart. A little curd here or a little ganache there can often save the day.

Luscious lemon or lime coconut curd

GLUTEN FREE / DAIRY FREE / EGG FREE / VEGAN
MAKES 1½ CUPS

This is beautiful to fill little cupcakes or to spread between the layers of a larger cake. It will keep incredibly well in the fridge — just press a round of baking paper onto the surface. I've adapted the recipe from Coming Home To Eat, *adding a little more cornflour to give it a creamier consistency.*

90 ml (3 fl oz) freshly squeezed and strained lemon or lime juice
1¼ teaspoons agar powder
2½ teaspoons cornflour (cornstarch) or kudzu (kuzu)
250 ml (9 fl oz/1 cup) coconut milk
60 ml (2 fl oz/¼ cup) maple syrup
60 ml (2 fl oz/¼ cup) brown rice syrup
½ teaspoon natural vanilla extract
2 teaspoons finely grated lemon or lime zest
tiny pinch of ground turmeric, if using lemon juice

BAKING NOTES

• Lemons and limes are highly acidic, and this will affect the set of the curd. This has been taken into account here, but you may find the set will vary with the seasons. Using meyer lemons can be different again since they are less sharp so you will need to reduce the amount of sweetness you add.

• Because you are dealing with a small amount of liquid in the beginning, make sure you only have a gentle simmer or you will evaporate off some of your juice.

• If you can tolerate dairy, then you must try the recipe for Tahitian Lime Curd (see page 219), which in my opinion is possibly the best lime curd ever.

Place the lemon or lime juice and agar in a small saucepan and whisk together until the agar is well combined with no clumps. Place over very gentle heat for about 5 minutes, stirring often, then increase the heat and bring to a gentle boil. It will be very thick, but will thin out as the agar dissolves. Immediately reduce the heat a little and continue to cook at a very gentle simmer for 5–8 minutes, stirring often to avoid the agar sinking to the bottom and sticking.

Meanwhile, place the cornflour in a bowl with 60 ml (2 fl oz/¼ cup) of the coconut milk and mix to a smooth slurry. Mix in the remaining coconut milk, the syrups and vanilla extract. Remove the agar mixture from the heat and add the coconut mixture, whisking constantly. Return to the heat and stir constantly until boiled. Do not overboil.

Remove from the heat and whisk in the zest (and turmeric, if using — taking care not to use too much as the colour can be a little too bright). Set aside to cool, then refrigerate for 1 hour or until set. Store in an airtight container in the fridge for up to 5 days.

Dark chocolate and coconut ganache

CAN BE DAIRY FREE IF DAIRY-FREE CHOCOLATE IS USED
MAKES A GENEROUS ¾ CUP — ENOUGH TO POUR OVER A 20–24 CM (8–9½ INCH) CAKE;
OR TO MAKE 24 SANDWICHED BISCUITS

This is a dark, luscious ganache, made all the better by using coconut milk rather than cream. Not only is it less rich, but it allows the dark bitterness of the cocoa to come through, and the cocoa is softened by the maple syrup and coconut. It's very good. The quality of coconut milk for ganache is very important — some brands (especially organic) can be quite watery — look for one that is creamier and is made without emulsifiers. I think the Ayam brand is very good. If you'd like to replace the coconut milk with coconut cream, use the same amount.

100 g (3½ oz) dark chocolate (70%), finely chopped
140 ml (4½ fl oz) coconut milk
2–3 teaspoons maple syrup, or to taste

Finely chop the chocolate and add to a small mixing bowl. Bring the coconut milk to the boil, pour it over the chocolate and stir until the chocolate is completely melted. Add the maple syrup and stir through.

If using to pour over a cake Leave to cool for a bit and firm up just a little before using.

If using as a filling Leave in a cool place (the fridge is fine) to set — this will take a few hours. Once the ganache sets, it will be a perfect spreading consistency and will keep in an airtight container in the fridge for 1–2 weeks. When you need to soften it — for spreading (if it is too hard) — bring it out to come to room temperature. If it is freezing cold or you want to pour it over a cake, set the bowl in a small saucepan of hot water and leave it to sit for a few minutes. As it starts to soften, it will look as if it is splitting a little, but once it has all melted, you can stir it together and it will be perfect. Let it cool for a minute or so before pouring over the cake.

If using to pipe There is a temperature sweet spot for this ganache. It is best soft, but not at all melted and will have a slight shine to it; the smaller the nozzle you use (such as a 5 mm/¼ inch star nozzle), the more important this is.

BAKING NOTE

• The amount of maple syrup you use depends on how you want to use the ganache. As an icing on the Bittersweet Banana, Chocolate and Quinoa Cake (see page 139), I prefer a strong chocolate taste, with a marked bitterness to offset the sweet banana beautifully.
• If you're wanting to use it as a ganache to spread between biscuits, or in a cake, you can increase the amount of maple syrup to 1–2 tablespoons.

Glorious fruit

A cake or biscuit most certainly does not need icing or frosting to make
it delicious — it can be equally wonderful served with ripe, organic fruit
in season. I love it, and use it wherever I can — baked into muffins and
cakes, whipped into buttercream icings, and also served with cakes in
any number of forms: baked, stewed, grilled or formed into a simple jam.
I cannot imagine this book without fruit or homemade jam. Even the
most simple baking, a scone say, is elevated to true wonder when served
with high-quality cultured cream (see pages 250–251) and homemade
jams and preserves from ripe, organic seasonal fruits. With a few bits
of leftover Génoise Sponge Cake (see page 151), Gluten-Free Almond
Butter Cake (see page 163), or Vanilla and Almond Cake (see page 166),
cream and the best seasonal fruit, you can have a dessert of wonder
in a matter of minutes.

Jam

The only fruit to use is that which is ripe, preferably organic and in season — this applies to all baking not only jam-making. Fruits such as this are bursting with natural sweetness, colour with enormous complexity and luscious flavour. We have become very accustomed to fruits available all the year round, but you will find they have nowhere near the same level of flavour. Fruits are fleeting, lasting only a few weeks, but there is a way to capture that moment — jam.

The jam (it's a universal recipe) in this chapter relies less on sugar, and more so on technique to capture the true complexity and glory of fruit flavour — it is a snapshot of the fruit at its best and the season. This is the technique used to make the cumquat jam in the Holiday Fruit Cake (see page 148). Jams are very easy to make, and will store in the pantry for up to one year. On a cold winter's day, when you take that batch of scones out of the oven, you will thank yourself for your stash of homemade jams and the colour and taste of summer will lift your spirits.

Technically, the object of preserving is to slow down the process of decay. Food spoils from the continued activity of natural enzymes in all fruits and vegetables and the continued work of microorganisms in the form of moulds, yeasts and bacteria present in the food and air.

Sugar, pectin and acid

Jam relies on sugar to saturate the natural moisture of the fruit and thus preserve it. I am often asked if something other than sugar can be used to make jam — the answer is complex. Many of the sugar-free jams you see are made with white grape juice concentrate, use pectin and have been processed in a boiling-water bath. Because there is not enough sucrose to saturate the fruit and preserve it (and this is true of many other non-sucrose based sweeteners, such as stevia, agave and brown rice syrup), the boiling-water bath is the preserving method. I have only included a recipe for jam made with sugar and the method recommended in My Universal Low-Sugar Jam (see page 271) is only for use with sugar (not other sweeteners).

I prefer to use one of the semi-refined organic raw sugars (not rapadura, which is too low in sucrose and too strong in flavour) in the smallest possible amount. Most jam recipes call for equal quantities of sugar to fruit by weight. You need about 60–70 per cent sugar for good gelling to occur naturally (sugar, pectin, acidity). I find this way too much sugar and prefer a ratio of 20–40 per cent sugar to fruit, but this will vary with the fruit — tart fruit will require more, and sweet fruit will require less. Because the holy trinity of sugar, pectin and acid is disrupted, this will result in a softer 'set', which I happen to prefer.

Pectin is a carbohydrate that helps to 'set' jam. It is particularly concentrated in the skins and cores of fruit. The conversion of the pre-curser substances to pectin occurs naturally during ripening but can also be forced by long cooking, as in the traditional methods of making jam without added pectin. Fruits vary in how much pectin, or pectin pre-cursers, they contain. Pectin produces structure and a kind of stiffness in jam by forming a water-holding network within the crushed fruit. Before gelling starts, individual molecules of pectin are surrounded and isolated from each other by water molecules. If the surrounding solution is acidic enough, the pectin loses some of its attraction for these isolating water molecules. Sour fruit will normally provide enough acid to take care of this step. If the acid content of the fruit is low, lemon juice can be added to make the fruit mixture more acidic. Once the pectin has loosened its hold on the water molecules, something more attractive must pull the water away from the pectin — this is the role of sugar. With its water stripped away, pectin opens out into a structure that links readily with other pectin molecules to form a three-dimensional network — a gel.

Fruits with high natural pectin and acid content include:

* blackberries
* crab apples
* cranberries
* plums
* quinces
* sour apples

Fruits with low natural pectin and acid content include:

* apricots
* blueberries
* figs
* grapes
* guava
* peaches
* pears
* prunes
* raspberries
* rhubarb
* strawberries

Low-pectin fruits benefit from the addition of lemon, to boost the acidity and thus setting. Unripe fruit (sour) will also increase acidity. Jam is best made with a good percentage of fruit that is not overripe because as the fruit ripens, the pectin breaks down and you will not get a good set.

Pick the right pot

The right pot is critical to making low-sugar jam. Mine is a traditional French copper preserving pan that is shallow and wide. It's about 12 cm (4½ inches) high, 36 cm (14¼ inches) across the base and 39 cm (15½ inches) across the top, with a 10 litre (350 fl oz) capacity. The wide surface area encourages evaporation and reduction, thus cooking the jam quickly. It is extremely difficult to make jam in a deep pot with a small surface area — tall pans are a major cause of runny jam.

However, you can make smaller amounts in your average large domestic saucepan. You can use a simple stainless steel pan — just make sure it is not too deep. A wider and more shallow pan with less capacity (for example, a sauté pan with a 5 litre/175 fl oz capacity and a depth of 8 cm/3¼ inches) is better than a pot with a 10 litre/350 fl oz capacity, but a depth of 16–18 cm (6¼–7 inches). It will mean you can only make small amounts at a time — about 2 kg (4 lb 8 oz) of fruit, but your jam will be more successful. You can also use a 20–24 cm (8–9½ inch) typical domestic saucepan, but keep the amount of fruit to 1 kg (2 lb 4 oz).

Never make jam in large quantities — another cause of runny jam — and never crowd your pan. How much fruit you use (the weight) will depend on the size of your pan — for mine, I use 4 kg (9 lb). A good guide is to only fill your pan two-thirds full of fruit.

Jars and lids

Always use tempered jars that can withstand the temperatures involved in sterilising, jam-making and storage. Some jars manufactured for products such as coffee, peanut butter and mayonnaise are not tempered and do not have strong seals on the lids. Jars must not be cracked, chipped or damaged in any way, and lids must not be scratched or dented. Jars can be re-used, but lids are good for one use only.

Sterilising your equipment

Your jars, lids, ladles and funnels must all be sterilised. This is easy to do in an oven at 120°C (235°F/Gas ½) for 20 minutes. Jars and lids must be sterilised, dry and warm. Once sterilised, turn the oven off and leave in the warm oven until the jam is ready. Equipment can also be boiled for 12 minutes in a large saucepan of water, then dried in the oven at a low temperature.

Putting the jam into the jars

Bottling technique is the other very important part of making low-sugar jams — the jam must be spooned with a sterilised ladle through a sterilised funnel into warm jars (as hot jam into cool or cold jars will cause the jars to break) as soon as it is ready. Make sure the sterilised jars are warm (from sterilising and then being kept warm in the oven) and sit them on a wooden surface or on towels (so they don't crack when the hot jam is added). This process will ensure the jars seal properly and that the jam does not spoil.

After ladling the jam into the jars, make sure there is no spillage as this will hinder a seal being formed. Gently wipe any spillage, taking care not to touch the sterilised lip of the jar. Place the lids on, taking care to touch only the outside of the lids. Holding the jars with a damp cloth (for a good grip), turn the lids until firm.

Let the jars sit until fully cool — do not move them for 12 hours or you can disrupt the vacuum process. A concave dip in the middle of the lid indicates a vacuum seal. If there is no concave dip, store the jam in the fridge and use straight away.

Once opened and the seal is broken, the jam begins to deteriorate and must be kept in the fridge.

My universal low-sugar jam

GLUTEN FREE / DAIRY FREE / EGG FREE

Jam made from 4 kg (9 lb) fruit with 30 per cent sugar in a 10 litre (350 fl oz) jam pot (with the dimensions described on page 269) will take about 1 hour from beginning to end. Using 1 kg (2 lb 4 oz) fruit in a smaller 20–24 cm (8–9½ inch) saucepan will take about 45 minutes.

This is how I make jam, but you can equally cut the fruit up and macerate it with the sugar overnight — this will give you a quicker cooking time the day after. If doing so, stage 1 will happen very quickly.

The technique described here is not suitable for preserving jam made without sugar, or jams made with vegetables, fish or animal products as these products are too low in acid and need to be processed appropiately in a boiling-water bath to eliminate the risk of botulism.

> 4 kg (9 lb) fruit (weighed whole)
> 800 g (1 lb 12 oz) (20% ratio) to 1.6 kg (3 lb 8 oz) (40% ratio)
>   organic raw sugar
> 1 medium lemon, skin on, cut into 8 bits

Preheat the oven to 120°C (235°F/Gas ½).

Sterilise your jars and lids (opposite), place on a baking tray lined with a clean tea towel and keep warm in a low oven.

Wash the fruit (there is no need to dry it) and cut into smaller portions. Discard any stones (as in apricots, et cetera). As a general guide, leave blueberries and small strawberries whole, but chop larger strawberries; cut apricots and plums into halves or quarters; and cut figs into quarters or smaller segments.

Place the fruit in your jam pot, together with the sugar and lemon and gently stir the sugar through.

Stage 1
Place the pot over very low heat, allowing the sugar to dissolve — this takes about 15 minutes, or a bit longer, depending on the size of your pot.

Stage 2
Once the sugar is visibly starting to dissolve, increase the heat slightly until you see a gentle bubbling. Stir frequently. It is at this stage you taste and add sugar as needed. Continue to cook for 15 minutes (or longer if using a deeper pan) — the juices will have weeped out from the fruit, thus increasing the amount of liquid in the pot.

Stage 3
Increase the heat to very high and boil until a 'set' is achieved. As you are now cooking at a high boil, you need to stir frequently to check the feel of the jam and to make sure it isn't

BAKING NOTE

You may be concerned that weighing fruits with stones in will ultimately end up weighing less (and thus ultimately will result in a higher ratio of sugar). I don't worry about this, as I only start with 20 per cent (800 g) and adjust it from there. The finished ratio of sugar will most often sit somewhere between 25 and 30 per cent, no matter how your fruit started out.

sticking to the base (wearing a long-sleeved shirt is good here). As the jam reduces, it will thicken. You may need to reduce the heat to a slower boil as the jam thickens but keep stirring frequently. This stage should take about 30 minutes, but the deeper the pot, the longer it will take. It should take about 10 minutes if using a small 1 kg amount.

Set is generally considered to occur when the jam reaches 105°C (221°F) for a 60% sugar jam. But this doesn't hold for low-sugar jams, where the relationship between sugar, acid and pectin has been disrupted (neither does it hold at a higher altitude, where set point can be at considerably lower temperature). You need to rely on other techniques to judge when your jam is ready. I go by appearance and 'feel' and cook the jam until it is fairly thick. The bubbles also, become more volcanic and flat. Placing a small amount of jam on a saucer or dish and chilling it is another good method for checking the consistency: when cool, run your finger through the middle — you want to see a clear line of plate underneath. Any juices that flow into the line should look like lovely liquid jam, and not at all watery, and should have body.

If you are sterilising by boiling, about 30 minutes before your jam is ready, bring a large pan of water to the boil, or place in the oven as described on page 270. Sterilise your funnel and ladle by boiling for 12 minutes. While they are boiling, remove the jars and lids from the oven, keeping them on their trays. Remove the funnel and ladle from the boiling water and shake a little to remove the water, allowing the air to dry them off. As soon as the jam is ready, ladle the warm jam through the funnel, into the warm jars. Seal the lids tightly, then leave to sit until totally cool. There should be a concave dent in the middle of the lid; if there isn't, store the jam in the fridge and use it straight away — never a hard thing to do.

Fruit accompaniments

Other than jam, these are some of my favourite fridge and pantry staples to have on hand for adding flavour and sweetness to my baking. You'll also find plenty more on poaching and baking fresh fruit in *Wholefood for the Family: Coming Home to Eat* and *Wholefood for Children*.

Vincotto cherries

WHEAT FREE / DAIRY FREE / GLUTEN FREE
MAKES 1 GENEROUS CUP

Deep and darkly flavoured, this is a wonderful treatment for plumping up dried red cherries, and they match exceptionally well with wholemeal flours. I've used these in the Cherry and Vincotto Wedges (see page 177) and they are a wonderful option in the Upside-down Jewelled Pudding (see page 177) or even as a quick dessert with a slice of the Pretty Buttermilk Cake (see page 172) and Crème Fraîche (see page 250). They keep for weeks refrigerated and just get better with age.

40 g (1½ oz/1 cup) dried cherries
1 teaspoon natural vanilla extract
2 tablespoons vincotto

Organic dried cherries tend to have some pits left in, so check them carefully and remove if found. Place the cherries and 125 ml (4 fl oz/½ cup) of water in a small saucepan. Gently simmer over very low heat for 10–15 minutes, then add the vanilla extract and vincotto and simmer for another 5–10 minutes or until you have about 2 tablespoons of liquid left. Place in a small container with a lid, and leave to sit overnight in the fridge for the flavours to fully develop. Store in an airtight container in the fridge for up to 4 weeks.

Dried peach and nectarine spread

WHEAT FREE / GLUTEN FREE / DAIRY FREE / EGG FREE
MAKES 1 CUP

Thanks to the maple syrup and vanilla, this is a fragrant spread and a great way to use dried peaches and nectarines. The spread complements the flavours of barley so well and I've used them in the Peach and Nectarine Oat and Barley Scones (see page 74), but it would be equally delicious in a bowl with a scoop of cultured cream (see pages 250–251). I'd be more than happy to use it as a shortcut in A Rustic Tart of Quince and Dried Fruit Compote With Goat's Cheese (see page 211) and a small amount in the Holiday Fruit Cake (see page 148).

75 g (2½ oz/½ cup) roughly chopped dried peaches
50 g (1¾ oz/½ cup) roughly chopped dried nectarines
2 tablespoons maple syrup
1 teaspoon natural vanilla extract

Place the dried fruit, 1 tablespoon of the maple syrup and the vanilla extract in a small saucepan with 250 ml (9 fl oz/1 cup) of water. Cover with a lid and cook at a very gentle simmer for 20 minutes. Remove from the heat and set aside for 30 minutes.

Transfer to a food processor with the remaining maple syrup and blend into a chunky purée. If necessary, add a little more water to make a moist, spreadable consistency. Store in an airtight container in the fridge for up to 2 weeks.

Honey-roasted figs

GLUTEN FREE / EGG FREE

I can't think of anything I love more, and these are especially good when served with the Walnut and Yoghurt Cake for Easter (see page 140). You can also roast with fresh thyme.

1–2 ripe figs per person
40 g (1½ oz) unsalted butter or ghee (see page 279)
2 tablespoons raw honey
a large pinch of ground cinnamon

Preheat the oven to 220°C (425°F/Gas 7).

Quarter each fig lengthways without cutting through the base. Squeeze them gently at the bottom to open them out a little and place in a baking dish. Dot the butter around the figs, drizzle with the honey and sprinkle over the cinnamon. Roast for 10–15 minutes.

Berry glaze

WHEAT FREE / GLUTEN FREE / DAIRY FREE / EGG FREE
MAKES 125 ML (4 FL OZ/½ CUP)

250 g (9 oz) fresh, ripe berries
½–2 tablespoons golden caster (superfine) sugar

Wash and if required remove any leaves from the berries. When using strawberries, I cut them into rough pieces, so more surface area will be exposed, but very wet berries, such as raspberries, black, young and logan, can be added whole. Add the berries to a small saucepan, along with 2 tablespoons of water and ½ tablespoon sugar. Cover with a lid and cook over a very gentle heat for 10–15 minutes or until it looks nice and juicy. If it tastes extremely tart at this stage, add a little more sugar, but remember the juices become concentrated.

Remove the lid and cook over high heat for about 2 minutes or until it looks syrupy — you need to boil it enough so it's not watery. Check for sweetness and add extra sugar as desired. Strain and discard the berries and allow the syrup to cool before using.

Passionfruit glaze

WHEAT FREE / GLUTEN FREE / DAIRY FREE / EGG FREE
MAKES ABOUT 185 ML (6 FL OZ/¾ CUP)

125 ml (4 fl oz/½ cup) passionfruit pulp (from about
    3–4 passionfruit)
1–2 tablespoons golden caster (superfine) sugar
¼ teaspoon agar powder

Add the passionfruit pulp to a 250 ml (9 fl oz/1 cup) measure and add enough water to make it up to 250 ml. Place in a small saucepan with 1 tablespoon sugar and whisk in the agar powder. Place over medium heat and bring to a low simmer, stirring frequently — as the agar begins to dissolve, it will sink to the base of the pan and stick. Once it comes to the boil, continue simmering for 6 minutes, stirring frequently. Taste after the first 2 minutes and add the extra sugar as needed. Remove from the heat and set aside.

Foundations

Kefir milk

GLUTEN FREE
MAKES ABOUT 435 ML (15¼ FL OZ/1¾ CUPS)

Kefir grains look like little cauliflowers, and you can buy them on the internet, or get them from someone who has some extras to spare. Each 'grain' is actually a little colony of friendly bacteria and yeasts. You use the grains to culture milk — as the bacteria grow, they consume much of the milk sugar (lactose) and protein, the longer it's left, the more it consumes making the milk more easily digestible. When ready, you strain the grains (putting them aside for another batch), and use the kefir milk. Many people consider kefir milk to have a broader spectrum of good bacteria than yoghurt, and to be superior. Culturing is aerobic, that is, it needs oxygen, so it does not require a lid, but does need to be covered with muslin.

1 tablespoon kefir grains
500 ml (17 fl oz/2 cups) full-cream, non-homogenised milk

Place the grains in a clean jar, pour the milk over them, and cover the top of the jar with a small piece of muslin (cheesecloth).

Leave to culture in a warm place. The rule here is: the warmer it is, the quicker it will culture. The longer it cultures, the more sour the taste becomes. Thus, in summer it may only take 5 or so hours and in winter it may take 24 hours or more. As the culture develops, it will begin to separate into curds and whey. I prefer my kefir milk when the curds and whey are not too pronounced, but rather just beginning to separate and the texture is more like yoghurt. I find the taste a little too sour when it has fully separated.

Place a sieve over a jug and tip the entire contents of the jar into it. Use a stainless steel spoon to gently push the grains to the sides, allowing the liquid to seep through the sieve, until you only have grains left in the sieve. What is in the jug is yours to drink or use. Wash out the jar, then add the kefir grains with some new milk — you are ready to go again.

Place the cultured milk in a clean bottle and store in the fridge. At this stage the bacteria continue to proliferate and consume lactose and protein — this is known as ripening. As the milk ripens, it will become increasingly sour, but it will still be delicious. It will keep for 3–4 days in the fridge. You will easily be able to tell when it is off, as it will smell nasty.

BAKING NOTES

- **Why is my kefir milk sometimes stinky and awful?**
  Invariably, your first kefir milk batch is made with a small amount of grain — about 1 tablespoon. If you give it too much milk, it can't make enough lactic acid to preserve the milk, and putrefying bacteria will proliferate more quickly. If you only have a small amount of grain, start with just a little milk and you will be fine. The grains grow very, very quickly and before you know it, you'll have plenty. This problem is also much more common when pasteurised milk is used, and rarely happens with raw. Approximately 250 ml (9 fl oz/1 cup) milk to 1 tablespoon kefir grains is a good place to start.

- **How do I store my kefir grains if I don't want to make kefir milk regularly?**
  As your grains grow, you can end up with rather a lot of them—all demanding to be fed and loved, just like your children. One can only use so much cultured milk and this is what I do when I want to slow down the production of my kefir milk: when you have strained the milk and are left with the kefir grains, place them in a smaller jar with just enough milk to cover them. Cover the jar with muslin and place in the fridge. When ready to use them, place them in a sieve and rinse with filtered water until clean. Place the clean grains in a jar and you're ready to go.

- **How do I keep my kefir grains 'alive', if I'm going away?**
  Follow the above procedure. The kefir grains might be a bit cheesy when you get back, but they're hard to kill. Many people also give them to a friend to look after and enjoy.

Almond milk

GLUTEN FREE / DAIRY FREE / VEGAN
MAKES 375 ML (13 FL OZ/1½ CUPS)

I prefer to blanch my own almonds for making almond milk, but you may like to buy them already blanched. Never use store-bought almond meal (ground almonds) as there is a world of difference between almond milk made with a conventional meal and biodynamic whole almonds. Almond milk doesn't keep well under warm and hot conditions.

80–120 g (2¾–4¼ oz/½–¾ cup) raw almonds, skins on
¼ teaspoon sea salt, if soaking almonds (optional)

If soaking almonds, place the almonds and salt in a bowl and pour in enough water to cover the nuts well. Set aside at room temperature overnight.

Strain and rinse well. The skins should now slip off easily, but if you find they don't, you will need to blanch them.

If using unsoaked almonds, place the almonds in a heatproof bowl and cover with boiling water and set aside for 3–5 minutes. The skins should slip off easily; if not, drain and repeat the process.

For both soaked and unsoaked almonds, place the almonds in a blender with 435 ml (15¼ fl oz/1¾ cups) of water and blend very well until smooth.

Peg four layers of muslin (cheesecloth) onto a jug or bowl and pour the almond milk through. Pick up the muslin and twist to squeeze out the remaining milk. Use immediately or store in a clean jar in the fridge for up to 2 days. After a time, the almond milk will separate, so just give it a stir before using.

BAKING NOTES

- 80 g (2¾ oz/½ cup) almonds will make perfectly good almond milk, but often in dessert work I prefer to make it richer and use 120 g (¾ cup).

- Many people ask if the meal left in the muslin (cheesecloth) can be used for baking. It's not the best thing, and gives a poor result. Better to use it as the base of a face cleanser (many of the best organic brands do) or as a body exfoliator.

- Soaking the almonds will optimise the goodness you get from them by breaking down the enzyme inhibitors. Ayurveda believes they should always be soaked to make them more digestible. It also recommends removing almond skins as they're considered irritating to the stomach.

Ghee

GLUTEN FREE / CASEIN FREE
MAKES ABOUT 225 G (8 OZ/1 CUP)

250 g (9 oz) butter, preferably unsalted

Melt the butter gently in a small saucepan over low heat. Once melted, increase the heat so there is a gentle simmer — as the water evaporates, there will be a gentle gurgling sound and the butter will be covered with white foam. Skim off and discard throughout. Continue to simmer uncovered, for 20–25 minutes or until the milk solids start to brown on the base of the pan — tilt it to check — and there is little foam left on top of the butterfat. The time will vary for different butters as they contain differing water and fat ratios; be careful not to leave it unattended towards the end as it can burn.

Remove from the heat and leave to cool until any milk solids left on top have sunk to the bottom. When cool, spoon off any remaining milk solids floating on the top. Gently pour the butterfat into a bowl, stopping as you get to the solids at the base of the pan. Discard the solids. To make sure all the milk solids are removed — this is especially important for people who are intolerant to the milk protein, casein — strain the ghee through two to three layers of muslin (cheesecloth).

Store in an airtight container in the fridge until needed. Ghee will keep indefinitely refrigerated.

Balsamic onions

WHEAT FREE / DAIRY FREE / GLUTEN FREE
MAKES ABOUT ½ CUP

This recipe is used as added flavour in the Roasted Pumpkin, Balsamic Onion and Feta Muffins (see page 116), but you may like to double the recipe — it keeps extremely well, and is a great addition to many meals.

½ teaspoon brown mustard seeds
1 tablespoon extra virgin olive oil
1 medium–large red onion, very thinly sliced
sea salt and freshly ground black pepper, to taste
1 tablespoon rapadura sugar
1 tablespoon balsamic vinegar

Place the mustard seeds in a heavy-based frying pan over medium heat and shake until the seeds begin to pop — take care not to burn the seeds. Immediately reduce the heat to low, add the oil and onion and cook, stirring frequently, for 10–15 minutes or until well wilted.

Add a little salt and pepper, the rapadura and vinegar. Stir through and cook for 10–15 minutes or until thick and the mixture does not look at all watery. Make sure you stir frequently, especially towards the end of the cooking period.

Store in a clean, airtight glass jar in the fridge for up to 4 weeks.

Roasted nuts

WHEAT FREE / DAIRY FREE / GLUTEN FREE

your choice of raw unsalted nuts

Preheat the oven to 180°C (350°F/Gas 4).

Place the nuts on a baking tray and leave until lightly roasted, fragrant and the skins are splitting. Roasting nuts depends on your oven and whether or not the nuts have skins and their size. It is always better to roast nuts slower than quicker. Most will take 8–10 minutes, and you should only cook them until light and fragrant.

If roasting almonds or pistachios, I don't bother to take the skins off. To remove the skins off other nuts, pour the hot nuts into a clean tea towel and rub the nuts together to loosen the skins. Pick out the clean nuts (you won't get it all off — don't worry about that) and leave them to cool a little before using or grinding.

Conversions and weights

almond meal	1 cup	100 g	3½ oz
amaranth flour	1 cup	125 g	4½ oz
barley flakes	1 cup	130 g	4½ oz
barley flour	1 cup	110 g	3¾ oz
besan flour	1 cup	135 g	4¾ oz
buckwheat flour	1 cup	140 g	5 oz
coconut flour	1 cup	130 g	4½ oz
coconut palm sugar, granulated	1 cup	140 g	5 oz
golden caster superfine sugar, unrefined	1 cup	210 g	7½ oz
golden icing confectioners' sugar	1 cup	150 g	5½ oz
maize meal	1 cup	110 g	3¾oz
millet flour	1 cup	150 g	5½ oz
oat flour	1 cup	97–100 g	3½ oz
oatmeal	1 cup	135 g	4¾ oz
oats, rolled	1 cup	100 g	3½ oz
polenta	1 cup	140 g	5 oz
potato starch	1 cup	160 g	5¾ oz
quinoa flakes	1 cup	100 g	3½ oz
quinoa flour	1 cup	120 g	4¼ oz
rapadura sugar	1 cup	150 g	5½ oz
rice flour, brown	1 cup	160 g	5¾ oz
rice flour, white	1 cup	155 g	5½ oz
spelt flakes	1 cup	130 g	4½ oz
spelt flour, unbleached white	1 cup	130 g	4½ oz
spelt flour, wholemeal	1 cup	145 g	5¼ oz
teff flour	1 cup	140 g	5 oz
true arrowroot	1 cup	120 g	4¼ oz
wheat cake flour, wholemeal	1 cup	130 g	4½ oz
wheat cake flour, unbleached white	1 cup	135 g	4¾ oz
wheat flour, plain (all-purpose) white	1 cup	150 g	5½ oz
wheat flour, plain (all-purpose) wholemeal	1 cup	150 g	5½ oz

Index

Acknowledgements

It remains an incredibly privileged and honoured position to be able to write books — you read me, cook from me and invite me into your home and lives. With an open heart I say thank you — we are building a brave new world where we care about how we grow, produce and prepare our food, and we're doing it together. But a book is never the work of one person, rather, requiring a multitude of blessings for it all to come together. And I am certainly blessed with friends and family who love and support me, and publishers that support my dreams of real, whole and good food to heal, nourish and delight. I'd like to introduce you to some of them — if you've read my other books, you will recognise their continued presence.

First and foremost is my daughter, Nessie, who encourages and supports all I do, who rolls her eyes when she thinks I've gone too far, and gives honest feedback to what I cook — it's not always positive! My dear friend Jeanie still keeps me sane with her passion for excellence and great brain, but more so because she is selfless in her friendship, and her daughter Violet showers me with hugs and kisses, and trust. Nene, my Best Friend Forever, always tells me how proud she is of me, cooks amazing meals and afternoon tea — cakes of stunning deliciousness and is probably the only other person I know in the world who shares my love of the colour pink. My beloved cousin Fran and her children Josh, Zac and Charlie love me wildly and abundantly as I do them and I can't imagine my life without them. Mum, Lisa, Kim, Peter, Kate, Pip, Anne and Mark are my close and loving family and continue to be there in so many ways. Indeed, Mark has newly married into the family and was put to work immediately, taking many cakes to his work for testing and providing meticulous feedback — detailed notes with ratings from the many people at work; the apple cake is only as good as it is (and it is) because Mark and his co-workers kept pushing me to make it better. Denise, Julie and Peter are my loving extended family and continue to be there for me in every way that counts. You might not have met Holly Davis — one inspiring woman making a huge difference, but I'm lucky to count her as my friend, too, along with another inspiring woman, Katrina Lane. I must have the best neighbours on the planet: John and Jenni, Corine and Pete — not only are they gorgeous and have great taste in music, but they bravely take plates for testing and keep my garden watered when I'm interstate. Vanessa, Dean, Nola, Tess, Gabrielle and Alan are also still there behind the scenes — making me laugh, caring, listening and encouraging — being good friends. Blessed, indeed.

All at Murdoch Books continue to passionately support my work and I'm again blessed to have worked with such talented people. Feedback often comes my way that the recipes work — this is due to the eagle eyes of Christine Osmond and Belinda So — I couldn't imagine doing a book without them. Cath Muscat and Kate Nixon did a glorious job creating such beautiful photographs, with 2010 Whole and Natural Foods Chef Training graduate Angie Cowan keeping us fed, and getting the cakes out of the kitchen.

Many continue to inspire and thus nourish me — I remain incredibly grateful to the work of Anne Marie Colbin, Dr Thoms Cowan, Heidi Swanson, Jessica Prentice, Myra Kornfeld, Peter Berley, Holly Davis, Sophie Zalokar and Katrina Lane.

Published in 2013 by Murdoch Books Pty Limited

Murdoch Books Australia
83 Alexander Street
Crows Nest NSW 2056
Phone: +61 (0) 2 8425 0100
Fax: +61 (0) 2 9906 2218
www.murdochbooks.com.au
info@murdochbooks.com.au

Murdoch Books UK Limited
Erico House, 6th Floor
93–99 Upper Richmond Road
Putney, London SW15 2TG
Phone: +44 (0) 20 8785 5995
Fax: +44 (0) 20 8785 5985
www.murdochbooks.co.uk
info@murdochbooks.co.uk

For Corporate Orders & Custom Publishing contact Noel Hammond,
National Business Development Manager Murdoch Books Australia

Publisher: Sally Webb
Designer: Miriam Steenhauer
Photographer: Cath Muscat
Stylist: Kate Nixon
Project Managers: Livia Caiazzo, Laura Wilson
Editor: Belinda So
Food Editor: Christine Osmond
Production Manager: Karen Small

A cataloguing-in-publication entry is available from the catalogue of the National Library
of Australia at www.nla.gov.au.

A catalogue record for this book is available from the British Library.

Printed by 1010 Printing International Limited, China

IMPORTANT: Those who might be at risk from the effects of salmonella poisoning (the
elderly, pregnant women, young children and those suffering from immune deficiency
diseases) should consult their doctor with any concerns about eating raw eggs.

OVEN GUIDE: You may find cooking times vary depending on the oven you are using.
For fan-forced ovens, as a general rule, set the oven temperature to 20°C (35°F) lower
than indicated in the recipe.

We have used 20 ml (4 teaspoon) tablespoon measures. If you are using a 15 ml (3 teaspoon)
tablespoon add an extra teaspoon of the ingredient for each tablespoon specified.